# REMAINS
## Historical and Literary
### CONNECTED WITH
### THE PALATINE COUNTIES OF
# Lancaster and Chester

VOLUME XXXIX – THIRD SERIES

MANCHESTER

Printed for the Chetham Society

1994

# The Rise and Fall of Parkgate, Passenger Port for Ireland 1686–1815

Geoffrey W. Place, M.A., Ph.D.

General Editor: P. H. W. Booth

MANCHESTER
Printed for the Chetham Society
1994

The society gratefully acknowledges the financial assistance
from Lancashire County Council towards the publication
of Volume 38 of the Third Series.

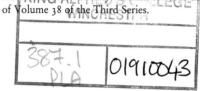

The Rise and Fall of Parkgate,
Passenger Port for Ireland, 1686–1815
by Geoffrey W. Place

Copyright © The Chetham Society, 1994
Text copyright © Geoffrey W. Place, 1994

Published for the Society by Carnegie Publishing Ltd,
18 Maynard Street, Preston
Typeset in Linotype Stempel Garamond by Carnegie Publishing
Printed and bound in the UK by Cambridge University Press

**British Library Cataloguing-in-Publication Data**
Place, Geoffrey W.
  Rise and Fall of Parkgate, Passenger Port
  for Ireland, 1686–1815.—(Chetham Society Series;
  ISSN 0080-0880; Vol. 39)
  I. Title  II. Series
  387.1094275
  ISBN 0-948789-93-X (HARDBACK)
  ISBN 1-85936-023-8 (SOFTBACK)

# Contents

# Abbreviations

| | |
|---|---|
| B.L. | British Library, London |
| *Cal. S.P. Dom.* | *Calendar of State Papers (Domestic)* |
| Cheshire R.O. | Cheshire Record Office, Duke Street, Chester |
| Chester City R.O. | City of Chester Record Office, Town Hall, Chester |
| H.M.C. | Historical Manuscripts Commission (publications of the Royal Comission on Historical Manuscripts) |
| *J.C.A.S.* | *Journal of the Chester Archaeological Society* |
| Mostyn (Bangor) | University College of North Wales, Bangor, Mostyn MSS |
| POST | Post Office archives, Freeling House, 23 Glasshill Street, London |
| P.R.O. | Public Record Office, London |
| QJF | Cheshire Record Office, quarter sessions files |
| Record Soc. L. & C. | Record Society of Lancashire and Cheshire |
| R.Y. | Royal Yacht |
| *T.H.S.L.C.* | *Transactions of the Historic Society of Lancashire and Cheshire* |
| U.C.N.W. | University College of North Wales, Bangor |
| U.C.W. | University College of Wales |

# Illustrations

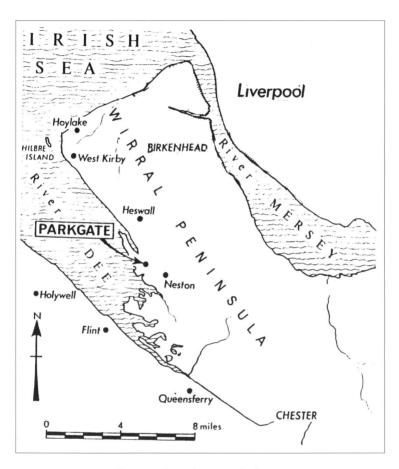

Figure 1. Location map, Parkgate.

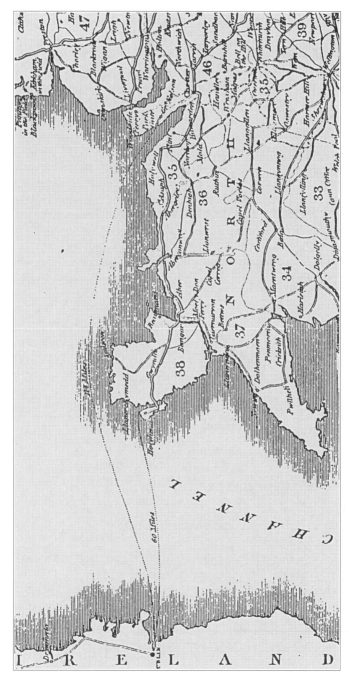

Figure 2. *The crossing from Dublin to Holyhead and to Parkgate*,
from *Paterson's Roads* (16th edition, 1822). The map is a version of the one engraved by Russell for the 13th edition (1803).

# Introduction –
# Parkgate and the Dee Estuary

During the eighteenth century, Parkgate's location would have been known to every educated Englishman. As the schoolboy Thomas De Quincey wrote to his sister in 1800:[1]

> We shall get to Dublin on or before Wednesday night and shall sail by the first Parkgate packet. I suppose you have enough geography to know that Parkgate is situated near Chester on the River Dee, twice as far from Dublin as Holyhead.

At the present day, not only have ships long left Parkgate, but so has the water, and the visitor standing on its sea wall can see several square miles of grass. Although most places have been subject to the winds of change, the feeling of change is particularly strong at Parkgate, which entered and left the public eye in little more than a hundred years. This is the story of its brief period of fame.

Parkgate stands at the north-west corner of Cheshire, on the Wirral peninsula, which juts between the estuaries of the Dee and the Mersey. The village is roughly half way down the English side of the Dee estuary, facing the Welsh hills, some twelve miles by road from Chester and about the same distance, by the modern tunnel under the Mersey, from Liverpool. It is a settlement of recent origin, having first been known as an anchorage in the early seventeenth century, and having emerged as a village only at the end of the same century. It served as an outport for Chester, to which city the navigation was often unsatisfactory, and its speciality was as a port for passengers to Dublin.

It is possible to trace passengers at Parkgate from 1686 to 1815. During this period Holyhead was the port for the Post Office packets across the Irish Sea at a much narrower point, as De Quincey

---

[1] Thomas De Quincey, letter of 3 Sept. 1800, in A. H. Japp, ed., *Memorials*, I (1891), p. 36.

pointed out: 60 miles rather than the 120 miles from Parkgate. We shall examine the growth of the Post Office packet service in Chapter Five. But Holyhead was a long way from any centre of civilised comfort – over 90 miles from Chester – and until the middle of the eighteenth century it was not accessible to wheeled traffic. In addition, Chester had a long mercantile connection with Dublin, so that passengers were likely to find a freight vessel preparing to sail. For reasons to be discussed in Chapter Five, Liverpool was slow to attract passenger traffic, and when it did in the 1780s there were enough travellers to keep all three ports busy. The easy access to Parkgate from Chester and the well-established and therefore well-equipped road from London to Chester encouraged the nobility, gentry and government officials whose business was most likely to be in the south of England to travel through Parkgate. The road connections are discussed in detail in Chapter Nine. The many passengers at the other end of the social scale, particularly harvest labourers who would walk to London, found that Parkgate was an easier place to start their land journey than Holyhead or Liverpool, not least because they had no river to cross.

There are no surviving clues from the seventeenth century to the size or population of Parkgate. The first certain evidence that anybody was actually living there derives from the houses, a string of conventional signs indicating a landmark for mariners, shown on Greenvile Collins' survey of 1686.[2] It is not until 1711, when a list of pew-holders in Neston church was made, that we have any idea of the likely population.[3] Although the settlement at Parkgate lies across the boundary between the townships of Great Neston and Leighton, the pew-allotment lists Parkgate separately. Out of a total of 227 pew-holders in all eight of the parish's townships, 23 lived in Parkgate and 57 in Great Neston. Although it may reasonably be argued that the number of pew-holders would be less, perhaps considerably less, than the total number of households, nevertheless the total of 227 compares fairly closely with the number of families in the parish, 275, noted by Bishop Gastrell in 1717. The bishop went on to record that 'Some houses upon the waterside in Great Neston are called Park Gates'.[4]

[2] Greenvile Collins, *Great Britain's Coasting Pilot* (1693), plate 30.
[3] Cheshire R.O., P.149/6/1.
[4] Francis Gastrell, *Notitia Cestriensis*, ed. F. Raines (Chetham Society o.s., 8, 1845) pp. 165–6.

From the pew-allotment of 1711 we might hazard the guess that there were roughly 30 households in Parkgate, representing perhaps 150 people. It is also worth noting that the number for Parkgate was about a third of the number for Neston.

It is clear from the lease books of the Mostyn estate that considerable development was going on in the 1720s and early 1730s. It is possible that Parkgate had doubled in size between 1711 and 1747, when Mrs Delaney recorded that Parkgate consisted of 50 or 60 houses, suggesting a population of 250 to 300.[5] In between the two, there is the evidence in 1732 of the Mostyn estate map.[6] This shows every building in Parkgate, but the corresponding Field Book, which names the tenants, survives only for that part of Parkgate that lay in Great Neston, and not for the part that lay in Leighton.[7] The Field Book names 26 tenants of houses in Parkgate, and the map suggests that there were a similar number in the Leighton half. This evidence suggests that Parkgate did not grow much between 1732 and 1748 when Mrs Delaney made her estimate.

For the nineteenth century, for which the census figures may be studied, there arises the problem that Parkgate had no official boundaries, and the figures for the separate townships of Great Neston and Leighton do not tell us much about Parkgate unless an assumption of Parkgate's size relative to Neston is made. When in 1841 the actual names of individuals can be counted, a decision must still be made about what constitutes Parkgate. The census takers included under 'Parkgate' the houses on Moorside, which are considered locally to be part of Neston. Making the subjective decision therefore that 'Parkgate' should mean only those houses on or near the Parkgate waterfront, the number of inhabitants in 1841 was 590, roughly one-third the number for Great Neston. The ratio of one-third was also tentatively applied in 1711. This ratio suggests that in 1801, when Great Neston's population was reported in the census as 1,486, Parkgate had nearly 500 inhabitants.

The only other clue comes from an estimate, made shortly before 1810, that Parkgate then contained 'above 130 houses'.[8] This sounds

[5] *The Autobiography and Correspondence of Mary Granville, Mrs Delaney*, ed. Lady Llanover (6 vols, 1861–2) 2, p. 457.
[6] Mostyn (Bangor) 8699.
[7] Mostyn (Bangor) 6086.
[8] Daniel and Samuel Lysons, *Magna Britannia* (6 vols, 1806–22) 2, part 2 (1810), p. 715.

rather a lot, even if the houses on Moorside were included, particularly as the population of Neston went down after 1800 (to revive in the 1820s) rather than up.

During the period 1700 to 1841, the population of England and Wales increased nearly three times, from perhaps 5½ million to nearly 16 million.[9] Parkgate seems to have doubled its population between 1711 and 1748, and doubled it again by 1841.

The character of the village during this period must have altered with its increasing size. As an appendage of Neston, which was the only town in the Wirral peninsula, Parkgate already had access to basic urban facilities, and needed to respond only to its raison d'être: to serve the waterfront. Its earliest institution was the Custom House, and we shall see that the establishment of the Customs there in 1688 played a large part in the establishment of a village and a passenger station. The first residents must have been mariners and Customs officers, followed by the support services needed by the ships – ship-repairers including carpenters, painters, anchor-smiths – and by the passengers – innkeepers, horse-hirers, inn servants. After about 1760 the seabathing craze enabled Parkgate, like many similar places, to offer its visitors something to do other than wait impatiently for the wind to turn. As the quality traffic built up, luxury trades such as perruque-makers, Assembly House and bathhouse keepers, were needed in the village. Nevertheless, both travel and seabathing were seasonal, there could be long delays in sailing caused by adverse weather, and Parkgate often seems to have relapsed into a somewhat dormant state.

Apart from its own increasing size, Parkgate was bound to reflect some of the great changes in eighteenth-century England. Traffic across the Irish Sea was susceptible to wars which were endemic for much of the period. It was not just the population of England which was growing rapidly: that of Ireland at least doubled during the century.[10] The increasing population was just one of the factors making for more travellers. Because Chester was a well-established city, it was less influenced by the national trend towards urbanization which encouraged Liverpool, as a fresher and more open-minded community, to enlarge rapidly. From an estimated population of between 5,000 and 7,000 in 1700, Liverpool grew to

---

[9] Basil Williams, *The Whig Supremacy 1714–60* (1939), p. 119; E. L. Woodward, *The Age of Reform 1815–70* (1938), p. 578.
[10] K. H. Connell, *The Population of Ireland 1750–1845* (1950), pp. 4, 25.

about 18,000 in 1750, 25,000 in 1760, 60,000 by 1793 and 83,000 in 1801. The huge increase in the final twenty years of the century matched a great growth in trade. During the same period, Chester's population grew not at all, being estimated as 14,700 in 1774 and recorded as 15,100 in 1801.[11] Chester's static situation helped to depress its share of the region's trade and Parkgate's need to specialise as a passenger station was enhanced thereby. Finally, we shall see in Chapter Nine that the industrialization of Britain towards the end of the century brought its dividend to Parkgate, when a visitor exclaimed in lengthy verse that he came to the resort to escape the poisoned atmosphere of Birmingham.

It was about 1195 that Lucian, a monk of St Werburgh's abbey in Chester, described the city as keeping 'the keys of Ireland', *claves Hibernorum*.[12] By reason of its situation, Chester became closely involved with the trade of Ireland, especially with Dublin: at the start of the sixteenth century, two-thirds of Chester's imports and nine-tenths of its exports, were with Ireland, and most of this trade was with Dublin.[13] Lucian mentioned two aspects of the maritime traffic of the Dee estuary. He said that the tides used to shift the sandbanks; and that his abbey provided shelter for travellers to and from Ireland.[14]

The shifting sands of Dee mentioned by Lucian have been the cause of continuing navigation problems in the part of the river, from Chester to the sea, known as Chester Water. The origins of the shape of the estuary are obscure, and geologists have speculated on a number of different reasons why so little water should occupy so large a basin. It has been suggested that at one time the waters of the Severn flowed into the Dee,[15] or that the waters of the Mersey flowed

---

[11] For Liverpool: Richard Brooke, *Liverpool as it was during the last quarter of the eighteenth century* (1853), pp. 159, 529; Ramsay Muir, *A History of Liverpool* (1907), pp. 180, 243; H. Peet, *Liverpool in the Reign of Queen Anne* (1908), p. 16. For Chester: G. L. Fenwick, *A History of the Ancient City of Chester* (1896), p. 473.

[12] Lucian, *Liber Luciani de Laude Cestrie*, ed. M. V. Taylor (Record Soc L. & C. 64, 1912), p. 45.

[13] D. M. Woodward, *The Trade of Elizabethan Chester* (1970), pp. 5–7.

[14] Lucian, *Liber Luciani de Laude Cestrie*, pp. 46, 58.

[15] L. J. Wills, 'The development of the Severn valley in the neighbourhood of Ironbridge & Bridgnorth', in *Quarterly Journal of the Geological Society of London*, 80 (1924) pp. 77–86.

into the Dee.[16] A more recent theory proposes that the estuary was formed, not by any action by water, but by an 'ice-way' which was thrust southwards by the pressure of an ice-cap over the Irish Sea.[17] Whatever the actual origin may be, the waters of the Dee have never in recorded times been sufficient to scour out an adequate navigable channel through the deep glacial deposit of silt which underlies its course to the sea.

If Parkgate's history has been a tale of constant change, much of this change has taken place in the Dee estuary. We shall learn that the city of Chester made many complaints about the state of the navigation between their quays and the sea, but that these claims were open to exaggeration and difficult to substantiate. The more important changes in the Dee have been induced by man, starting with the Dee mills of the earls of Chester. At one time these operated eleven water wheels and included a weir across the river at Chester which reduced the tidal limit and hence the scour of the river.[18] A number of schemes were put forward in the seventeenth century to channel a part of the river below Chester into a canal and so bypass the sandbanks which had gathered at the head of the estuary. These proposals resulted in the New Cut, opened in 1737, which took the river five miles below Chester to emerge on the Welsh side, and not the English side as it had done before. The river then reverted to its old course at Parkgate, but gradually, again helped by man, the water swung to the Welsh side all the way to the sea. Extensive land reclamation beside the New Cut further reduced the tidal scour and increased the silting. All these changes are examined in Chapter Two. Today, even the water flowing down the river is closely monitored and controlled, so that Chester, Birkenhead, Liverpool and other places may be supplied with water.[19]

An important factor for change over the years was the size of ships. Improved designs of hull and rigging were constantly making it possible to use larger ships, and we shall examine one particular technological development, the yacht-type, which was borrowed

---

[16] J. P. Bethell, 'The Dee estuary: a historical geography of its use as a port' (M.Sc. thesis, U.C.W. Aberystwyth, 1953), p. 14.

[17] R. Kay Gresswell, 'The origins of the Dee and Mersey estuaries', *Geological Journal*, 4, part 1 (Liverpool, 1964), pp. 77–86.

[18] B. E. Harris, *Chester* (1979), p. 135.

[19] *The Dee Regulation Scheme* (undated pamphlet c.1986), Welsh Water Authority, Dee & Clwyd Division.

from Holland and then developed by English shipwrights. After about 1680 most ships outside the coastal and cross-Channel trades were three-masted, and the dividing line between two and three masted vessels rose from about 60 tons in 1720 to about 150 tons in the 1760s: and by the 1760s, ships of 300 to 400 tons were common in the transatlantic trade.[20] We shall see that most ships anchoring at Parkgate were two-masted, and that 200 tons was about the limit for a ship which could safely enter the estuary. It follows that the increasing size of ships effectively limited Chester Water's vessels to the coastal and Irish trades. In 1672 there were 30 ships belonging to Chester Water (17 on the Cheshire side, 13 on the Welsh side) while there were 65 ships belonging to Liverpool.[21] But Liverpool, with its deep water anchorages, could exploit the Atlantic trade, initially with sugar and tobacco, later with slaves and cotton. Liverpool's ships numbered 220 in 1750 and 796 in 1802. Chester's shipping, however, had remained the same, there being 32 ships belonging to the estuary in 1792.[22] The freight ebbed to Liverpool, and the Dee was left with passengers.


Passengers, first mentioned by Lucian in the twelfth century, were always an important part of the economy of trade across the Irish Sea. The majority of travellers to Dublin before the 1780s seem to have passed through Chester, though they did not always sail in or out of the Dee. The numbers were probably small until the movement of large bodies of soldiers about the year 1600, which stirred rivalry between Chester and Liverpool.[23] It was at about this time that we hear of some individual travellers at Neston, like two Catholic boys who tried to sail to France in 1595; they 'dranck and dranck' with 'a frenchman laden by way of marchandize for frannce'.[24]

The first hint of a regular passenger service was in 1615, when John Bedson of Little Neston (the next township up river from Great

[20] Ralph Davis, *The Rise of the English Shipping Industry in the Seventeenth and Eighteenth Centuries* (1962), pp. 76–9.
[21] John Rylands Library, Mainwaring MSS 149.
[22] R. Stewart–Brown, *Liverpool Ships in the Eighteenth Century* (1962), p. 18.
[23] J. J. McGurk, 'The recruitment and transportation of Elizabethan troops and their service in Ireland, 1594–1603', (Ph.D. thesis, Liverpool 1982); H.M.C., *Salisbury MSS* (1906) xi, pp. 465–7.
[24] P.R.O., SP12/253/22. See also K. R. Wark, *Elizabethan Recusancy in Cheshire* (1971), p. 113.

Neston) described himself as 'a man that useth to travel betwixt England and Ireland with many passengers'.[25]

However, at such a date the technical ability of ships to manoeuvre out of the estuary was limited, and the services available for passengers were primitive:[26]

> . . . passengers for Ireland sometimes wait a quarter of a year together for a wind . . . passengers are obliged to go to the country houses or to the local gentry.

Throughout the seventeenth century there are scattered accounts of travellers coming through Neston, sometimes with a caution which we will hear echoed in later years, by John Wesley amongst others – this one was William Temple in 1671:[27]

> I would not engage myself to any master, knowing their tricks, but told them we would be in readiness for the first that sailed.

A little earlier, in 1666, Matthew Anderton addressed a letter from 'Park Gate, Chester Water' while waiting to sail to Dublin.[28] We shall examine in detail in Chapter Three how the Royal Yachts are known to have brought passengers to and from Parkgate in 1686.

The subsequent growth in travel resulted in the emergence of Parkgate as primarily a passenger station. It is scarcely possible to estimate the numbers involved, except in certain special cases such as vagrants, nor to quantify their importance to the local economies. In the case of Parkgate, which subsisted largely on the passenger traffic until seabathing provided another source of income in the 1760s, the existence and development of the village form in themselves valuable evidence of the economic importance of this form of trade.

Travel within England had been stimulated by the introduction of the coach, and in 1607 the London watermen were complaining about the competition from coaches. Their popularity in the capital led to the establishment of public stage-coach routes out of London by 1650.[29]

[25] Cheshire R.O., QJF 43/4/30.
[26] *Cal. S.P. Dom., Eliz & James I Add. 1580–1625* (1872), pp. 612–13, 25 May 1619.
[27] *Cal. S.P. Dom., 1671* (1895), p. 349.
[28] *Cal. S.P. Dom., Charles II 1665* (1894), p. 599, item 125.
[29] J. H. Markland, 'Some remarks on the early use of carriages in England', *Archaeologia* 20 (1824), pp. 443–77; pp. 465–71.

The increased demand for travel facilities led to road improvements through the Turnpike Acts, the first being passed in 1663 although not followed by other Acts until the 1690s.[30]

At the same time that technical improvements were taking place with overland travel, complemented as we shall see by improvements to sea travel, there was political and economic stimulation for movement on the routes to Ireland. The civil wars of the 1640s which had left Ireland devastated, had also provoked more of that suspicion of travellers which had often inhibited easy movement. The official suspicion of travellers eased after 1660 and almost entirely evaporated after the 1715 rebellion had been resolved. The growing prosperity of Ireland during the eighteenth century was reflected in the increasing brilliance of Dublin as a capital city.[31] This brilliance gave rise to political, social and cultural reasons to travel to and from Ireland, especially through Dublin, and Parkgate flourished in response to those needs. The growing populations of both countries encouraged the migration of harvest labourers, since the Irish needed the cash and the English farmers needed the labour. Eventually the pressure of travellers allowed the use of specialist passenger vessels, still further stimulating the flow, and Parkgate reached its zenith in about 1790.

Parkgate therefore emerged as a passenger station because of specific developments which are discussed on the following pages. Further developments were to end its prosperity very soon after its zenith. Dublin lost its status as a capital city after 1800; improved road access to Holyhead ended Parkgate's advantage of cosy nearness to Chester; the human interference with the River Dee eventually drove the main channel away from Parkgate; and once Parkgate was floored by events, the introduction of steam ships gave the advantage to Liverpool and ended any hope of recovery for a passenger station in the Dee.

---

[30] Joan Parkes, *Travel in England in the Seventeenth Century* (1925), pp. 26–7.
[31] Constantia Maxwell, *Dublin under the Georges* (1936), pp. 83–113.

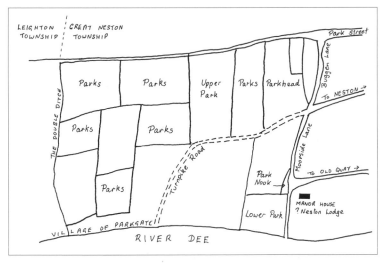

Figure 3. Neston Park. Its apparent boundaries, showing field names, taken from the Mostyn estate map, 1732, and the tithe map, 1847.

# 1  *The Origins of Parkgate*

Parkgate was first used as the name, not of a settlement, but of an anchorage in the Dee estuary, and described that part of the long Neston anchorage which lay beside Neston Park. This medieval deer park was originally enclosed by Roger de Montalt, who was baron of Mold (Monte Alto) from 1232 to 1260, and who was lord of the manor of Neston. His enclosure is known by a grant in 1258 which Roger made to the abbey of St Werburgh in Chester, to which his uncle Ralph had given Neston church in the previous century,[1] of

> certain lands in Neston which he had earlier given to Neston church in exchange for some lands, belonging to the church, which were enclosed within his park at Neston.[2]

The park seems to have been formed, therefore, about the year 1250. Its northern boundary can be determined from the evidence given to Special Commissioners at Neston in 1569,[3] and its extent can be deduced from field names which survived into the eighteenth and nineteenth centuries.[4] The park had a river frontage of some 1,000 yards, and it was on part of this land that the village of Parkgate later developed. It is known that a herd of deer was kept in the park,[5] and while the deer were preserved there could be no human settlement. But the land was sold in 1599 by the earl of Derby and settlement then became possible.[6]

---

[1] J. Tait, *Chartulary of Chester Abbey, part 2* (Chetham Society, N.S. 82, 1923), p. 302.
[2] *ibid*, p. 306.
[3] P.R.O. CHES 2/234, 14 & 15 Elizabeth, e.g. at end of f.7; see also *Cheshire Sheaf*, 3rd series 20 (April 1923), p. 28, item 4751.
[4] For a detailed description of the boundaries of Neston Park, see G. W. Place, 'Neston Park', in *Bulletin of the Burton and South Wirral Local History Society* 5 (1984), pp. 15–20.
[5] *Calendar of Inquisitions post-mortem*, 2 (1906), p. 83; rent roll of the Earl of Derby, see *Cheshire Sheaf*, 3rd series 4 (April 1902), pp. 36–7, item 613; *Cal. S.P. Carew MSS*, p. 220 (15 July 1594).
[6] Mostyn (Bangor) 6853 (see bibliography).

Before that happened, and before Parkgate was recorded as a place-name, there were occasional references to the anchorage at 'Neston' and in 1349–50 this anchorage was listed as 'Neston park'.[7] It is ironic, in view of the Customs establishment at Parkgate which later laboured to keep out illegal imports, that the place-name is first recorded in an enquiry into illegal exports. The exports concerned calfskins, which had long been a bone of bitter contention amongst the merchants of Chester. As a protectionist measure, the export of leather without a licence had been illegal since 1558 [8] but in 1584 the Chester merchants were granted a licence to export calfskins in compensation for heavy losses from pirates.[9] Before that there had been trouble with a cargo of skins which was being loaded by night, ready to be taken downstream to a ship waiting at Neston.[10] A similar ploy was attempted in 1610 by Robert Berry.

Robert Berry was a contumacious merchant who, despite being one of the few traders who controlled the monopoly of calfskins licences,[11] tried to avoid the terms of his licence. He had already been imprisoned for losing his temper before the mayor of Chester when questioned over a matter of importing wine.[12] In 1610 a sailor gave evidence that Berry had hired him to take a boat, at night, laden with 'packe skins and other Comodities', 'from the watergate to the parkegate'.[13] Berry refused to appear to answer the charge, and was disfranchised.[14]

That is the first recorded mention of Parkgate as a place-name. In the following two years Parkgate was twice recorded as an anchorage, of the *Gift* of London in 1611, and of the *Unicorn* of Leighton in 1612.[15]

Until the final two decades of the seventeenth century there seems to be no surviving evidence that anybody was actually living at Parkgate. The few references to the place that have been found all

[7] K. P. Wilson, ed., *Chester Customs Accounts* (Record Soc. L. & C., 1969), pp. 21, 31, 33.
[8] 1 Eliz. cap. 10.
[9] D. M. Woodward, 'Chester leather industry', *T.H.S.L.C.*, 119 (1967), p. 85.
[10] D. M. Woodward, *The Trade of Elizabethan Chester*, p. 62.
[11] *ibid*, p. 59.
[12] *Cheshire Sheaf*, 1st series 1 (July 1878), p. 51, item 177.
[13] Chester City R.O., QSE/9/47.
[14] Chester City R.O., AB/1/f.311.
[15] Chester City R.O., QSE/11/10; QSE/13/16.

mention it as an anchorage; and as an anchorage it has to be understood as a part of the Neston waterfront.

The vexed question of the state of the River Dee and the problems of interpreting the evidence for its varying condition will be examined presently when we study its navigation. For the present, suffice it to say that the estuary presented 'an area of ever-changing submarine morphology',[16] where the shifting sands constantly altered the channels and adjusted the extent and depth of the anchorages.

The Dee estuary was often known as 'Chester Water', and although the Mersey was occasionally called 'Liverpool water', Chester Water was a much more common term. It was a useful name because a ship nominally bound for Chester, and which might actually reach the city on high tides, might anchor at any of a variety of points within the estuary.

An early example occurs in the charter-party of the *Grace* of Neston in 1572, whereby Thomas Mylner contracted to take his barque 'from the river of Chester water' to Waterford and back.[17] We do not know whether Mylner sailed from the New Haven at Neston, which will be described in the next section and which is the most likely point at that date. Sometimes the general direction is given an added precision, as when the Royal Yacht *Monmouth* left Dublin on 19th April 1690, 'sailed for Chester water', and anchored at Parkgate' on the 22nd.[18] Sometimes the term seems to imply an anchorage which was not necessarily a landing-place: in 1686 the R.Y. *Portsmouth* landed passengers at the Beerhouse (just below Parkgate) on 14th July, 'rode in Chester Water' for the next week and 'weighed from Parkgate' on the 22nd.[19] Captain Wright of the *Portsmouth* often 'rode in Chester water' and it is not clear whether this is another way of saying that he remained at Parkgate, or whether he landed passengers and moved to deeper water before mooring. In 1702, for example, when the river-bed conditions had

[16] A. H. W. Robinson's phrase in *Marine Cartography in Britain* (1962), p. 141.

[17] B.L., Harleian MS 2004 f. 137; see *Cheshire Sheaf*, 3rd series 19 (April 1922), p. 31, item 4542; also D. M. Woodward, 'Charter party of the Grace of Neston' in *Irish Economic & Social History* 5 (1978), pp. 64–9.

[18] P.R.O., ADM 51/574.

[19] P.R.O., ADM 51/3943.

no doubt altered, Captain Breholt often landed passengers at Parkgate and then moved to deeper water downstream at Dawpool.[20]

By ellipsis, 'Chester' was often given as a direction, either to mean Chester Water, or to indicate that Chester was the end point for the cargo, whatever the precise anchorage used. A recurrent literary puzzle concerns the embarkation point of Edward King, whose subsequent death in 1637 inspired Milton's poem 'Lycidas'.[21]

> This worthy gentleman, Mr Edward King, was a fellow student with Milton and Cleveland in Christs College in Cambridge: who having sailed from Chester, the ship that he was in foundered upon a rock on the Irish seas. Some escaped in the boat, and great endeavours were used in that great consternation to get him into the boat, which did not prevail. So he and all with him were drowned except those only that escaped in the boat.

In view of the many writers who have incautiously attributed his embarkation or drowning to Parkgate, the point is important.[22] Did he literally sail from Chester? It is possible that he did, for as late as 1707 the City Council was claiming that vessels drawing nine feet of water could reach Chester at all spring tides.[23] This draft would allow ships of perhaps 70 tons to reach the city; and 70 tons was the burthen of the Post Office packets sailing between Holyhead and Dublin in the eighteenth century.[24] But it is more likely, in view of the date, that he sailed from Neston Key. It was this Key which was visited in 1621 by certain Chester shoemakers who went to Neston 'to viewe certayne Irishe lether'.[25]

'Chester' as a direction must be treated with great caution. In 1674 a correspondent at Chester wrote that 'the Mary yacht is arrived

---

[20] P.R.O., ADM 51/186.
[21] *Obsequies to the Memorie of Mr Edward King Anno Dom. 1638*, preface to the 1694 edition. See J. K. Fransson, 'The fatal voyage of Edward King, Milton's Lycidas', in *Milton Studies* 25 (Pittsburg, 1990), pp. 43–67.
[22] e.g. P. Sulley, *The Hundred of Wirral* (1889), p. 190; M. Hardwick, *A Literary Atlas and Gazeteer of the British Isles* (1973), p. 95; *The Oxford Literary Guide to the British Isles*, ed. D. Eagle and H. Cannell (1st edn, 1977), p. 278, but corrected *me instante* in the 2nd edition (1981); H. E. Young, *A Perambulation of the Hundred of Wirral* (1909), p. 137. Both Sulley and Young state that King was travelling the wrong way, *from* Dublin.
[23] H.M.C., *Appendix to 8th Report* (1881), pp. 394–5.
[24] POST 1/10 p. 44.
[25] Chester City R.O., GB/4 p. 47.

here', but 'here' turned out to mean Dawpool, some fifteen miles down river from the city.[26] The shipping lists in newspapers often mention Parkgate but also often mention Chester, partly because Chester might be the port of registration. The entry 'Racehorse of Chester, Norman, to Chester with passengers'[27] might conceivably mean that the vessel had sailed up the New Cut to Chester; except that Joseph Norman's brig *Racehorse* was well known as a Parkgate regular. There were several years in the 1740s when a great many ships carried soldiers from Dublin to 'Chester', yet after one such draft we are told that everybody 'landed safe the next day at Parkgate, without losing one man or horse, or any one ship running foul of another'.[28] In general, the evidence overwhelmingly suggests that passengers for Chester or Chester Water in the eighteenth century were making for Parkgate; in the seventeenth century there can be no such probability.

Other sources similarly use 'Chester' at times without further particulars. *Lloyd's Lists* rarely mention Parkgate before 1768 and tended to say 'Chester' instead. The brig *Active* was a regular trader between Dublin and Parkgate from 1774 when it was built, as the Customs accounts show;[29] it was described in *Lloyd's Register* as 'Dublin to Chester constant',[30] and when the *Active* was granted a pass to go to Marseilles in 1775 by the admiralty, it was said to be 'in River Dee'.[31]

Parkgate slowly emerged during the seventeenth century as the most useful part of the long Neston anchorage: very slowly, for after the initial references in 1610–12 very few mentions of Parkgate have been found before 1686. By the Neston anchorage is meant the 3,000 yards (about 1¾ miles) between Neston Key and Beerhouse Hole, all of which lies within the ancient parish of Neston.

[26] *Cal. S.P. Dom., 1673–75* (1904), letters from Matthew Anderton, 12 & 19 Dec. 1674, pp. 459, 472.
[27] *The Dublin Journal*, 6 April 1753.
[28] *ibid*, 25 Feb. 1744. The troop movements were in 1742, 1744, 1745.
[29] The Customs Account book of Humphrey Read (the 'Parkgate Account') held by H.M. Customs & Excise library service.
[30] *Lloyd's Register of Shipping* (1782), no pagination.
[31] P.R.O., ADM 7/100, August 1775.

Neston Key was the name often given to Chester's New Haven, built in the mid-sixteenth century. When it was mooted in 1541 it was called 'the New Haven' and it was referred to as 'the haven' in the accounts of money paid for the construction of the pier by Chester city companies in 1557 and 1559.[32] It was also referred to as 'the New Key' throughout its working history;[33] and it was called 'Neston Key' or 'the Key at Neston'.[34] When Chester's canalization of the River Dee, or New Cut, was opened in 1737, another New Quay on the Welsh shore was formed at its outer end, at Golftyn, and is shown as 'New Quay' on Boydell's map of 1771.[35] This latter place had received its present name, Connah's Quay, by 1784.[36] But long before that, by 1743, Neston Key had become known as 'the Old Quay'.[37] This plethora of names for a single place has confused many researchers since.

Neston Key was a stone pier which was built into the river, at right angles to the shore, on the boundary between the townships of Great Neston and Little Neston. Although often cited as twelve miles from Chester, which is the distance by road, the sailing distance by the old course of the Dee was nearer ten miles, and the Key was nearly another ten miles from the Hoylake anchorage just outside the mouth of the estuary. The distances were also often under-estimated:[38]

> By reason of the flatts and shallows which in this day are in the river of Dee, nere to Chester, the cytyzens of Chester are constreyned to make them a wharf, 8 myle of, where shyps may in more safety ride, as at more convenency be a flete, for at low water they are on ground also. But this which usually they call a wharf is rather a faced pere.

[32] Edna Rideout, 'The Chester Companies and the Old Quay', *T.H.S.L.C.* 79 (1927), pp. 148, 159.
[33] e.g. in 1551, R. H. Morris, *Chester during the Plantagenet and Tudor Reigns* (1894), pp. 459–60; Richard Blome, *Britannia*, p. 54 (in 1673).
[34] e.g. in 1679, Chester City R.O. Crownmote records, c/1; in 1690, P.R.O. T1/11/69/.
[35] Thomas Boydell, *Plan of the lands and premises . . . of the River Dee Company* (1771).
[36] *The Chester Chronicle* mentions 'Connah's Quay' on various dates in 1784, e.g. 19 June.
[37] Cheshire R.O., DHL 27/4, 29 Dec. 1743.
[38] 'Certain verie rare observations of Chester', *Cheshire Sheaf*, 3rd series 22 (July 1925), p. 47, item 5232, quoting B.L., Harleian MS 473, c.1574.

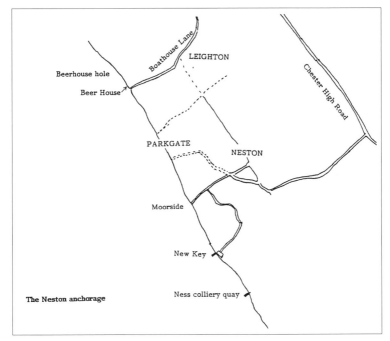

Figure 4. The Neston anchorage.

The construction and necessary repairs of the Key were a burden on the city of Chester, which declined to spend any more money on it after 1604.[39] Nevertheless, it was still in use until the end of the seventeenth century. Sir Richard Grenville, while waiting to sail with a troop of thirty horse to Ireland in 1642, wrote from the New Key to explain the weather's delays.[40] In 1679 Robert Wood was crushed while trying to launch a boat at the Key at 'Nesson'.[41]

In 1691 Charles Hewitt, customs officer at Neston, listed thirteen ships and their crews which were 'belonging to the Chester Water now at home at Neston Key and the Parkgate near adjoining'.[42] After the 1690s the Key was not mentioned specifically as an anchorage

[39] Chester City R.O., Assembly Books order, 10 Oct. 1604; Rideout p. 150 (see note 32).
[40] Cheshire R.O., DCC 14/28.
[41] Chester City R.O., Crownmote records, 10 June 1679.
[42] P.R.O., TI/11/69–76.

again, although, occasionally and exceptionally, ships still found themselves there very much later, in the following case eighty years later:[43]

> The Martha, Liverpool to Aberdovey with tobacco, groceries etc, ran before a storm and came to the Old Key in Chester Water.

However, all that has been said about Chester as a direction can also, in its smaller way, be said about Neston. 'Neston' was often used to describe some point on or near the long Neston anchorage, and whether Neston Key is meant, or some point down river from it, remains uncertain, as the landfall may well have been uncertain at the time. For example [44]

> Captain Sir William Vaughan. He brought over this regiment into England at Christmas 1643, landed at Nesson in Worral behind Chester.

Thirty years later,[45]

> The Countess of Meath went hence to Neston intending to go aboard the Swan, but met there with the dogger, which immediately sailed thence with her to Dublin.

Immediately next to the Key was the Key House, a brick building which served as a prominent landmark. The following diary extract suggests that the Royal Yacht *Portsmouth*, which is known four years later to have usually visited Parkgate, was expected at Neston Key but could not anchor there:[46]

> 1st May [1682]: My Lord and Lady Derby went to Neston to meet the Duke [of Ormonde] attended by the troop wherein all the gentlemen marched, dined at the Key hous. About 5 at night the yact appeared, the Duke, Duchess, Lord Ossory landed 4 miles beyong where we met them and came to Chester.

---

[43] Glegg Account book (see bibliography, University of Liverpool), 20 July 1763.
[44] Richard Symonds, *Diary of the Marches of the Royal Army during the Great Civil War*, ed. C. E. Long (Camden Soc. 1859), p. 255. This landing may have been part of the larger force which landed 'in Cheshire' on 7 Feb. 1644—see Peter Young, *The English Civil War Armies* (1973), p. 39.
[45] *Cal. S.P. Dom.*, 22 Jan. 1676; *1675–76* (1907), p. 525.
[46] Diary of Sir Willoughby Aston (Liverpool City Record Office), 1 May 1682.

Similar references to the Neston anchorage can be found for the next twenty years. The last one so far found is in 1704:[47]

> His Grace left Dublin on Monday at 4 and arrived at Neston at noon yesterday. The Seaford convoyed us, in which I came with my family.

The war that made the *Seaford*'s protection necessary was to last until 1711. As shipping began to return to normal, Parkgate had emerged as the usual anchorage for any shipping entering Chester Water, and Neston was never mentioned again.

In the course of the long decline of Neston Key, another point in the river, at the opposite end of the Neston anchorage and down river from it, was becoming a popular mooring. this was known as the Beerhouse hole.

At the north end of the modern village of Parkgate, its link with the outside world is Boathouse Lane. Until the 1840s when the north end of the shore road, the Parade, was built,[48] the lane ran downhill and into the river. At its foot was an inn, known until at least the mid-eighteenth century simply as the Beerhouse. It existed as an inn in 1613,[49] became known as the Ferry House or Boat House by the start of the nineteenth century[50] and was finally called the Pengwern Arms[51] before it was closed after storm damage in 1881 and demolished.[52] The building was, like the Key House, a landmark, and so was recorded as 'the Brew House' by Andrew Yarranton in 1674 and as 'Beerhouse' on Greenvile Collins' chart of 1686.[53]

A stretch of the river near the Beerhouse was known as Beerhouse hole. It was not recorded by that name on any chart of the estuary, but Collins marked the anchorage with a conventional sign and indicates slightly deeper water there. At certain periods of the river's history, it seems that ships visiting Parkgate would have to beach themselves on the shore, but could ride afloat in Beerhouse hole about a thousand yards down river. As the anchorage was recorded

[47] *Cal. S.P. Dom., Anne vol. 2, 1703–4*, p. 579, 22 March 1704.
[48] *Chester Chronicle*, 14 May 1841.
[49] Cheshire R.O., Index of Wills, James Gertrie of Thornton Hough, 1613.
[50] *Chester Chronicle*, 17 June 1814.
[51] *ibid*, 2 April 1847.
[52] *ibid*, 22 Oct. 1881, 4 March 1882.
[53] Andrew Yarranton, *England's Improvement by sea and land* (pub. 1677 but surveyed 1674), p. 191; Greenvile Collins, *Great Britain's Coasting Pilot*, plate 30 (1693). For his survey date of 1686, see the next section.

before there were any signs of a village, it may well be that the Beerhouse gave rise to the first settlement at Parkgate.

In 1642 Sir Richard Grenville was at Puddington, and later at the New Key, waiting to take a troop of cavalry to Ireland:[54]

> Such wonderful stormy weather hath beene here abouts yesterday, that oure shipping hath generally had some losses and hurtes, of which the Providence Mr Johnson's shippe sprunge a planke and tooke a leake by it, that filled her with water and so spoyled all the goods aboard her; two shippes more by the Beer house are sunke, whereof one is the Samuell of Nesson . . .

By far the best description of the Beerhouse anchorage was by a French visitor, Jorevin de Rochford, who was travelling in the late 1660s:[55]

> Chester may be reckoned among the good seaports, since it is the ordinary passage of the packet boat, messengers and merchandize going from England to Ireland. The first thing I did on my arrival at Chester, was to learn when the packet-boat would sail for Dublin; it had set off some days before; but I found a trading vessel laden with divers merchandizes, in which I took my passage for Ireland. This vessel was at anchor in the gulf, near the little village of Birhouse, eight miles from the town. Here are some large storehouses for the keeping of merchandize to be embarked for Ireland . . .

If de Rochford observed accurately [56] and there was a cluster of buildings around the Beerhouse, then this is the earliest record of houses on approximately the Parkgate waterfront. The Beerhouse was in the township of Leighton, not Great Neston, and a number of ships had earlier been listed as 'of Leighton'.[57]

---

[54] Cheshire R.O., DCC 14/21, 4 Feb. 1641 OS.
[55] By internal evidence, during the reign of Charles II, and estimated at 1666–8 by Constantia Maxwell, *The Stranger in Ireland* (1954), p. 98.
[56] Jorevin de Rochford, 'Description of England and Ireland', part of his travels printed in Paris, 1672, 'very rare' in 1809 when an extract was published in *The Antiquarian Repertory*, ed. F. Grose (1809) 4, pp. 549–622.
[57] e.g. *Unichorne* of Leighton, 1612 (Chester City R.O., QSE 13/16); *Guift* of Leighton, 1658 (*Cheshire Sheaf*, Nov. 1878 p. 115 [1st series, vol. I] item 371).

The anchorage appears in an unexpected form as 'Briethouse' on a French chart of 1693.[58]

From the following letters of the earl of Arran to the duke of Ormonde one may suppose that the Beerhouse could be used as a landfall when Neston Key, perhaps, could not:[59]

> 1682, 2 May: I conclude your Grace may be landed at Neston this day . . .

> 6 May: I had an account on Thursday night that your Grace was landed the Monday before at the beerhouse, which I was very glad to hear, for as the wind stood with us, we all judged you could not land before the afternoon tide the next day.

The first detailed sailing record within the estuary to have survived is the journal, or captain's log, of the Royal Yacht *Portsmouth* in 1686:[60]

> 12 April: At 10 in the forenoon wee came up to the Bear house hole and landed our passengers, anchored in seven fathoms at high water.

During the next eighteen months, Captain Wright often landed his passengers or moored at Beerhouse hole (his spelling varied between Beer, Bear, Bar and Barr): his log names it ten times to Parkgate's eight times.

Beerhouse hole is occasionally mentioned during the next century, presumably when the shifting sands made it once more a deep anchorage. The R.Y. *Dorset* anchored there in 1803 and 1812 to await the tide to carry her to Parkgate.[61] It also provides one of the last occasions when any merchant ship visited Parkgate, albeit unwillingly, in 1822:[62]

> The cheese brig Britannia, John Neild master, dragged anchor and sank in Beer-house hole, below Parkgate. She carried 105

[58] Carte de la Rivière de Dée ou de Chester, an inset on Carte Générale des Costes d'Irlande at des Costes Occidentales d'Angletere, levée et gravée par ordre exprez du Roy, 1693.
[59] H.M.C., *Marquis of Ormonde*, NS 6, pp. 359, 361.
[60] P.R.O., ADM 51/3943.
[61] P.R.O., ADM 51/1443, 2260.
[62] *Chester Chronicle* and *Chester Courant*, 13 Dec. 1822.

tons of cheese from Chester, 29 tons of ginger, 10 tons of raisins etc from Liverpool, bound for London.

Before we leave this account of the changing situation on the Neston anchorage from which Parkgate emerged, it may be salutary to suggest that, during the seventeenth century, all parts of it were capable of use as landfalls at any given time. But Neston was pre-eminent: in 1673 Richard Blome wrote:[63]

> The chief [gate of Chester] is Water-gate, where great ships in time past at full sea did come; but the channel is now so choaked up with sand that it will scarce give passage to small boats, insomuch that all ships now come to a place called the New-key about 6 miles distant.

In 1686 Captain Greenvile Collins, the King's Hydrographer, gave the city of Chester a copy of the chart he had just made of the Dee estuary. As this was the first chart of Chester Water ever made, the city was suitably grateful:[64]

> It is ordered by unanimous consent that twenty guineys lately given by the Treasurer of this citty to Captain Collins by the direction and appointment of the Mayor and Justices of the Peace as a gratuity for his the said Captain Collins paines in surveying the river gieving the city a map thereof shall be allowed in the Treasurers account.

The importance of this chart to our story is that it literally put Parkgate on the map for the first time.

'My inclinations from youth had been bent on discoveries,' wrote Collins about his first known voyage in 1669, which set out to explore the west coast of America.[65] He is next heard of as sailing master or navigating officer of the *Speedwell*, a ship sent to find a north-east passage to the orient. No passage was found and the

---

[63] Richard Blome, *Britannia* (1673), p. 54.

[64] Chester City R.O., AB/3, 19 Nov. 1686. Unfortunately the city does not still have this gift.

[65] James Burney, *Voyages and Discoveries in the South Seas and Pacific* (1803–17), cited by S. Mountfield, 'Captain Greenvile Collins and Mr Pepys', *Mariner's Mirror* 56 (1970), p. 85.

*Speedwell* was wrecked,[66] but Collins' account of the voyage reached the king. Samuel Pepys[67]

> received His Majesty's particular directions in favour of Mr Collins from whom and his journal His Majesty hath received so much satisfaction.

This royal approval was to provide him with his later career as a hydrographer: meanwhile it gave him preferment in the fleet of Sir John Narbrugh which sailed to curb the pirates of Algiers. He acted as sailing master on four ships in the next three years, finally on the admiral's flagship, and the drawings he made show his keen eye for cartographic detail.[68]

On his return home in 1679, Collins gained his first command, of the frigate *Lark*. But his reputation was as a navigator, and for reasons to be discussed when we examine the royal yachts, this skill made him particularly suitable for these small vessels. 'He never attained any very considerable rank in the service,' wrote Charnock, 'having scarcely ever commanded any other vessel than a yacht.'[69]

At this time the only sea charts of British waters readily available were Dutch, based on the work of Lucas Janszoon Waghenaer whose *Sea Mirror* was published in 1584, to appear four years later in English as *The Mariner's Mirrour*. In 1671 John Seller published a new sea atlas called *The English Pilot*, but nearly all the charts were of Dutch origin.[70] In the 1680s Pepys[71]

> decided to collect from Mr Seller a list of sea charts and books on navigation printed in English, shewing how the books of charts under several titles borrow all from Waggoner.

A new and English survey was called for, and Collins was chosen for it, possibly recommended by Admiral Narbrugh to the King, who will have remembered Collins' work:[72]

---

[66] *ibid*, p. 88.

[67] J. R. Tanner, ed., *Naval MSS in the Pepysian library* 3 (1909), p. 260.

[68] F. E. Dyer, 'The Journal of Grenvill Collins', *Mariner's Mirror* 14 (1928), pp. 197–209.

[69] John Charnock, *Biographia Navalis* (1794) 2, p. 60.

[70] A. H. W. Robinson, *Marine Cartography in Great Britain* (1962), pp. 34–39.

[71] J. R. Tanner, ed., *Samuel Pepys' Naval Minutes* (1926), p. 224.

[72] *Cal. S.P. Dom., 1680–81* (1921), p. 328, 23 June 1681.

After reciting that he had chosen Capt. Collins, commander of the Merlin yacht, to make a survey of the sea coast of the kingdom by measuring all the sea coasts with a chain and taking all the bearings of the headlands with their exact latitudes, the true plots of all harbours, roads, bays, creeks, islands, soundings and the setting and flowing of tides, which will tend much to the security of navigation . . .

The King's commission emphasised the need to measure from the land. Dutch charts tended to inaccuracy because they relied on observations of an often hostile coast from the sea, where distances were hard to measure.

And so Collins' great survey began. For the first two seasons, 1681 and 1682, he used the *Merlin* yacht, but in 1683 he transferred to the R.Y. *Monmouth*, probably because this vessel could more easily be run ashore.[73] His survey took seven years, until 1688, and in that year he returned to R.Y. Merlin,[74] so apparently most of the survey was done in the *Monmouth*. It was in the *Monmouth*, then, that Collins surveyed Chester Water. There is no record of his itinerary during those seven years, and some observers have been misled by the dates of the printed versions of some of the charts. His chart of 'The River Dee or Chester Water' is dated 1689,[75] yet we know that he gave a copy to the city of Chester in 1686. When the map was engraved he probably added 1689 because he dedicated it to William III. That was indeed a tactful move, because Collins had just served in the fleet which sought to oppose William's landing in England, and he was about to obtain the job of commander of the king's personal yacht. We can be reasonably certain that the survey of the Dee took place in 1686, and not before, because Captain Wright on the R.Y. *Portsmouth* twice saw the *Monmouth* in these waters, in July 1686 while sailing to Liverpool, and in October while entering Dublin harbour.[76] Collins had been reappointed commander of the *Monmouth* in April 1686,[77] and Chester's payment of £20 was confirmed in November.

---

[73] See the chapter on The Royal Yachts (Chapter 3) below.

[74] 'Journal of Captain Greenvile Collins', 17 Jan. 1688, printed in H.M.C. *15th Report app. 1, MSS of the Earl of Dartmouth* 3, p. 54. Notice that Charnock (see note 69) misread Merlin as 'Martin'.

[75] Greenvile Collins, *Great Britain's Coasting Pilot* (1693), plate 30.

[76] P.R.O., ADM 51/3943.

[77] John Charnock, *Biographia Navalis* 2, p. 60.

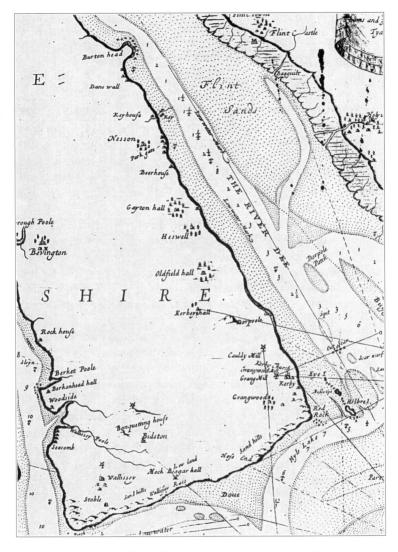

Figure 5. Greenvile Collins' chart of the Dee, surveyed in 1686.

In October 1688, his survey finished, Collins was summoned from the ship he then commanded (*Young Spragge*) to be sailing master for Lord Dartmouth's flagship, the *Resolution*, in the fleet which failed by reason of the wind to intercept the convoy bringing William of Orange to Torbay. Collins is next heard of as commander of the

R.Y. *Mary* when she carried William III from Hoylake to Ireland in 1690, and he remained with the *Mary* for the next three years. In January 1694 he transferred to the *Fubbs* yacht and then died, apparently in March.[78]

Collins' survey was the first large-scale survey of British waters by any Englishman.[79] It was criticised at the time: Trinity House (Deptford), which was responsible for charts but which had been bypassed in this matter by Charles II, ignored Pepys' urging to send an observer—Pepys thought the task was too great for one man.[80] Trinity House complained of Collins' 'ill-performance of his book of carts', but they remained in use for a good hundred years. Published in 1693, they went through twenty editions, with the last reprint in 1792.[81]

The importance of Collins' chart of Chester Water to the city of Chester was related to some proposals for an improvement in its maritime fortunes. In 1687 Andrew Barry petitioned James II, saying that the Dee's navigation for eight or nine miles below Chester had been lost: he wanted a lease to reclaim land.[82] This was the first skirmish in a long battle to control the river, and the new chart was a potent weapon in that battle.

For Parkgate, which was named for the first time on any map, the chart provided evidence that its anchorage must have been in regular use in the mid 1680s, evidence confirmed by the journal of the R.Y. *Portsmouth* which we shall examine later. Five conventional signs for houses are shown on the shore, with one at the Key House and one at the Beer House, indicating the extremes of the Neston anchorage. The five houses at Parkgate do not imply that Parkgate was five times bigger than Neston, which is shown with a single house sign, but that a line of houses on the shore formed a landmark for mariners. They do mean, of course, that the anchorage had become a settlement.

---

[78] F. E. Dyer (see note 68), p. 218.
[79] G. P. B. Naish, 'Hydrographic surveys by officers of the Navy under the later Stuarts', *Journal of the Institute of Navigation*, 9 (1956), p. 51.
[80] J. R. Tanner, ed., *Samuel Pepys' Naval Minutes* p. 388.
[81] A. H. W. Robinson, *Marine Cartography in Great Britain*, p. 161.
[82] *Cal. Treasury Books*, 10, part 3, pp. 1219–20: 1693–96.

The village of Parkgate grew up at the point where the northern boundary of Neston Park came down to the river, some eight hundred yards upstream from the Beer House. This boundary was also the dividing line between the townships of Great Neston and Leighton, both being townships in the ancient parish of Neston. In formal usage, therefore, Parkgate had no official identity and its residents could be identified by the parish or township, just as the Parkgate anchorage could be referred to as Neston. Gradually the settlement became large enough to merit its own name, as a locality in its own right, and this occurred roughly in the first decade of the eighteenth century.

From the 1660s there were regular mentions of the anchorage, but apart from the buildings shown on Collins' chart, the first evidence of a Parkgate resident was recorded in 1694, when John Rylance, yeoman of Parkgate, was issued with a licence to marry Elizabeth Richardson.[83] This source, the marriage licences, yields only two more references to Parkgate in the eight years following.

Parkgate was named in the Neston churchwardens' accounts in 1702, when payment was made for 'carrying boards and spars from Parkgate to the schoolhouse'.[84] But the parish register did not name Parkgate until as late as 1711, with the record of the baptism of Alice Hancock.[85]

Apart from Customs activities, to be examined later, the only other record of residents so far found before 1710 is in the diary of Henry Prescott, who had a 'plentifull dinner' after a Confirmation service at Neston:[86]

> We sitt past 4, mount, call at Park Yate, where after 2 bottles good claret, remount, ride by the seaside . . .

Perhaps he visited the *White Lion*, which was said to have had a date tablet of 1708 on it.[87]

By these halting steps can the emergence of the village be traced. The growth must have been considerable: a pew allotment list of 1711 shows twenty-three names for Parkgate, over one-third of the

---

[83] W. F. Irvine, ed., *Marriage Licences granted in the Archdeaconry of Chester, 8, 1691–1700*, Record Soc. L. & C., 77 (1924), pp. 64, 109.

[84] Cheshire R.O., P 149/9/1.

[85] Cheshire R.O., P 149/1/2.

[86] John Addy, ed., *The Diary of Henry Prescott, 1*, Rec. Soc. L. & C., 127 (1987), p. 180.

[87] *Cheshire Sheaf*, April 1898, p. 46, item 204 (3rd series, vol 3).

number given for Great Neston and one-tenth of the whole parish of eight townships.[88] It is noteworthy that, on this list, Beerhouse is listed separately, with a single name.

By 1732, when we have for the first time an estate map for Neston and Parkgate, the village had between fifty and sixty houses, nearly half the size of its parent town.[89] Its success as a port for passengers had caused it to flourish.

### RESTRICTIONS ON TRAVEL

Although at common law the subject had a theoretical right to travel freely, the king had the power to prevent his subjects from leaving the realm without licence. This power was bolstered by statutes and orders from time to time, and until the control of foreign travel lapsed in the early eighteenth century, travellers to Ireland other than mariners would usually have needed a licence.[90]

The farmer of these licences in Wirral in 1634 was Patrick Craford, who complained that

> by the obstinate disobedience of owners and masters of ships, passengers are transported beyond seas, without taking the Oath of Allegiance or their names being registered.

He wanted to be able to bind shipmasters in £50, and innkeepers in £10, to ensure he got the names, and he wanted to keep the office of Clerk of the Passes in Neston.[91] Six years later his successor as Clerk of the Passes, Thomas Braddock, was accused of failing to send in the names of passengers or to pay his £50 a year.[92]

The restrictions on travellers were not solely legal ones, especially in troubled times. In 1645 [93] a traveller

> got as far as Neston on my way to Ireland. Our goods came down in boats, but have been here seized by a warrant . . . The reason is information that we were bringing some malignants' goods from Chester, which I protest to God we did not.

---

[88]  Cheshire R.O., DHL 12/1.
[89]  Mostyn (Bangor) 8699.
[90]  William Holdsworth, *History of English Law*, 10 (1938), p. 390.
[91]  *Cal. S.P. Dom., 1634–35* (1864), p. 146, 14 July 1634.
[92]  *Cal. S.P. Dom., 1640–41*, p. 367, para. 55.
[93]  H.M.C., *Earl of Egmont*, 1 (1905), p. 252, 28 April 1645.

A would-be supporter of James II,[94] just after that monarch had fled his country,

> rode over the sands to Chester, which is thirteen miles from Holywell . . . At Chester I alighted at the post-house, having found the gates of the city locked, and much difficulty in getting in . . .

From about 1690 there seems to have been less attempt at the regular control of travellers, but times of war could soon induce official nervousness: in 1710 there were fears of [95]

> French men and other suspicious persons going beyond the sea without passes from the Principal Secretary of State. You are to give orders to the Customs Officers not to suffer any passengers to go beyond sea without such a pass.

This order produced confusion and

> the stop of a great number of passengers at Parkgate bound for Ireland

who could get such a pass only in London.[96]

And so, as travellers steadily grew in numbers, the fact of travel became less suspicious and official attempts at control were allowed to lapse. It may be significant that the emergence of Parkgate as a village coincided with the easing of restrictions on travel, so that it was favourably placed for the explosion in the numbers travelling.

There was, however, at least one later occasion when passes were needed for travel: during the Jacobite invasion of 1745. An Irish adventurer called Bradstreet got himself employed as a government spy, initially to report on his fellow Irishmen in England but later, if he is to be believed, on the rebel army:[97]

> I waited on Mr St—e at the Cockpit, to get proper passports, without which there was no travelling. I got a pass, as a private gentleman, to go to Ireland, and to make Chester [where the rebels were supposed to be going] my road.

[94] R. H. Murray, ed., *Journal of John Stevens, 1689–91* (1912), p. 9.
[95] *Cal. Treasury Books* 24 part 2, p. 517 (25 Nov. 1710).
[96] P.R.O., T1/127 (19 Dec. 1710).
[97] G. S. Taylor, ed., *The Life and Uncommon Adventures of Captain Dudley Bradstreet* (1929), p. 118.

Figure 6. Anchorages on the Wirral shore of the Dee,
superimposed on Speed's map, 1612.

# 2 *The Dee Estuary and its Navigation*

In 1732, when Kinderley's Bill to improve the navigation of the Dee was presented to Parliament, the existing state of the river was the subject of many complaints:[1]

> For some time past the navigation hath been so lost, that ships have been forced to stop at Parkgate, eight miles below Chester towards the sea, and all goods and merchandizes exported and imported from and to Chester, are sent to and from Parkgate . . .

How long ago, from the evidence put forward in that year, had the navigation of the river to the city of Chester been 'lost'? How long was 'for some time past'? Apparently quite recently:[2]

> . . . of late the tides and west-winds have brought in such vast quantities of sand into the harbour, that it is choak'd up, and ships can get no further than Parkgate . . .

A witness to a Committee of the House of Commons was a little more specific:[3]

> Within their memory, no vessels besides boats could come to Chester but at the time of spring tides; but they have been told by ancient people that formerly ships of 100 or 150 tons could come to Chester.

So when were these times that the 'ancient people' remembered? Further back than forty-five years, apparently. In May 1687, Andrew Barry and others petitioned James II,[4]

---

[1] 'The Case of the Inhabitants of the County of Chester', B.L., 357 C.1.37.
[2] 'The Case of the Citizens of Chester', B.L., 816 M.8.38 (1732).
[3] Evidence of Captain Bell, *Journal of the House of Commons* 21 (24 Feb. 1733), p. 812.
[4] *Cal. Treasury Books* 10 part 3 (4 Oct. 1695) p. 1219.

setting forth that the River Dee was formerly navigable inso-
much that vessels of good burthen came up to the walls of
Chester Castle, but that by the violence of the tides of late years
great quantities of earth have been washed into the channel and
the same thereby rendered wholly incapable of navigation for
above 8 or 9 miles below Chester to the ruin of the trade of
that city . . .

Similarly, when Andrew Yarranton surveyed the estuary in 1674 he
reported:[5]

. . . finding the river choked with sands that a vessel of twenty
tuns could not come to that noble city, and the ships forc'd to
lye at Nesson in a very bad harbour . . . that the trade of
Chester is much decay'd, and gone to Leverpool . . .

Perhaps we should go back a hundred years, to a time when the New
Quay was being built:[6]

By reason of the flatts and shallows which in this day are in
the river of Dee, nere to Chester, the cytyzens of Chester are
constreyened to make them a wharf, 8 myle of, where shyps
may in more safety ride . . .

It does not matter how far back we go; we shall run into the recurring
myth of the golden age of the port of Chester. K. P. Wilson has
demonstrated the skilful use which the city of Chester made of this
myth in the fifteenth century, when a series of petitions managed to
elicit charters which successively cut the fee-farm due to the Crown
from £100 a year to £20.[7] These charters variously attributed the
decay of the port, due to the silting of the river, to forty years before
1445, sixty years before 1484, two hundred years before 1486.[8]
    The question of whether, indeed, Chester ever had a golden age as
a port, is beyond the scope of this study; yet to appreciate the

---

[5] Andrew Yarranton, *England's Improvement by Sea and Land* (1677),
p. 191.
[6] 'Certain verie rare observations of Chester', *Cheshire Sheaf*, 3rd series 22
(July 1925), p. 47, item 5232.
[7] K. P. Wilson, 'The port of Chester in the fifteenth century', *T.H.S.L.C.* 117
(1966), p. 1.
[8] R. H. Morris, *Chester in the Plantagenet and Tudor Reigns* (1894), pp.
511–12, 518, 521–2.

development of Parkgate we need to compare the ascertainable facts with the modern version of the myth, which runs something like this: in Roman and Norman times, shipping had open access to Chester itself, but that progressive silting of the river had caused the nearest anchorage to move downstream, to Shotwick, to Burton, to Neston and finally to Parkgate.[9]

The earliest surviving records of Dee anchorages in use over a considerable period suggests that all these places, and many more, were in use together, without any apparent shift downstream. The Chester Customs accounts, 1391–1566, show that wine or iron landed at Chester, Portpool (just outside Chester), Shotwick, Burton, Denhall, Neston, Gayton, Heswall, Redbank (identifiable as the anchorage later called Dawpool), and Point of Air.[10] So far from shifting down river, the most commonly used anchorages go the other way: from 1353 to 1492, Redbank was most commonly used; from 1488 to 1539, Burton and Denhall were the most popular.

It was at that time, the 1540s, that Chester began to build the New Haven at Neston in the vain hope of finding shelter on the exposed Wirral shore. It is noticeable that when Collins made his survey in 1686, he marked five anchorages inside the Dee estuary: at Dawpool, Beerhouse, Parkgate, Neston Key (if the rather obscure mark on his chart at this point is indeed an anchor) and Denhall. A list of ships taken in 1690 showed that then 'at home' there were ten ships at Denhall and thirteen ships at Neston Key and Parkgate.[11] The emergence of Parkgate in the seventeenth century, and its pre-eminence as a Dee anchorage in the eighteenth century, must be explained in terms other than the progressive silting of the estuary as a whole.

A much more accurate key to the navigation of the Dee is likely to be that provided in the preamble to the Act to Recover and Preserve the Navigation of the River Dee, 1732:[12]

> The said river not being navigable is chiefly owing to the breadth of the said sands, and to the shifting of the chanel from one side thereof to the other, as the winds and tides vary.

[9] For an example of this kind of reading, see Dorothy Sylvester, *A History of Cheshire* (1971), p. 52. She also supposes that the New Quay and Old Quay were two different places.
[10] K. P. Wilson, ed., *Chester Customs Accounts 1301–1566*, III, (1969), pp. 20–61.
[11] P.R.O., T1/11/69–76.
[12] 6 Geo II c.30 (1732), para. 1.

This is not to say that the river did not silt up, for anchorages like Portpool and Shotwick clearly fell out of use. But it is to suggest that the theory of the river progressively silting from Chester to Neston is not supported by satisfactory evidence, and that a more likely explanation is that the Dee always was a shallow and unpredictable river, which became of less value to the Chester economy with the secular increase in the size of ships; and that the constantly shifting sands of Dee altered the suitability of different anchorages from time to time.

Despite the jeremiads, there was the possibility that ships could reach Chester itself, as we have seen when considering Edward King and the Earl of Clarendon. According to petitioners in 1689,[13]

> Vessels of about 200 tuns do come up with the tide within a league or thereabouts of the city of Chester, and boats of about 15 or 20 tuns come constantly up to the very walls of the same.

Two hundred tons was large for the Dee at any time, and larger than those which normally used Parkgate in the eighteenth century. If a league is taken to be three miles, that would be just outside Blacon Head, possibly the anchorage known as Portpool, and much nearer Chester than Shotwick. At roughly the same time, Celia Fiennes visited Chester:[14]

> there they have a little dock and build shipps of 200 tunn I saw some on the stocks.

A more accurate guide to the normal state of navigation at Chester may be given by a document already referred to, a list of seamen and sometimes their ships as well, taken in Chester Water in 1690.[15] 353 men are named altogether. At Chester itself were 24 men, of which 19 are 'labourers in lighter boats belonging to the river at Chester'. 80 men were listed as living on the Welsh side, from Bagillt to Llanasa; 55 men on ten ships were at Denhall; 101 men on thirteen ships were 'at Neston Key and the Parkgate near adjoining'; and 104 men were listed for various townships in Wirral, including a further ten for Neston.

[13] 'The Case of the Gentlemen, Freeholders and other the Inhabitants of the County of Flint', B.L., 1888 c.11.1.
[14] C. Morris, ed., *The Illustrated Journeys of Celia Fiennes 1685–c.1712* (1982), p. 157.
[15] P.R.O., T1/11/69–76.

This evidence suggests that, except perhaps on the highest tides, goods for or from seagoing ships were carried on lighters between Chester and one of the anchorages. We have seen that this happened with calfskins in 1610, and it was the normal practice in 1732:[16]

> . . . all goods and merchandizes exported and imported from and to Chester, are sent to and from Parkgate, either by land carriage at an expence of 6s. per ton, or by small boats at an expence of 2s. per ton.

It was to alter this situation that Chester sought to control the flow of the river, culminating in Kinderley's New Cut, opened in 1737.

If, therefore, Parkgate was one of several anchorages in use in the late seventeenth century, why did this particular one flourish and support a substantial village? Was it because it provided a good harbour, particularly suitable for passengers? The answer appears to be a resounding no, for Parkgate was just as poor and exposed an anchorage as any other in the estuary. Andrew Yarranton described Neston as 'a very bad harbour, where the ships receive much damage'.[17] In 1707 the Chester City Council applied [18]

> to the Commissioners of her Majesty's Customs that a place may be appointed for landing and discharging of goods on this side of Burton Head, where ships might be more secure under shelter of the Head, than they usually do at Parkgate.

Notice the striking implication that it was apparently quite possible to anchor ships and land goods, as late as 1707, on the Chester side of Burton Head, and that the reasons for not doing so were administrative rather than navigational. We shall examine the role of the Customs later.

Three weeks later the City Council expressed its opinion of Parkgate in even stronger terms:[19]

> This House, taking up their consideration that the place called Parkgate by the removal of the sands which heretofore were a

---

[16] See note 1 (above.)
[17] Andrew Yarranton, *England's Improvement by Sea and Land*, pp. 191–2.
[18] Chester City R.O., AB/3/154, 16 Sept. 1707.
[19] *ibid*, 5 Dec. 1707, AB/3/155; ML/4/630 (26 Jan 1708).

safeguard for the ships lying there, is now become a very dangerous place for ships to lie in for lading and unloading of goods.

And this was on the eve of Parkgate's superiority as a port. Nor did things get better, for twenty-five years later this evidence was given by Captain Stevens, and confirmed by Captain Samuel Bell, to a House of Commons committee:[20]

Parkgate is a very bad and dangerous harbour for ships to lie at, they being very much exposed to the winds, and their bottoms are often damaged by running on ground, the same being a hard sort of marle: and that one of the times it cost him £60 to launch her and take out her lading . . .

A later witness, Captain John Matthews, said,[21]

Vessels cannot harbour with safety at Parkgate, the channel being uncertain and shallow.

We shall see when we examine the role of the Royal Yachts in the estuary's history, that there were only two places in the Dee where the water was deep enough for ships to ride at anchor at low tide: Dawpool and Beerhouse hole, which were two of the five anchorages on Collins' chart. The other three anchorages were above the low water mark, so that ships using the Dee not only had to be of a small size, but of a special construction. In 1689 the Treasury ordered the Customs to clear ships in the king's service free of charge, and to prevent fraud,[22]

directed the Commissary of the Provisions for the Army at Chester to order the ships employed in the King's service to take in all their stores at Parkgate, New Quay or Denwall and to present their bills of lading there.

The collector of Customs at Chester pointed out that this order was not practicable for all the ships concerned, because[23]

for ships of great burthen which cannot when laden lie aground without prejudice, Parkgate is not so convenient. But that ships

---

[20] *Journal of the House of Commons*, 21 p. 812 (24 Feb. 1732).

[21] *ibid*, 22, p. 44 (16 Feb. 1733).

[22] *Cal. Treasury Books* 9, part 1 (1931), p. 284 (17 Oct. 1689).

[23] *ibid*, p. 300 (12 Nov. 1689).

of Chester, Liverpool and Whitehaven are not of the [said] sort, for they are built chiefly for the coal trade and are used to lie aground and for such ships Park Gate is most convenient . . . He therefore desires that a proviso be added to the order that such ships as cannot so lie aground, by reason of their burden or fashion of build, they may take their lading to Hoylake.

This is why ships too large for the Dee such as Naval men o' war awaiting convoys, and the large fleet movements to Ireland in 1689–90, used the deep water anchorage at Hilbre or Hoylake, just outside the mouth of the estuary.

A century later a similar warning accompanied the chart of Liverpool Bay by Laurie and Whittle, in 1794:[24]

Vessels must lie aground on the beach below the houses [at Parkgate] to be safe; for though there is 2½ fathoms in the channel off the town, and 3 fathoms a little above the town, yet the stream of the tide is so strong, and the anchor-ground so weak, that the strength of the stream would make a vessel drag her anchor.

The need to be able to lie aground governed the choice of the *Monmouth* rather than the *Merlin* yacht for these waters in 1675.[25] When the passenger packet the *King George* was wrecked on Hoyle Bank in 1806, local opinion was said to hold that her build was too narrow or 'crank' for these waters, since 'she could not take the ground with any degree of safety'.[26]

However, the unsuitability of Parkgate as an anchorage is relative to the suitability of other places, for the North West was not well provided with natural harbours. The Lords Justices of Ireland did not think much of Liverpool in 1691:[27]

. . . wee have ordered Captaine William Wright, Comander of the Monmouth yacht, to sayle to Chester water . . . in regard it may be inconvenient for their Majesties' service that she should put into the harbour of Leverpoole for fear of being

---

[24] Admiralty, Hydrographic Department, chart no. 682 Dg. The sailing directions quoted by C. Armour, 'The Trade of Chester and the State of the Dee navigation 1600–1800' (Ph.D. thesis, London, 1956), p. 106.
[25] See the next chapter on the Royal Yachts.
[26] *Cheshire Sheaf*, 1st series II, p. 269, item 1574 (April 1881).
[27] *ibid*, p. 133, item 2200 (April 1884).

wind bound therein, wee therefore think fitt hereby to desire that you will as soon as possible cause a small vessel to be sent about to Chester water with such stores as aforesaid, to prevent any such inconvenience or prejudice which may happen to the Monmouth yacht by her saileing into the harbour of Leverpoole.

Nor was Holyhead necessarily considered to be much better. In 1660 Captain Samuel Sharland of the *Fox* complained, when ordered to sail between Chester Water and Holyhead, that [28]

Holyhead Bay is a very bad and dangerous place to ride in at any time.

It was just as necessary for a ship to lie aground at Holyhead as at Parkgate, and we shall see more presently of Pepys' remark that [29]

the Merlin [is] judged not fit through the rankness of her keel to lie on ground at Holyhead.

Even in 1808 when Holyhead harbour was [30]

one of the rude accommodations of nature, in which the helping hand of man has not interfered,

the packet captains complained that when the wind blew in certain directions they had to run aground in the inner harbour, while the engineer George Taylor reported that Holyhead was [31]

a very inconvenient and dangerous place for passengers and their baggage at all times of the tide as the packets cannot come to a quay.

During the eighteenth century, Holyhead no more had a quay than did Parkgate.

In 1670 leave was granted to Chester to bring in a bill to improve the river navigation, following a petition by the mayor and citizens

---

[28] *Cal. S.P. Dom., 1659–60* (1886), p. 546 (16 April 1660).
[29] J. R. Tanner, ed., *Naval MSS in the Pepysian Library*, 3 (1909), pp. 44–7.
[30] George Nicholson, *The Cambrian Traveller's Guide* (1813), pp. 647 ff.
[31] M. Elis-Williams, *Packet to Ireland* (1984), p. 28. The report was in 1808.

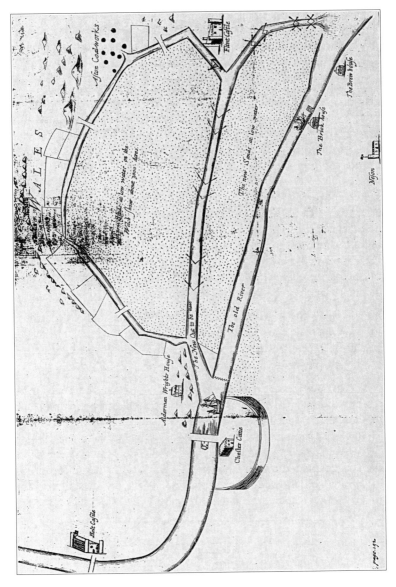

Figure 7. From Andrew Yarranton, *England's Improvement
by Sea and Land*, 1677.

in 1666.[32] Andrew Yarranton seems to have been the first person to suggest how the river could be tamed, in 1677:[33]

> And if it were made to Chester navigable by a New Cut, as is in the map prescribed, there would be three thousand acres of land gained out of the sea, and made rich land . . .

The river then, of course, ran on the English side of the estuary. His map proposed a canal to be cut across the sands in the direction of Flint Castle, with another waterway going round Saltney Marsh and serving Aston coalworks. The map is of interest to Parkgate (which is not named on it) because it shows Neston Key and 'The Brick House' or Key House next to it, while further down the river is shown 'The Brew house'. In every other respect the map is a mere sketch and does not represent a serious proposal; the short paragraph referring to the Dee forms the last page of a book which seeks to defeat the Dutch without fighting, through bolstering Britain's economy. Yarranton's proposed method of doing so was to improve the navigation of her rivers. But the paragraph does highlight the aspect of land reclamation. In 1689 those who claimed freehold of the sands or marsh land on the Welsh side stated that [34]

> They may inclose as much of the Commons and soil of the said freeholders as may come to £30 or £40,000 per annum, which will be more profitable to Mr Gell and the City of Chester, than the navigation.

The proposal to implement some such plan as Yarranton's by Andrew Barry in 1687 has already been noticed, but he relinquished his claim to a London merchant called Francis Gell, and in the course of all this, an inquiry was held at Neston in February 1693 which determined that the land overflowed by tides on the Wirral side of the river belonged to the Crown.[35] Gell's petition obtained an Act in 1700 which allowed the mayor and citizens of Chester to make the river navigable, but although 'several considerable sums of

---

[32] *Cal. S.P. Dom., 1670* (1895), p. 87; *Cal. S.P. Dom., Charles II 1665–66* (1864), p. 436, 11 June 1666.
[33] Andrew Yarranton, *England's Improvement by Sea and Land*, pp. 191–2.
[34] See note 13 above.
[35] *Cal. Treasury Books* 10 part 3, pp. 1219–20. This decision was overturned by the Act of 1732 (see note 37).

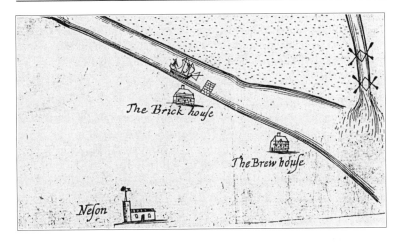

Figure 8. The Brick house (Quay house) and the Brew House
(Beerhouse) from Andrew Yarranton's map, 1677.

money have been laid out and expended', the permitted time of
twenty-one years ran out with little accomplished.[36]

It was Nathaniel Kinderley, an engineer from Lincolnshire who
had constructed drainage in the Fens, that devised the scheme which
was actually carried out. Published in 1732, 'An Act to Recover and
Preserve the Navigation of the River Dee', appointed him and his
successors[37]

> to make and keep the said River Dee navigable from the sea to
> a certain point within the Liberties of the City of Chester called
> Wilcox Point, in such a manner that there shall be 16 foot of
> water in every part of the said river at a moderate spring tide,
> for ships and vessels to come and go to and from the said City.

Although the depth of sixteen feet proved too much to achieve, a
depth of twelve feet or so at ordinary spring tides was provided, an
immense improvement on anything that Chester had known, perhaps ever. Telford wrote in 1823:[38]

---

[36] Gell's Act was 11 & 12 William III c.24, and is summarised in the preamble
to Kinderley's Act of 1732 (6 Geo II c.30).
[37] 6 Geo II c. 30.
[38] F. Webster, 'The River Dee reclamation and the effect upon navigation',
*Transactions of the Liverpool Engineering Society* 51 (1930), pp. 80–1.

Upon the whole the progress of the river improvement, as regards navigation, seems to have proceeded with all the success that could either have been expected or hoped for.

If from a navigational point of view, seen from Chester, the undertaking was successful, so was the parallel aim of land reclamation. Apart from duties payable on goods sent by way of the New Cut, Kinderley and his successors were granted 'all that sand, soil, ground, marsh and salt grass' known as the White Sands, between certain named points about Chester and the sea. The River Dee Company, formed in 1740, began the task of enclosure in 1744, and by 1916 the total land reclaimed from the estuary amounted to 18½ square miles.[39]

Seen from Parkgate, however, Kinderley's proposals seemed in 1732 to be ominous. Thirty-five masters of ships and traders living at or near Parkgate, including for example John Wolstenholme, the landlord of the Beerhouse, and Samuel Ansdell, ship carpenter, went to the expense of making a petition to parliament. It may have been very expensive—the Corporation of Liverpool was shocked to receive a solicitor's bill for £240 for their own petition.[40] The Parkgate petition said,[41]

That there is a Bill now depending in this Honourable House to recover and preserve the navigation of the River Dee, which if it passed into a law and any thing be done in consequence thereof to alter the channel as proposed by the said Bill, your petitioners apprehend that the greatest part of the water will be thereby diverted from Parkgate which is at present the safest and most convenient place on the said river for ships and vessels to lie or anchor in, and that the passage thereto will be choaked and destroyed to the great prejudice of the navigation of the said river and the ruine of your petitioners.

Their landlord, Sir Roger Mostyn, was involved in two petitions; one with twenty-five other landowners because 'a new method of determining property [is] introduced', and one with Liverpool because

[39] G. Lloyd, 'The canalization of the River Dee in 1737', *Flintshire Historical Society Transactions* 23 (1967–68), p. 40.
[40] Sir James Picton, ed., [Liverpool] *Municipal Archives and Records* (1836, reprinted 1886), p. 92.
[41] House of Lords Record Office, 1732 petitions.

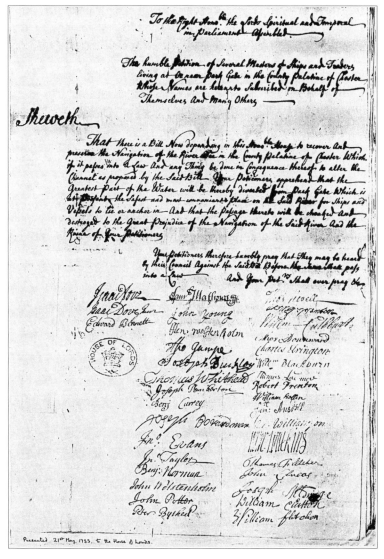

Figure 9. The Humble Petition of Several Masters of Ships and Traders living at or near Park Gate, 1733 (reduced; reproduced by kind permission of the Clerk of the Records, House of Lords).

they feared the Cut would prejudice the trade of Liverpool and Parkgate and destroy Hoyle Lake.[42] As well as these petitions against the bill, three witnesses with experience of Parkgate were heard in its favour: these were Captains Stevens, Bell and Matthews, whose evidence that Parkgate was an unsatisfactory anchorage we have already examined. The chief allies of the inhabitants of Parkgate in opposing the bill were the cheesemongers, who did not want to pay increased tolls. They had been accustomed to loading cheese on to ships at Parkgate and Dawpool, as indeed they continued to do, and [43]

> it is apprehended the new intended navigation will very much spoil the usual loading places at Parkgate and Dawpool, and render it unsafe if not impossible for ships to ride there.

Apart from those whose interests were at stake, opposition came from expert observers who thought that the results of such a major alteration to the natural water flow would be disastrous. Thomas Badeslade argued from his experience of the Kent towns Lympne and Rye that the new canal would be insufficiently scoured by fresh water or tide, and [44]

> it will soon be silted up to the height of the other sands, insomuch that in a year or two's time no ship can be brought to Parkgate.

A chart made by John Mackay of the Dee in 1732 as evidence against the bill had written on it,[45]

> Between Chester, Flint and Parkgate, 7,000 or 8,000 acres are proposed to be gained from the sea, by which means no less than two hundred millions of tuns of tyde will be prevented from flowing there (twice in 24 hours) which on the reflex acquireth the greater velocity to scour and keep open the lake and bar. Whether these ill consequences (which must certainly attend the present undertaking) are not more likely to destroy the present navigation in Hyle Lake and the River Dee, rather

[42] Mostyn (Bangor) 7263.
[43] B.L., 357 C.1.37. The 'cheesemongers' were a loose confederation of London merchants. See G. E. Fussell, 'The London cheesemongers in the 18th century', in *Economic History* I (1929), p. 395.
[44] B.L., 190 D.15.1.
[45] Bodleian Library, Gough maps 3; F. Webster, 'River Dee', p. 79.

than recover or preserve a better, is humbly submitted to the Right Hon. the House of Lords.

These submissions were of no avail: the bill passed the Commons in May 1733, the Lords in June and received the Royal assent on 13th June.[46] There were political overtones to the passage of the River Dee Bill:[47]

> They write from Chester on the 19th, that the day before Hugh Williams Esq. coming down from London, was met and ushered into town by vast numbers of gentlemen and citizens, who thanked him for his services in getting the River Dee Bill pass'd.

Hugh Williams, M.P. for Anglesey and a sponsor of the Bill, attempted twice, vainly, to be elected for Chester in the Whig interest, in 1722 and 1734. His stage-managed return to Chester represented a hopeless attempt by the local Whigs to use the Bill, ostensibly a cross-party measure, as a lever to oust the Tories from the control of Chester—'Down with the Grosvenors and hey for the Navigation!'[48]

Not only the Whigs, but the citizens of Chester heralded a new dawn of Chester's trade and prosperity. The work of construction took three years, and the water was turned into the New Cut on 3rd April 1737.[49]

The immediate result was that the water, released from its new course at Golftyn on the Welsh side, came straight across the estuary to Parkgate where it resumed its former course. While that course persisted, which it did for between sixty and seventy years, Parkgate was safe. However, the route of the river across the estuary was unstable: a description just after the New Cut was opened said,[50]

---

[46] *Journal of the House of Commons* 22, p. 136; *Journals of the House of Lords*, 1733, vol. 24, pp. 304, 310.

[47] *Dublin Journal*, 30 June 1733.

[48] S. W. Baskerville, 'The establishment of the Grosvenor interest in Chester 1710–48', *J.C.A.S.*, 63 (1980) esp. pp. 71–80; W. R. Williams, *The Parliamentary History of the Principality of Wales, 1541–1895* (1895), p. 6. For an account of a similar Whig cavalcade into Chester three months earlier, see Henry Taylor, 'An unpublished diary of the Rev. Peter Walkden in 1733–43', *J.C.A.S.*, new series 3 (1888–90), p. 154.

[49] G. Lloyd, 'Canalization' p. 36.

[50] S. Fearon and J. Eyes, *A Description of the Sea Coast of England and Wales* (1738).

> From Parkgate to the entrance of the new river leading up to Chester the channel is so subject to alter, that no description can be given that will be of any use.

When John Eyes drew a chart of the Dee and New Cut in 1740, the only anchorage marks he showed inside the estuary were three at Parkgate, though none at Beerhouse hole which seems to have been temporarily out of use, and one at Dawpool.[51] The object of the River Dee Company's engineers was henceforth to rationalise the channel through the lower estuary so that it flowed through the Mostyn deep, towards the Welsh shore, and away from Parkgate. The first attempt was a stone causeway from the end of the original training bank to the New (Connah's) Quay, which can be seen on Boydell's map of 1771.[52] This may have helped to stabilise the channel but did not affect the flow to Parkgate. Further groynes were put in place, after 1800 principally under the direction of Thomas Telford, but the details have not survived.[53] Between 1819 and 1823 considerable works were undertaken, including cutting away part of the natural rock at Connah's Quay and continuing the stone wall, again by Telford; but before then the damage to Parkgate had largely been done. There are no charts or written references to register these navigational changes, which can be inferred only, and uncertainly, from the gradual drift of shipping away from Parkgate. As there were other factors contributing to Parkgate's decline, which probably took effect sooner, it is safer to suggest that the deliberate alteration in the course of the river finally put paid to the Parkgate anchorage by 1815. As Hanshall wrote in 1823,[54]

> About fifteen years ago Parkgate presented every appearance of the bustle of a seaport, there being at that time five or six stoutly-built packets, besides other vessels, engaged in the trade with Ireland. At the present time this, as a packet station, is completely neglected, and no vessels of burthen can come within a considerable distance of the quay, although but a few years ago they rode alongside it.

[51] John Eyes, *A Survey of the River Dee* (1740).
[52] Thomas Boydell, *A Plan of . . . the Lands and Premises of the River Dee Company* (1771).
[53] F. Webster, 'The River Dee reclamation', p. 88.
[54] J. H. Hanshall, *History of the County Palatine of Cheshire* (1823), p. 641.

In 1775 a disaster struck at Parkgate when two of its ships were lost in a great storm. From this disaster there stemmed the Act for Erecting a Lighthouse near the Port of Chester, which also provided for the licensing of pilots in the Dee; and the register of pilots provides useful clues, in the shift from English to Welsh pilots, to the relative decline of Parkgate.

The ever-changing sands of the unreliable Dee had probably always made a pilot desirable for those masters who did not have local knowledge. There were pilots before the 1776 Act, but they were not regulated and our knowledge of them is scanty. In 1724 an unnamed man, 'a stranger, a pilot, who dyed at Mr Urmston's at Parkgate', was buried at Neston.[55] A group of surviving Acts of Protest from the 1760s, in which ships' masters made sworn statements to a magistrate as evidence of damage to cargo or ship, contains several references to pilots. Two of them are named: the master of the *Northern Lass* of Dublin, Robert Hudson, had taken coal on board at Ness Colliery before taking a pilot, George Norman, to conduct him from the colliery to Dawpool, where he was to load further cargo before sailing for Philadelphia. Norman succeeded in running the ship ashore at Dawpool and received the master's blame.[56] The brig *Providence* had sailed from Dublin to Chester in ballast, intending to load lead, when the pilot, Alexander Cavan, 'wilfully ran the vessel on to the Welsh shore' whence he came to Parkgate, much damaged.[57]

The two ships lost in 1775 were the *Trevor*, Captain William Totty, and the *Nonpareil*, Captain Samuel Davies, and their loss caused a commercial as well as a personal tragedy at Parkgate:[58]

> Captain Davies . . . sailed with Major Caulfield and family and several other families; it is thought not less than a hundred persons in all besides the major's coach and horses. Mrs Davies says her husband went out in very low spirits as he did not like the appearance of the weather, but the major and some other passengers pressed him to put out; which he did and was twice put back but got off a third time. We are just told that captain Davies' boat is taken in with many dead bodies.

[55] Neston parish register, 6 Sept. 1724.
[56] John Glegg, 'Acts of Protest, 1762–68' (University of Liverpool, Sidney Jones Library, Special Collections), p. 58 (19 Aug. 1764).
[57] *ibid*, p. 126 (12 Nov. 1767).
[58] *Freeman's Journal*, Dublin, 27 Oct. 1775.

But life had to go on, without much delay. Two weeks later this advertisement appeared:[59]

> Ann Davies, of Parkgate, widow of Samuel Davies, late master of the Nonpareil, begs leave to inform the nobility and gentry travelling between England and Ireland by way of Parkgate, and the public in general, that she continues the business of an inn at her house, the sign of the King's Arms, in Parkgate.

Terrible though the loss of a hundred passengers was (and they included forty-three vagrants from the Neston House of Correction[60]) the loss of the *Trevor* with thirty lives and an extremely valuable cargo caused a greater stir. She had on board East India goods which had come from London by land,[61]

> also £6,000 in specie, besides silks, woollen cloths, jewels and other things, to the amount of between £30,000 and £40,000.

The estate steward who organised the collection of the cargo as it washed ashore on the Lancashire coast, James Standen, earned so much gratitude that he was granted the freedoms of both Chester and Dublin. On the other hand, nineteen persons were arrested for robbing the bodies of the dead cast on to the Flint shore.[62]

The same storm of 1775 caused the loss or distress of many other ships, including the *Sally* and the *Elizabeth* which were damaged at or near Parkgate. As the *Nonpareil* was lost on Hoyle Bank and the *Trevor* near the Lancashire coast, neither would have benefited from any navigational aids. Yet the disaster was taken as the opportunity to provide such aids, which in turn could be expected to restore confidence in Dee shipping.

Four sea-lights had already been erected on the Wirral peninsula, at Leasowe in 1763 and at Hoylake in 1764, whilst a lighthouse was built at Bidston in 1771.[63] For fear of confusion with these lights, the mayor of Liverpool opposed the building of a lighthouse on the Dee.[64] That was the proposal put to a public meeting on 24 November 1775 in

---

[59] *Chester Chronicle*, 11 Dec. 1775.
[60] Cheshire R.O., QJF 204/1.
[61] *Chester Chronicle*, 30 Oct. 1775.
[62] *ibid*, 4 April 1777; 6 Nov. 1775.
[63] G. I. Hawkes, 'The Point of Ayr Lighthouse', *Maritime Wales* 9 (1985), p. 32. Two lights were provided at each place.
[64] *ibid*, p. 35.

Chester, chaired by Alexander Schomberg, the commander of the R.Y. *Dorset*, and attended by seven ships' captains amongst others. A board was formed to obtain an Act of Parliament for the provision of two lighthouses, buoys and landmarks. The proposal [65]

> has met with great encouragement at Parkgate and Neston, by a handsome subscription in aid towards applying to parliament for an Act.

The Act was duly passed in 1776 [66] and a lighthouse at the Point of Ayr was opened in September 1777.[67] The lighthouse itself does not further concern our story except as regards its name. Alexander Schomberg, in accepting the command of the lord lieutenant's yacht, had set aside his chance of further promotion in the Royal Navy.[68] He was the leader in obtaining the Lighthouse Act and he seems to have regarded it as his chance of immortality. He was knighted by the lord lieutenant in 1777, but he hoped that his name would become a geographical one:[69]

> my patience is quite exhausted. There has been no step yet taken to name the Light of Air as it was intended and recommended by the Earls of Sandwich [First Lord] and Buckingham [Lord Lieutenant] . . . I intreat you will send an official letter or order to the Committee at Chester that the light may be named on the charts, in the writings and by the navigators, the Schomberg Light and Lighthouse.

The committee in Chester supported him, Trinity House raised no objection, and while Sir Alexander continued to sail in and out of Parkgate, the lighthouse was known as the Schomberg Air Light. He died in 1804, and after this, perhaps when the original lighthouse was replaced by Trinity House in 1819, it became the Point of Ayr Light and Schomberg's name was dropped. As well as the lighthouse, the Trust was concerned with buoys and pilots. Buoys were necessary on the unstable channel between Parkgate and the New Cut:[70]

[65] *Chester Chronicle*, 18 Dec. 1775.
[66] 16 Geo III c.61. The Act appointed trustees to implement its provisions.
[67] G. I. Hawkes *op. cit.*, p. 36.
[68] See the next chapter, on the Royal Yachts.
[69] Point of Air Lighthouse Trust, Minute Book (Chester City R.O., QAP/1, July 1779.) The modern spelling is 'Ayr'.
[70] *ibid*, 19 Dec. 1775.

for the banks shift so often the pilots are obliged to fix empty casks as temporary buoys before they dare venture to bring up any large vessels.

The trustees were also given the power to regulate the use of pilots. The Parkgate pilots may not have been in good public standing at that time, as one of them, John Wright, was tried though acquitted of murder in 1775.[71] The Act gave the trustees the right to examine and license pilots in the Dee, to fine anyone acting as a pilot without their licence, and to require ships entering the estuary to use pilots or to pay them instead. If a master refused a pilot's services, the pilot was nevertheless required to lead the vessel with his boat as far as Dawpool or Parkgate. There was one important exception:[72]

This Act shall not extend to prevent or hinder the master or other person having the command of any ship or vessel in the coast-trade, or trading to or from Ireland, from conducting or piloting his own ship or vessel into or out of the said port of Chester, without being subject to the payment of the said rates for pilotage . . .

The majority of the ships in the Dee fell into these categories.

The first pilots to be licensed, in 1776, were all from Parkgate and all named Wright: Joseph, John, William and Samuel. During the next thirty years most of the pilots came from Parkgate or Chester, with a few from Dawpool. The first pilot from the Welsh side was licensed in 1803, from Connah's Quay. By 1823 the great majority of the pilots lived on the Welsh side.[73]

An interesting relic of the Parkgate pilots survives in Liverpool, at the offices of the Mersey Docks & Harbour Company. It is a glazed earthenware jug, holding ten pints, typical of Liverpool's Herculaneum pottery. On one side is painted the boat of a Dee pilot, single-masted, cutter rigged with a yellow hull. It is flying the official pilot's flag: four lines through the centre divide it into eight parts, coloured blue and white alternately—'a flagg gyronny of eight argent and azure'. (The Liverpool pilot's flag, established after the Liverpool Pilot Act of 1766, was halved horizontally, white and red.) Below the spout is painted:

---

[71] *Chester Chronicle*, 7 Aug. 1775.
[72] 16 Geo II c.61 (p. 1414).
[73] Chester City R.O., QAP/1.

Banrad Rilton
Pilot 1805
Parkgate

The jug commemorates Barnard Relton or Railton (perhaps the pottery painter could not read), mariner of Parkgate, born about 1755, who was first licensed as a Dee pilot in 1787. He was regularly re-licensed every three years until 1807, and died within the two years following. No reason for honouring him with this jug in 1805 has yet emerged, either from the Trust Minute Book or the *Chester Chronicle*.

To understand Parkgate's emergence and pre-eminence in the eighteenth century, we must look at the other anchorages in use in the Dee at the same time, their function, and any reasons that can be suggested for a failure to develop as Parkgate did. We shall now consider Neston Key and Denhall, Dawpool and Hoylake.

Neston Key and Denhall are similar in that both were in use at the end of the seventeenth century as Parkgate was emerging; both disappeared from the records as Parkgate became established in the first years of the eighteenth century; and both were prevented from any possible recovery by the New Cut in 1737 which sealed the fate of any anchorage up river from Parkgate on the Cheshire side, with the exception of Ness Colliery quay. No houses grew up round Neston Key except one: the Key House. The spelling 'quay' came into use in the early eighteenth century, following the French 'quai' (which represents the earlier pronunciation in English), no doubt to distinguish the word from the key that locks.[74] In Cheshire we find 'key' in general use until about 1760, when 'quay' becomes usual in educated use. A wood-frame version of the house existed in 1599,[75] but it was the brick version, marked on Yarranton's map as 'Brick House' in 1674, which seems to have been an inn in the 1680s:[76]

---

[74] *Oxford English Dictionary.*
[75] The wood-frame house, Chester City R.O., TAO/1, pp. 141–2; Yarranton (see note 5, above).
[76] Col. T. Bellingham's diary, 12 Nov. 1689—*Cheshire Sheaf*, 4th series, 3 (July 1968), p. 25.

Figure 10. The Parkgate pilot jug (reproduced by permission of the Mersey Docks and Harbour Co.)

> We made a very fayre passage, and landed at Nesson about 7
> att night, and lay at the Key House, at George Eaton's.

Unlike the Key itself, the Key House did not belong to the City of
Chester which owned no land on the shore. The house belonged to
the Cottinghams of Little Neston. When Peter Ryder, son-in-law of
the George Eaton who seems to have been an innkeeper in the
quotation above, took a lease of the building in 1700, the owner
Charles Cottingham imposed a covenant not to erect any building
within a hundred yards.[77] There would seem to have been a policy
of non-development which contrasts with the active development by
the Mostyn family which we shall see at Parkgate. One may suppose,
too, that building a stone pier into the river at right angles to the flow
of water was certain to cause silting beside it. At Parkgate no sea wall
or landing stage was built until its great shipping days were nearly
over. The chief advantage of Neston Key, that it was near the town
of Neston, was just as true of Parkgate; and as the Key lost its
advantage by man-induced silting, so was Parkgate gaining it by
development, with the added advantage of proximity to Beerhouse
hole.

There may also have been a difficulty of land access. The map of
the Neston anchorage in Chapter One shows that to reach Chester
from the Key, one had to follow the winding road now called Old
Quay Lane. This route was necessarily winding because the road was
sandwiched between one of Neston's town fields on the inland side,
and swampy ground, known as The Moors, on the river side.

Very little has been recorded about the anchorage at Denhall. It
lies just down river from Burton, and as a locality it lies partly in
Burton township and partly in Ness. We have seen that both Burton
and Denhall (which probably represent two ends of the same
anchorage) were in constant use in the late fifteenth and early sixteenth centuries. Burton had been important enough to have gained
a charter for a weekly market and an annual fair in 1299,[78] while a
hospital existed at Denhall for the relief of 'poor men, travellers
arriving from Ireland, and others', between 1238 and 1495.[79] But

---

[77] Cheshire R.O., DHL 3/9, 11.
[78] *Calendar of Charter Rolls, 1257–1300*, see P. H. W. Booth, ed., *Burton in Wirral, a History* (1984), p. 10.
[79] H. E. Savage, ed., *The Great Register of Lichfield Cathedral* (1926), see P. H. W. Booth, *Burton*, p. 28.

Burton had long since dwindled to the predictable round of an agricultural village. One hears occasionally that ships were much higher up the river: in 1698 Robert Boswell of Dublin had some goods stolen from on board the *James Boat* while it lay at Great Saughall, halfway between Burton Head and Chester;[80] while a storm-blown ship was unloading at Shotwick as late as 1808.[81] In 1689 Denhall was mentioned with New Key and Parkgate as a place where ships in the Royal service should be cleared by Customs,[82] and the next year ten ships were listed as being there—six ships 'of Chester' and four from further away including London.[83] However, nothing further was heard of Denhall and it may be supposed that changes in the river channel made it less suitable. Collins showed it as an anchorage but Eyes in 1740 did not.

Dawpool is the most interesting of the alternatives to Parkgate because it was in use at the same time, but came to nothing. While known as Redbank, the anchorage had been in constant use between 1353 and 1492,[84] and Leland identified Redbank as approximately the place later called Dawpool:[85]

> About a 3 miles lower [than Neston] is a place caullid the Redde Bank. And ther half a mile withyn the land is a village caullid Thrustington [Thurstaston].

The actual distance along the shore is five miles. Dawpool was often mentioned from the mid seventeenth century when it offered the deepest water inside the estuary. In 1665, for example,[86]

> A Dutch caper anchored in Chester Water but Captain Rooth of the Dartmouth, being in Dawpool, has gone to look after him.

We shall see presently that the Royal Yacht *Mary* seems to have made Dawpool her regular anchorage. In 1670,[87]

---

[80] Cheshire R.O., QJF 126/4/41.
[81] *Chester Chronicle*, 14 Oct. 1808.
[82] *Cal. Treasury Books*, 9, part 1 (17 Oct. 1689), p. 284.
[83] P.R.O., T1/11/69–76.
[84] K. P. Wilson, ed., *Chester Customs Accounts 1301–1566*, 111 (1969), pp. 21–61.
[85] L. Toulmin-Smith, ed., *The Itinerary in Wales of John Leland*, c.*1536–39* (1906), p. 91.
[86] *Cal. S.P. Dom., 1664–65* (1863), p. 422 (12 June 1665).
[87] *Cal. S.P. Ireland, 1669–70* (1910), p. 1112 (23 April 1670).

Lord Berkeley arrived at Chester on Monday 18 April. On Tuesday morning, being anxious to get to his post as soon as possible, he left all his equipage, plate and goods to follow as they could, and went to Dawpool and on board the Monmouth and Mary yachts with his wife, children and gentlemen of his train.

A later yacht, the R.Y. *Charlotte*, also favoured Dawpool, and between 1701 and 1709 her commander, Captain Breholt, often landed his passengers at Parkgate before mooring in the deeper water at Dawpool.[88] For a while passengers used to land at Dawpool as an alternative to Parkgate, perhaps because one sometimes had to wait for the next tide to get between the two. In 1718 the primate of All Ireland landed at Dawpool from the R.Y. *Dublin* although she continued to Parkgate.[89] A similar thing in reverse was recorded by Henry Prescott in 1694:[90]

> I go to see the Bishop of Killaloe's family at Neston. Alderman Allen and I see the children on board the Pearl. Shee casts anchor and waits Mr Tenyson at Dawpool about 12. I go on board again, Mr Murry with us. We return by the Moon to Neston.

Apart from the passengers, Dawpool was a good place to take on goods because the ships could ride at anchor rather than be beached, and the cargo could therefore be stowed to achieve the correct balance. Lead, which was more usually loaded at Parkgate, was also loaded at Dawpool: in 1713, 106 tons of it were loaded on to the *Neptune* at Dawpool for Rotterdam.[91] In 1732 the cheesemongers of London referred to 'the usual loading places at Parkgate and Dawpool'.[92]

However, the shifting sands were not to be relied on here either. In 1738 it was reported of Dawpool,[93]

---

[88] P.R.O., ADM 51/186.

[89] P.R.O. ADM 51/260.

[90] Diary of Henry Prescott, 27 Aug. 1694—see *Cheshire Sheaf*, 3rd series 43, item 9226 (Dec. 1949).

[91] P.R.O., E 190/138/1, quoted by C. Armour, p. 191.

[92] 'The case of the cheesemongers', B.L., 357 C.1.28.

[93] S. Fearon and J. Eyes, *A Description of the Sea Coast of England & Wales* (1738).

Figure 11. The site of Dawpool (Dalpool)
from P. P. Burdett's Map of Cheshire, 1777.

It was the best place in the river, both for good lying and early coming to and from the sea; but now a bank lies where the best of the road was, which dries at low water.

Nevertheless, Dawpool continued to be used regularly for freight until at least the 1780s: Randall Padmore, a waiter, searcher and riding officer at Dawpool at least between 1782 and 1788 [94] and who died in 1792 [95] may have been the last Customs officer there. An example of cargo in this later period is leather: nine sloops from Chester with 1,270 bundles of leather were sent to Dawpool to meet the *Andalusa* for Leghorn, in 1763.[96] The Dee Lighthouse Act required the river pilots, as we have seen, to lead vessels to Parkgate or Dawpool from 1776.[97]

The alteration in the main course of the river, caused by the New Cut in the last years of the eighteenth century, was to destroy Dawpool utterly. The string of conventional houses shown on Burdett's map in 1777 had disappeared altogether by the time an estate map was drawn in 1817 and Greenwood's map of Cheshire was published in 1819.[98] A grandiose plan for an artificial harbour at 'Dawpool', in fact sited a mile further up the river, was drawn up by Telford in 1822, would have cost £30,000 and came to nothing.[99]

Dawpool may well have faded away in any case because its road connections were poor, there was little in the way of back-up services, and there was no alternative employment when it fell on hard times. Parkgate was to cope successfully with all these problems.

The last anchorage to be examined, Hoylake, was not inside the estuary at all, but provided deep water and shelter for ships using both the Dee and the Mersey. Occasionally passengers disembarked there— John Wesley in typical haste did so in 1773[100]—but this was unusual. In 1690 there were two houses and the King's storehouse there [101] and things were much the same in 1784 when Emma Hart wrote,[102]

[94] P.R.O. CUST 18/440.
[95] *Chester Chronicle*, 19 Oct. 1792.
[96] Cheshire R.O., QDN 1/5 (11 June 1763).
[97] 16 Geo III c.61.
[98] Cheshire R.O., DPB 2315.
[99] *Chester Chronicle*, 7 Sept 1821; 29 March 1822; Cheshire R.O., DPB/394.
[100] John Wesley, *Journal*, 5 July 1773.
[101] Gédéon Bonnivert's diary, June 1690—*Cheshire Sheaf*, 3rd series 8, item 1695 (Aug. 1910) quoting Sloane MS 1033.
[102] Alfred Morrison, ed., *The Hamilton & Nelson Papers* (1893), letter 124, 12 June 1784, 1, p. 85.

And High Lake has 3 houses in it, and none of them as is fit
for a Christian.

It was nine years later that a retired butler opened a hotel there.[103]
The chief reason for mentioning Hoylake here is that its use by
the English fleet in 1689–90 has sunk into the folk memory of
Parkgate, typified by a story about two anchors, once on the 'Donkey Stand' at Parkgate:[104]

> On either side of the bastion on the esplanade, two one-armed
> anchors lie . . . Collins marked them when he took his survey
> in 1684 [sic] yet, singularly, they are called William and Mary,
> and said to have been dropped by vessels when William III
> sailed for the Boyne!

These anchors can be seen on the letterhead of the Pengwern Arms
and were ten or twelve feet long. According to E. Barber, 'These
were not carried on the boats but were permanently buried in the
sands, and buoys fastened to them'.[105] Of course the anchor on
Collins' map is not meant to be a real anchor, but is a conventional
sign for an anchorage derived from the Dutch 'Waggoner' charts.

That William III's army in 1689 and the king himself in 1690 sailed
from Hoylake, is thoroughly recorded. The suggestion that the
anchors could have been dropped from a vessel of this fleet probably
relies rather uncritically on a statement by Daniel Defoe, published
over thirty years after the event, where he describes 'Nesson' as [106]

> the place where in the late war in Ireland, most of the troops
> embarked when that grand expedition began.

This apparently inaccurate account is not supported by con-
temporary evidence. The Rev. George Story recorded that in 1689
the army camped for a week at Neston before embarking at
Hoylake, ten thousand strong.[107] The following year Dr Rowland
Davies wrote that the king, with '400 recruits of horse', embarked at

[103] *Chester Chronicle*, 19 July 1793.
[104] Hilda Gamlin, *'Twixt Mersey and Dee* (1897), p. 260.
[105] E. Barber, 'Parkgate, an old Cheshire port', *J.C.A.S.*, new series 8 (1911),
p. 24.
[106] Daniel Defoe, *A Tour through the whole Island of Great Britain* (1724–6),
Letter VII, vol. 2, p. 467.
[107] George Story, *An Impartial History of the Affairs of Ireland* (1691), p. 6.

Hoylake.[108] These numbers needed the space of an extensive anchorage: Story said that he sailed in company with eighty or ninety vessels, while in 1690 Henry Prescott saw above three hundred ships at Hoylake.[109] The narrow and shallow river channel at Neston would have looked crowded with a dozen ships.

We shall see in the next chapter that at least one vessel that sailed into Hoylake in 1689, then came up river to Parkgate to haul out and have her sides washed. This was the R.Y. *Monmouth*, whose journal, particularly in 1690, gives further evidence that the troop movements as a whole went through Hoylake.[110] So it was, strictly speaking, possible that the two anchors could have been lost by a king's ship, if not necessarily in 1689–90. Captain Henry Lawson of the R.Y. *Dublin* was charged £20 in 1722 for the loss of two mooring anchors.[111] Could these have been the ones? They might have been, though losing anchors was common enough.

The anchors themselves probably went for scrap in 1940.[112] The survival, if not of themselves, of their legend illustrates both the continuity of local history and the relative status of Hoylake and Parkgate.

[108] R. Caulfield, ed., *Journal of the Rev. Rowland Davies, 1690* (Camden Society, 1857), pp. 109–17.
[109] Diary of Henry Prescott, 10 July 1690, in *Cheshire Sheaf*, 3rd series 33 (June 1938), item 7384.
[110] P.R.O., ADM 51/574.
[111] P.R.O., ADM 36/892.
[112] G. W. Place, 'William & Mary, the tale of two anchors at Parkgate', *Wirral Journal* (Autumn 1987), p. 10.

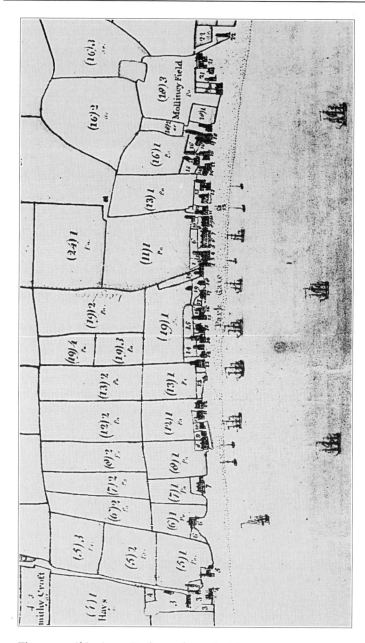

Figure 12. Shipping at Parkgate, from the Mostyn estate map, 1732, Mostyn (Bangor) 8699 (reproduced by permission of Lord Mostyn.)

# 3  The Royal Yachts
## on the Dublin Station

From the 1660s until the 1830s, the Royal Navy provided a yacht for the service of the lord lieutenant of Ireland. Because the yachts were much smaller than most other classes of naval fighting vessel, they were able to enter the shallow waters of the Dee estuary. In doing so, they were instrumental in stimulating the passenger traffic between Parkgate and Dublin.

Yachts were first introduced to Britain and to the Royal Navy in 1660. Before that, a small warship had been stationed in Irish waters and was known as 'Her Majesty's Irish Galley'.[1] In 1576 Lord Deputy Sidney asked for [2]

> one of her Majesty's ships to lie upon the Irish coast for the safe conduct of treasure.

He was sent the 90-ton *Handmaid*, which was replaced by the *Popinjay* in 1587 and the *Tremontana* in 1601. Where these vessels anchored on the English side is not recorded. In 1627 ten small vessels called *Lion's Whelps* were built, numbered one to ten, and two of them, the fifth and ninth, were employed in Irish waters.[3] The earl of Cork, lord justice of Ireland, sailed to England in 1629 from Youghall to Milford and returned via Beaumaris where he intended to hire a vessel. But there appeared a king's ship, a pinnace called the *Ninth Whelp*, sent to convey him to Ireland. However, the *Ninth Whelp* had to take refuge at Dawpool in Chester Water before sailing to Dublin.[4]

[1] T. Glasgow, 'The Elizabethan navy in Ireland, 1583–1603', *The Irish Sword* 8 (1965–6), p. 294.
[2] *Cal. S.P. Ireland 1574–85, Lord Deputy to Privy Council, 4 Sept. 1576*, p. 98.
[3] J. J. Colledge, *Ships of the Royal Navy* (1969), p. 321; John Wassel, 'The Lion's Whelp', *Mariner's Mirror* 63 (1977), p. 368.
[4] D. Townshend, *The Life and Letters of the great Earl of Cork* (1904), p. 176.

As well as the Royal Yachts, which from about 1661 were specifically at the disposal of the lord lieutenant, there were always naval vessels stationed in Irish waters and their duties were primarily defensive: to deal with privateers and to escort merchant vessels in convoy. In 1659, for example, the *Fox* and the *Paradox* were sailing between Dublin and Holyhead, Chester Water or Chester Bar.[5]

As time went by and ships generally became larger, men o'war became much too large for Chester Water. In the 1670s the *Norwich*, at 160 tons small enough to enter the Dee though not recorded there, was taking convoys from Dublin to Bristol or to Holyhead.[6] By 1704, however, the *Hector* (493 tons) and the *Valeur* (321 tons) were gathering ships for convoy to Dublin, Bristol or London.[7] But they were marshalling their charges outside the mouth of the estuary, in the deep-water anchorage at Hoylake. From then on the only regular vessels of the Royal Navy which could enter the estuary were the Royal Yachts.

On his return to England in 1660, Charles II was taken from Breda to Scheveningen, where his English convoy lay, on a Dutch yacht which he greatly admired. In Dutch 'jacht' derives from a word meaning hunt or chase. Yachts were light, fast-sailing vessels, suited to the shallow waters of the Netherlands. Their manoeuvrability made them useful for short journeys, and they were particularly suitable for the purpose encountered by Charles II: the carriage of nobility or officials whether on affairs of state or for pleasure.

The king's admiration so impressed the burgomaster of Amsterdam that he asked leave to present a similar vessel. This was the Royal Yacht *Mary*, sent to England on 12 August 1660 as a gift from the city of Amsterdam.[8]

[5] *Cal. S.P. Dom., 1658–59*, p. 504, and handwritten addition on p. 499 shown on Kraus reprint of this volume (1965); see also *Cal. S.P. Dom., 1659–60* p. 546.

[6] P.R.O., ADM 8/1, 'A list of ships', 1673, 1675, 1677.

[7] J. J. Colledge, *Ships of the Royal Navy*, pp. 261, 583; Chester City R.O., ML/4.

[8] C. G. 't Hooft, 'The first English yachts, 1660', *Mariner's Mirror* 5 (1919), pp. 109–11.

The *Mary*'s design was highly thought of in England, and two similar yachts, the *Anne* and the *Catherine*, were built in England in 1661. Sir John Evelyn recorded that he [9]

sailed this morning with his Majesty in one of his yaachts (or pleasure boats), vessels newly known among us, til the Dutch East India Company [sic] presented that curious piece to the King, and very excellent sailing vessels.

The Stuart kings were much taken by the sailing qualities of the yachts and no less than twenty-six had been commissioned by 1686. In 1700 there were still fifteen in service, and in those years they were used for general naval purposes which involved short journeys. These included ferrying people and dispatches across the English and Irish channels, surveying, and dockyard duties.[10] In the later eighteenth century when there were about nine yachts on the Navy List, five were for the personal use of the Royal family, one was at the disposal of the lord lieutenant of Ireland, and three were for dockyard duties. The yachts in the service of the king were often used together: there survives a sketch of five yachts ceremoniously grouped to witness the launching of H.M.S. *Grafton* in 1771.[11] by that time their 'hunting' attributes were no longer required, and Falconer's dictionary of 1769 describes a Royal Yacht as,[12]

A vessel of state usually employed to convey, princes, ambassadors or other great persons from one kingdom to another. As the principal design of a yacht is to accommodate the passengers, it is usually fitted with a variety of convenient apartments with suitable furniture, according to the quality or number of persons contained therein. They are in general elegantly furnished and richly ornamented with sculpture, and always commanded by captains in his Majesty's Navy. The Royal Yachts are commonly rigged as ketches, except the principal one reserved for the sovereign, which is equipped with three masts like a ship.

[9] Sir John Evelyn, *Diary*, ed. E. S. de Beer (1955) 3 p. 296. 'Newly' in this edition is read as 'not' by 't Hooft, Gavin and others.
[10] P.R.O., ADM 7/550 (ships' stations); W. E. May, 'The Royal yachts under George I', *Mariner's Mirror* 68 (1982), p. 69.
[11] See *Mariner's Mirror* 24 (1938), p. 355.
[12] William Falconer, *An Universal Dictionary of the Marine* (1776 edn), no pagination.

The yacht design was gradually adapted to English requirements by English shipbuilders. The original Dutch vessels were *yacht*-rigged, with a single mast, a mainsail, a square topsail and two headsails. The *Mary* had leeboards, looking like huge paddles attached to the sides, but the English copies of the yacht design omitted the leeboards. Of the Royal Yachts which visited Parkgate, the *Portsmouth* was certainly of this type as may be seen from a painting by Willem van der Velde made in 1674.[13] Gradually a second mast was introduced: a small mizzen-mast resulted in a *galliot*-rig, while a larger mizzen-mast produced a *ketch*-rig. Most of the yachts built after about 1680 were probably ketch-rigged. A drawing in William Sutherland's *Britain's Glory or Shipbuilding unveil'd* of 1717 showing a ketch-rigged yacht may represent the R.Y. *Dublin* which played an important part on the Parkgate to Dublin route.[14]

In a few cases the larger yachts were *ship*-rigged; that is, they had three masts and square sails. Falconer's reference to the sovereign's ship-rigged yacht refers to the R.Y. *Caroline*, built in 1749 with the large size of 252 tons. But the R.Y. *Dorset*, built in 1753 specifically for the Irish service, was also given three masts. They can be seen on the model of her hull in the National Maritime Museum at Greenwich, which also has a painting of her in 1788 by J. T. Serres.[15] This latter is a watercolour sketch, but Serres also painted a large oil called *Lighthouse in Dublin Bay* which shows the *Dorset*.[16]

The modern association of yachts with racing would have appealed to Charles II, who in fact was racing his *Catherine* against the Duke of York's *Anne* for £100 when Evelyn recorded the match in 1661. But the yachts on the Dublin station did not race, and the use and development of the type for private pleasure cruising was introduced by the formation of the Royal Yacht Squadron in 1815.[17]

---

[13] A. P. McGowan, *The Royal Yachts* (1977), plate 5.
[14] C. M. Gavin, *Royal Yachts* (1932), p. 250.
[15] Model: National Maritime Museum, catalogue no. 1753-1.
[16] The painting belongs to the Victoria & Albert Museum, London, but was seen while on loan to Heveningham Hall, Suffolk. This was probably the picture seen by C. M. Gavin (p. 269).
[17] C. M. Gavin, *Royal Yachts*, p. 21.

After his first enthusiasm for the *Mary* had died down, Charles II handed her over to the navy for the public service, apparently in 1661.[18] She was soon stationed at Dublin, possibly at once, and possibly by direct command of the king if Robert Lyle (who clearly was unfamiliar with the new word 'yacht') was correct when he wrote in 1663,[19]

> I was going on to catch the packet-boat at Holyhead, having found no convenience at Chester; but as I found here the Mary Jack (given by the King to the Lord Lieutenant) ready to sail, I am going over by her.

Her captain in that year is not recorded, but in 1665 James Sharland, who had earlier commanded the *Fox* and so was a specialist in Irish Sea navigation, was appointed captain.[20] The *Mary* was first recorded in Chester Water in 1666 when she was at Dawpool, landing Mrs Aldersey and awaiting moneys for Ireland.[21] From the Dublin end we learn how much: 'The Mary yacht, arrived here on Monday, brought £11,700 in her.'[22] This was the role, the transport of 'treasure', for which a naval vessel was ideal, and for which Lord Deputy Sidney had asked in 1576. Money was too valuable to be entrusted to the Post Office barks at Holyhead, and at this date was too heavy to be transported through the almost trackless hills of North Wales. As we shall see, the transport of money for the army was one of the tasks given to the R.Y. *Monmouth* in 1690–91.

During the 1660s the *Mary* seems to have been working in partnership with the *Harp* which we have already met and which was also briefly commanded by Sharland in 1664. The *Harp* frigate, ketch-rigged, had been built at Dublin in 1656 and at 75 tons was even smaller than the *Mary*'s 92 tons.[23] She carried ten guns to the *Mary*'s eight, so both were lightly armed against the dangers of the high seas. Not all the dangers of naval life were on the seas, however;

[18] P. W. J. McBride, part 2 of 'The Mary, Charles II's yacht' in *International Journal of Nautical Archaeology and Underwater Exploration* 2, 1 (1973), p. 61.

[19] *Cal. S.P. Ireland, 1663–65* (1907), 5 June 1663, p. 120.

[20] John Charnock, *Biographia Navalis* (1794). The State Papers refer variously to James, Samuel and Francis Sharland, between whom Charnock does not distinguish (vol 1, p. 45).

[21] *Cal. S.P. Dom., 1665–66*, p. 228.

[22] *Cal. S.P. Ireland, 1666–69* (1908), p. 164, 25 July 1666.

[23] J. J. Colledge, *Ships of the Royal Navy* 1, p. 254.

in 1667 both ships were at Dublin petitioning the Navy Commissioners for fifty-two weeks' pay[24]

> that their families may not be starved in the streets, and
> themselves go like the heathen, having nothing to cover their
> nakedness.

The usual task for the *Mary*, as it was to be for all her successors on the Dublin station, was to carry notable passengers to and from Dublin. In 1667 'the *Mary* yacht pleasure boat' (recalling Evelyn's description) was at Dawpool to receive Lady Ossory, and during 1669 she was taking passengers from Dublin to Milford Haven and to 'Chester'.[25] To Holyhead, that year, the Lord Lieutenant's 'yack' brought over Mr Dashwood, who was concerned in the farm of the Irish revenue, with two packets from the lord lieutenant to the lord keeper.[26]

The sailing qualities of the *Mary* must have impressed the Post Office agent at Holyhead. After one of his packet ships was lost in November 1670 he asked that its replacement should be a Dutch-built ship:[27]

> that sea is so short and broken that Holland-built ships are
> found the fittest for that passage.

What sort of vessel he got is not recorded but it certainly was not a Dutch yacht: more probably a dogger.

Such evidence that survives suggests that Dawpool was the *Mary*'s usual landfall in the Dee estuary. When the new lord lieutenant of Ireland, Lord Berkeley, was anxious in April 1670 to reach his new appointment, as quickly as possible, he left all his luggage to follow as it could, and went to Dawpool. There, with his family and household, he embarked on the *Mary* and *Monmouth* yachts for Dublin.[28] In 1674 it was at Dawpool that the *Mary* was paid off, 'some officers from the Navy Office having come hither for the purpose'. 'Last Wednesday the Mary yacht was paid forty-six months pay at Dawpool in this river and yet she is still sixteen months in arrears.'[29]

[24] *Cal. S.P. Dom., 1667*, 27 June 1667, p. 238.
[25] *Cal. S.P. Dom., 1667*, p. 457; *Cal. S.P. Dom., 1668–9*, pp. 163, 222, 399.
[26] *Cal. S.P. Ireland, 1669–70* (1910), p. 24.
[27] *Cal. S.P. Dom., 1671*, p. 203.
[28] *Cal. S.P. Ireland, 1669–70* (1910), p. 112.
[29] *Cal. S.P. Dom., 1673–75*, pp. 459, 472.

Clearly the cash-flow problems of 1667 had become worse. The lack of pay no doubt contributed to a scandal in 1672 when James Leslie, gunner on the *Mary*, accused his captain of being 'a drunken, idle, debauched fellow' who was cheating the king by forging seamen's tickets and selling the ship's gunpowder.[30] Although Sharland was eventually acquitted of these charges, he was removed from the ship, being replaced by William Burstow.

It was Burstow who was in command for the *Mary*'s last voyage in March 1675. She had sailed from Dublin bound for Chester Water, and so probably for Dawpool, when on a foggy night she struck a rock on the Skerries, off the coast of Anglesey near Holyhead. The *Mary*'s official complement was listed as twenty men in peacetime and thirty when at war.[31] On this voyage she carried a crew of twenty-eight, four of whom were lost including Captain Burstow. Of the forty-six passengers, thirty-one were lost, including the earl of Meath.

The fate of the earl of Meath highlights an important aspect of the yacht's duties on the Dublin station. It is likely that Captain Burstow had been ordered by warrant from the lord lieutenant to carry the earl and his party to England; but his party would not have consisted of forty-five persons. The remaining passengers were probably a mixture of those carrying official warrants and private travellers who had made their own arrangements with the captain. We shall look at the warrant system in more detail presently.

The loss of the *Mary* meant that Samuel Pepys, who had been involved with naval affairs since 1660 and was Secretary for the Navy from 1673, had to find a replacement. His problem was to find a vessel suitable for the conditions in the Irish Sea. He wrote first to Captain Baker of the R.Y. *Merlin* to say that it was his turn for Ireland, but that if he thought his vessel was too 'sharp', meaning that the section of her hull was relatively narrow so that the ship might roll over if she went aground, 'being thereby rendered less fit to lie on the ground for Ireland', the R.Y. *Monmouth* must go instead.[32]

The problem of ships using the Dee estuary having to lie aground we have already met, and it applied equally at Holyhead. Baker must

[30] *Cal. S.P. Dom., 1672*, pp. 518–19.
[31] J. R. Tanner, ed., *Naval MSS in the Pepysian Library* (1, 1903), pp. 294–5.
[32] J. R. Tanner, ed., *A Descriptive Calendar of the Naval MSS in the Pepysian Library*, 3 (1909), p. 43 (27 April 1675).

have claimed that the *Merlin* was unsuitable, for Pepys next wrote
to Morgan Kempthorne,[33] captain of the R.Y. *Monmouth*.[34]

> These are to tell him that either he or the Merlin is to attend
> the coast and service of Ireland in the room of the Mary, lately
> lost; and the Merlin being judged not fit through the rankness
> of her keel to lie on the ground at Holyhead, it will be for his
> vessel to go, but he may if he wishes exchange with the com-
> mander of Merlin.

Kempthorne chose to go himself and captured a French privateer on
his way to Dublin.[35]

The R.Y. *Monmouth*, built in 1666, had been briefly to Dublin
before, in 1669, when Captain William Fazeby was ordered to take
the earl of Orrery there from Milford. But Fazeby was unhappy
about the conditions:[36]

> If this yacht stays upon the coast she will be quite spoiled as
> she will not take the ground.

As we have seen, the *Monmouth* assisted the *Mary* to transport the
lord lieutenant from Dawpool to Dublin and then returned to the
English Channel where she remained until 1675. If Fazeby thought
the *Monmouth* unsuitable for lying aground, clearly the *Merlin* was
considered even less suitable. Perhaps this is the explanation for the
switch between the vessels by Greenvile Collins, who was appointed
to the *Merlin* in 1681 for his hydrographic survey, but who changed
to the *Monmouth* in 1683, apparently returning to *Merlin* when his
survey was complete.

It was the R.Y. *Monmouth*, therefore, which in 1676 brought the
countess of Essex, wife of the lord lieutenant, into the anchorage at
Neston under the command of Morgan Kempthorne.[37] This visit

---

[33] J. Charnock, in his *Biographia Navalis*, vol. 1, p. 397, doubts whether
Morgan Kempthorne was commander of the R.Y. *Monmouth* because he
would be too young, allegedly barely 16. Pepys listed both John and Morgan
Kempthorne (see note 32 above) as captains of the ship in 1673, and the
captain's log (P.R.O., ADM 51/4265) shows that Pepys was right and that
Morgan took over from his brother.

[34] Tanner, *Naval MSS 2*, 1 & 8 May 1675, pp. 44, 47.

[35] Tanner, *Naval MSS 2*, 10 Sept. 1675; 4, p. 219.

[36] *Cal. S.P. Dom., 1668–69* (1894), p. 300 (28 April 1669), p. 384 (28 June),
p. 520 (7 Oct.); 1670 (1895), p. 10 (7 Jan.).

[37] *Cal. S.P. Dom., 1676–7* (1909), pp. 56, 182.

provides the first recorded use of the Neston anchorage by a Royal Yacht. She remained on the Dublin station for another two years, by which time she was in need of repairs. As Pepys wrote [38]

> The Monmouth yacht be laid up as soon as she shall be brought back from the coast of Ireland, where she has long been.

Kempthorne became commander of the *Kingfisher* on which he was to die heroically three years later while fighting seven ships from Algiers. R.Y. *Monmouth* returned to the English Channel for a while until Collins took her for surveying, after which she returned to the Dublin station for the rest of her naval career.

Her replacement at Dublin was the R.Y. *Portsmouth*.[39] The *Portsmouth*, 133 tons, was built in 1674 and remained in the service of the lord lieutenant until 1687. The painting by Willem van der Velde of the *Portsmouth* when she was newly built (see note 13 above) shows the richly carved detail, painted and gilded, not only on bow and stern but along the sides as well, with wreaths round the gun-ports. This rich decoration was a feature of many, perhaps all the Royal Yachts and emphasised their dignity as vessels of state. In 1765 the R.Y. *Dorset* was to be 'carved and beautified in an elegant manner' at Parkgate.[40]

With the *Portsmouth*'s commander, William Wright, we encounter a specialist yacht captain. Wright was [41]

> remarkable for having never, through a very long service of near thirty years continuance, commanded any vessel except a yacht.

Wright had served in the *Bezant*, apparently another gift from the Dutch like the *Mary*, and in the *Kitching* before taking command of the *Portsmouth*, which he joined on the (English) Channel station before bringing her to Dublin in 1679. From the *Portsmouth* he was appointed to the *Monmouth* in 1687 and stayed with her on the Dublin station until she was sold in 1698.[42]

It is important to realise that, in the Stuart navy, the office in charge of a ship was not necessarily a professional seaman and may

[38] Tanner, *Naval MSS* 4 (1923), p. 611.
[39] P.R.O., ADM 8/1, 'List of Ships', July 1679.
[40] *Freeman's Dublin Journal*, 30 August 1765.
[41] John Charnock, *Biographia Navalis* 1, p. 277; 2, p. 213.
[42] *ibid*, p. 278.

not have had much or any knowledge of navigation. The navigator on a vessel was called the sailing master, often referred to as the master, and his was the responsibility for the technical conduct of his ship. For example, Collins described two courts-martial of masters whose ships ran ashore in 1689.[43] This situation was fast changing in favour of a professional navy in which the captain took full responsibility. The officer in charge of any ship, whether a naval or a merchant vessel, was given the title of captain, if only temporarily. The captain of a naval vessel was known as its commander, while the 'master' was his sailing master or navigating officer. On a merchant ship, however, the captain was customarily described as its master.[44]

The yachts, being small vessels and specialists in sailing qualities, needed commanders with strong technical abilities. Though they had sailing masters (when the *Mary* was lost, Captain Burstow was drowned but his master survived) they attracted officers who were good navigators and ship handlers. An example was Greenvile Collins, who was master of several ships before becoming a yacht commander, and was chosen as a hydrographic surveyor because of his navigating skills. In 1688 he was taken from the command of a ship to act as sailing master for Lord Dartmouth's flagship. Like Collins and Wright, Captain Sharland of the (first) *Mary* may have been a navigating specialist, because he applied for a post as pilot in Irish waters when he was removed from his command.[45] William Fazeby who commanded the *Monmouth* in 1668–71, also commanded eight different yachts up to 1688.[46] Finally, Wright's successor at Dublin, George Breholt, also seems to have been a specialist yacht commander.

Although R.Y. *Portsmouth* joined the station in 1679, almost no details of her service have survived before 1686. Then, for the eighteen months from March 1686 to September 1687, we have William Wright's journal or log book, so that for the first time we have exact details of a yacht's sailing pattern.[47]

[43] H.M.C., *15th Report Appendix 1 (Earl of Dartmouth, 3)*, p. 57.
[44] N. A. M. Rodger, *The Wooden World* (1988), p. 20; see also G. P. B. Naish, *Hydrographic Surveys*, p. 48.
[45] *Cal. S.P. Dom., 1672–3*, 4 Feb, p. 518; 1673, p. 563, 30 Sept.
[46] Tanner, *Naval MSS* 1 (1903), p. 349.
[47] P.R.O., ADM 51/3943.

The pattern had clearly changed. Whereas the *Mary* seemed, on the scattered evidence available, to have used Dawpool as a regular anchorage, the *Portsmouth*'s log mentions Dawpool only twice out of twenty-one landfalls in the Dee, and in each case Dawpool was a temporary halt before anchoring in Beerhouse hole, at the northern end of Parkgate. On one occasion both were used by passengers:[48]

> Landed Earl of Clarendon at Dawpool but continued to the Barr [Beer] House hole and landed rest of passengers there.

Clarendon was the retiring lord lieutenant.

In these eighteen months Beerhouse hole is mentioned ten times, Parkgate eight times and Holyhead eleven times. On several occasions the yacht anchored in Beerhouse hole but was later said to have weighed anchor from Parkgate, which is not surprising if they were virtually the same place. But not quite: one of the reasons why yachts came to Parkgate was to haul ashore and grave the hull: that is, clean its bottom. When the *Portsmouth* did that,[49]

> Made an end of graveing, hal'd off the wayes and fell down to the Beerhouse hole.

If the 'ways' were at the south end of Parkgate, it might have been over a mile down river to Beerhouse hole. The sailing pattern, then, indicates that the lord lieutenant's yacht was sailing between Dublin and either Chester Water (seventeen times) or Holyhead (ten times). The only variations were visits to Portsmouth to collect a new mast, to Liverpool to collect the earl of Derby and deliver him to Douglas in the Isle of Man, and to Beaumaris after a visit to Holyhead. No mention of carrying money occurs in the journal and the sole purpose of the voyages seems to have been to carry passengers:[50]

> At 10 in forenoon wee came up to the Bear House hole and landed our passengers, anchored in seven fathoms at high water.

In October 1687 Wright sailed the *Portsmouth* to London, and he left her for his new appointment in the R.Y. *Monmouth*.

---

[48] P.R.O., ADM 51/3943, 21 Feb. 1687.
[49] *ibid*, 14 May 1687.
[50] *ibid*, 12 April 1686.

William Wright brought the *Monmouth* back to Irish waters as a part of the fleet which sailed from Deptford to Hoylake in July 1689. The fleet entered

> into hoylak. So we anchored in wild rode till 4 afternoon in 8 fathoms water att ½ flood, and then way and sayled up chester river and anchored att parkgate in 4½ fathoms water ½ flood.

He hauled ashore, had the sides of the ship washed and returned to Hoylake. On 10th August,[51]

> This day the army began to imbarque for Ireland. God prosper their proceedings.

The yacht was then employed in both the passage of the army in 1689 and the king in 1690, a sequence which is described in Chapter 2. From July 1690 she was employed on the customary duties of the lord lieutenant's yacht, and this usually involved ferrying passengers. On one occasion the yacht left Parkgate for Dublin with 120 passengers on board, one of the rare occasions when the total number carried, as opposed to the name of a single celebrity, is recorded.[52] Money was carried over: fifty chests of it on one occasion, thirty on another.[53]

In 1691 there were three occasions when the *Monmouth* carried prisoners under guard, bound for Chester castle.[54] On one occasion while riding in Chester Water 'we began to press men' and the pressed men were put on board a ship at Hoylake.[55] But once 1691 was over, the duties returned to normal. The voyages were usually between Dublin and Parkgate, because it was in 1689 that James Vickers became contractor for the Post Office packets at Holyhead and, as we shall see, he insisted that Captain Wright should not interfere with Vickers' passenger traffic.

The fact that Wright therefore sailed to Parkgate except when his orders or the weather obliged him to visit Holyhead, must have been a major factor in the development of Parkgate as a regular port for passengers. Another attraction of Parkgate as an anchorage seems to have been that it was a suitable place to effect minor repairs, where

[51] P.R.O., ADM 51/574.
[52] *ibid*, 4 Oct. 1690.
[53] *ibid*, 3 Jan., 15 April 1691.
[54] *ibid*, 10 Jan., 13 Aug., Oct. 1691.
[55] *ibid*, 14 March 1691.

his own men could grave and tallow the hull, and there were carpenters who could caulk the seams. Whereas later yachts used to go to Plymouth as a rule for their refits, the *Monmouth* in these years was refitted at Liverpool.[56] The last duty of the R.Y. *Monmouth* on 2nd July 1698 was to land the earl of Athlone at Parkgate and have her hull washed before sailing to Deptford to be sold.

For the first four years of her stay on the Dublin station, the *Monmouth* was accompanied by another yacht, the R.Y. *Navy*, commanded by Phineas Pett, for which relatively little work was found.[57] Unusually for a Royal Yacht, she spent quite a long time at Liverpool on several occasions, spasmodically taking notables between Dublin and Holyhead and Parkgate. In June 1693 Captain Pett was brought a fresh ship, the R.Y. *Soesdyke*, which had just been purchased by the Royal Navy, but Pett was replaced as commander in 1694 by George Breholt.[58]

It was the *Soesdyke* under Breholt, therefore, which took over the role of lord lieutenant's yacht, performing the usual duties. Breholt's pattern of sailing for his first full year, 1695, shows that he visited Dublin twelve times, Parkgate ten times, Holyhead twice and Liverpool once. This pattern continued until the end of the century.

In 1696 James Vickers of Holyhead complained once more that [59]

> the yachts which are ordered to attend his Majesty's service between, Dublin, Holyhead and Chester do convey passengers, which were used to be carried in the pacquet boats, whereby he is a great sufferer.

The response of the Treasury lords was to desire

> that the like injunction may be given to all the captains of his Majesty's yachts as hath been formerly given to Captain Wright.

Yet it is difficult to see what Vickers had to complain about, as in 1695 the *Soesdyke* visited Holyhead only twice; in 1696 she visited Holyhead three times and Beaumaris once up to September, the date of Vickers' petition. Of course, Vickers' contract to carry the mail

---

[56] *ibid*, 25 Jan. 1691, 9 March 1693.
[57] P.R.O., ADM 51/3918.
[58] P.R.O., ADM 51/4344. 'Soesdyke', in modern Dutch 'Soestdijk', is the name of a royal palace near Soest, east of Hilversum, Netherlands.
[59] *Cal. Treasury Books* 9, 1696–97 (1933), p. 265.

gave him no monopoly of passengers, and his touchiness merely reinforced the tendency of the yachts, and therefore of the quality traffic, to visit Parkgate.

In 1701 Breholt exchanged the *Soesdyke* for another yacht the R.Y. *Charlotte*. This vessel was brought from Deptford by its commander, Thomas Marke, who then took charge of the *Soesdyke*, paid one visit in her to Parkgate, and returned with her to Deptford.[60]

The R.Y. *Charlotte*, 143 tons, was built in 1677 and served for a remarkable 84 years before being rebuilt in 1761 and finally broken up in 1771.[61]

An account of a journey by Mary Lovett in 1703 survives:[62]

> We are all well at Chester, from whence we hope to goe presently eight miles off and take shipping if we can get room, for they say it was never known the ships to be so full; there is 6 Ladys of Quality and a Lord gone down to wait there, ready for the ships to go off, with abundance more passengers; it is said there goods is worth at least thirty thousand pounds.
>
> It's so full that little or no convenience is to be had, besides having no convoy. If they do goe they will call at Holyhead, where is expected a convoy.

In the end Mary Lovett travelled overland to Holyhead and caught the yacht there. Convoys were necessary during the War of Spanish Succession, and in 1702 the city of Chester had petitioned the queen:[63]

> That the prosperity of the said Citty doth chiefly depend upon trade at sea and particularly to and from the Citty of Dublin and other parts of the kingdom of Ireland: That in the time of war, the Irish Channel is greatly infested with privateers, invited thither by the prospect of intercepting the coal fleetes, and other ships with persons of great quality and very valuable goods.

---

[60] P.R.O., ADM 51/4344, Dec. 1701 to Jan. 1702.
[61] J. J. Colledge, *Ships of the Royal Navy* I, p. 116.
[62] Margaret, Lady Verney, ed., *Verney Letters of the 18th Century* (1928) I, p. 193.
[63] *Cheshire Sheaf*, 1st series, I, Oct. 1878, p. 102, item 329.

They asked for a ship of war, as did William Allen a year later in a letter to the lord lieutenant:[64]

> we have a ship here called the Phenix of Chester, Thomas Maddock master, which is very richly loaden with Merchants goods for Dublin, worth severall thousand pounds, and dare not venture her to go without a convoy.

The response to these pleas was to provide H.M.S. *Seaford* which with 24 guns, compared to the eight on R.Y. *Charlotte*, could provide effective defence. In 1704 they patrolled together, with forty soldiers on board the *Charlotte*. They found a French privateer and a small bark taken by him; the *Seaford* chased the privateer.[65] Other men o'war were employed, including *Hector* and *Valeur*, already noted. In 1707 there were more warnings at Chester about privateers [66] and in the same year R.Y. *Charlotte* met a French privateer off Anglesey to whom H.M.S. *Arundel* gave chase.[67] On May 11th 1707,[68]

> My cosin John Freke landed saffe at Dublin affter he had bin fower days att sea from in the packett boatt from Chester. Whilst he was crossing the sea, were eleven ships taken by privateers from holly head.

The *Seaford* was still providing protection in 1709 when Captain Breholt 'went for London' to collect his new ship, specially built for the Dublin station, the R.Y. *Dublin*.[69]

For the next hundred years the story is taken up by two yachts: R.Y. *Dublin*, 1709–52, and R.Y. *Dorset*, 1753–1814. Both were specially built for service on the Dublin station, and both spent their entire careers at the disposal of the lord lieutenant of Ireland.

One small example of the impact which these yachts made on the local economy is shown by the names of the *Yacht Inn* at Woodbank, on the Chester High Road, roughly half way between Chester

[64] *Cheshire Sheaf*, 3rd series, 23, March 1926, p. 22, item 5330.
[65] P.R.O., ADM 51/186, 5 March 1704.
[66] Chester City R.O., ML/4/594, 608.
[67] P.R.O., ADM 51/186, 3 June 1707.
[68] M. Carbery, ed., *Mrs Elizabeth Freke, Her Diary 1671–1714*, p. 72.
[69] P.R.O., ADM 51/186, 6 June 1709.

and Parkgate. In 1722 this inn was referred to as *The Ship*, Wood-bank.[70] In 1757, 'the Half-way House, commonly known by the sign of the Dublin Yacht', was to let.[71] Ten years later,[72]

James Philips (late horsebreaker of Chester) has taken the Dorsetshire Yacht, near the Two Mills on the Heath, on the Parkgate road. He will continue to break horses.

In Chester itself there was the *Yacht Inn* in Watergate Street, described in 1856 as 'the most picturesque and curious of all our Chester inns', and where Jonathan Swift scratched satirical lines on a window pane.[73] There is also the *Dublin Packet Inn* in Northgate Street.

R.Y. *Dublin*, 148 tons and ten guns, was built at Deptford in 1709. At first she carried 45 men, but in 1713 her complement was altered to 40, and in 1737 to 50.[74] Her first commander was George Breholt who took charge on 13 August 1709, when 'the Dublin Yacht was launcht into the wet dock not being near compleated'.[75] In October she left Deptford for Milford in convoy under the protection of H.M.S. *Southampton*: shots were exchanged with several enemy ships near Penzance. She reached Dublin in January 1710 and resumed the sailing pattern which Breholt had established with the *Charlotte*.

In April 1711, Breholt was replaced by Captain Henry Lawson who remained commander of the yacht until he died. He was due for removal from command in 1732, but was retained at the request of the lord lieutenant, the duke of Dorset.[76] Lawson died at sea in April 1734.[77] His second in command was his sailing master, usually listed as mate or pilot, George Newman, who had sailed with Lawson since at least 1713 and who himself died in 1735.[78] The Royal Yachts carried only one commissioned officer, although a midshipman was occasionally carried; both Captain Weller Senior and Captain Schomberg were to carry their sons on

[70] Cheshire R.O., QJF 150/2.
[71] *Adam's Weekly Courant*, 22 Nov. 1757.
[72] *ibid*, 10 March 1767.
[73] Thomas Hughes, *The Stranger's Handbook to Chester* (1856), pp. 59–60.
[74] P.R.O., ADM 36/894; 36/898.
[75] P.R.O., ADM 51/280.
[76] *Dublin Weekly Journal*, 23 May 1732.
[77] P.R.O., ADM 51/4172.
[78] Neston parish register (burials), 6 Jan. 1735.

board as midshipman.[79] Sometimes if the commander was not aboard the master would command the ship.

After Lawson's death, the *Dublin*'s new commander was Captain John Weller (senior) who took command from May 1734 until he resigned in favour of his son, also John Weller, in 1751.[80] Perhaps the father was already unwell, for he died in January 1753:[81]

> He was cut for the stone six days before he died. As he was an experienced commander, a well-bred gentleman and a sincere friend, his death is much lamented.

John Weller junior remained with R.Y. *Dublin* until she was broken up in 1752, when he commissioned her successor. George Newman was followed as master by William Culbert, who made his mark in the parish of Neston by becoming the supposed father of Hannah, daughter of Margaret Howard whose husband was a Parkgate mariner.[82]

The usual purpose of the yachts in these years was to carry persons of importance by the permission of the lord lieutenant or, in his absence, a commission of three called the lords justices who acted as a vice-regal council. After the fourteenth century, the title of lord lieutenant or lord deputy (to the lieutenant) succeeded that of justiciar, which remained the title for an emergency appointment. For much of the eighteenth century the viceroy, usually termed the lord lieutenant in these years, came to Ireland for only a few months in alternate years for the parliamentary sessions. During his absence the lords justices held office and they were, typically, the archbishop of Armagh (as primate of all Ireland), the chancellor and the speaker of the House of Commons, although others might be appointed on occasions.

From 1767 to 1800 the viceroys were resident almost continuously.[83] Orders for the yacht, or permission to use it officially, were granted by warrant. The names of warrant-holders were entered into the yacht's muster roll, listed as 'supernumeraries' (that is, extra to the ship's complement) and were there stated to be carried 'by order

[79] e.g. for Weller, P.R.O., ADM 36/898, 1 Jan. 1738.
[80] *Dublin Weekly Journal*, 18 May 1751.
[81] *Faulkner's Dublin Journal*, 9 Jan. 1753.
[82] Neston parish register, baptism 15 July 1746.
[83] T. W. Moody, F. X. Martin, F. J. Byrne, eds., *A New History of Ireland*, 9 (1984) succession lists of Chief Governors by J. G. Simms, pp. 486, 493.

of the Lord Lieutenant' or 'by order of the Lords Justices of Ireland'. The entry usually added, 'borne for victuals only', which technically meant that they were entitled to meals, and of course carriage, but not wages.

Sometimes the yacht's captain was given direct orders:[84]

> wee have ordered Captain William Wright, Commander of the Monmouth Yacht, to sayle to Chester water, there to attend such further orders as he shall from time to time receive from us.

And similarly, the earl of Clarendon signed a warrant to the captain of the yacht to go to Beaumaris to collect his successor as lord deputy, Lord Tyrconnel.[85] Sometimes there was a request for the yacht's use:[86]

> The Master of the Rolls sent a message yesterday to the Lords Justices to desire that he might have the use of the yacht to carry him to Parkgate upon its return hither, for that he found himself strong enough to undertake a journey to Bath.

From the point of view of the captain, they were all orders:[87]

> The Dublin Yacht is to call at Holyhead to bring over the Rt Hon Sir Thomas Prendergast and his lady; and will immediately go to Parkgate for Cooly Westly Esq and his family.

In the year 1738, 111 warrant passengers were carried on fifteen voyages, eleven of them from Dublin to Parkgate and four trips from Parkgate to Dublin. No warrant passengers were carried to or from Holyhead or any other port in that year.[88] Often the passengers were noblemen, including Lord Lanesborough, Lord Forbes, earl of Granard, Lord Butterworth, earl of Thomond, earl of Anglesey, Lord Limerick, earl of Darnley, Lord Howth and the earl of Barrymore. Frequently the warrant passengers were gentry rather than nobility, or were soldiers: in two months in 1737 the yacht carried Brigadier-General John Ligonier and two servants from Holyhead

[84] 9 Jan. 1691, quoted in *Cheshire Sheaf* (April 1884), p. 133, item 2200.
[85] S. W. Singer, ed., *The Correspondence of Henry Hyde, Earl of Clarendon* (1828) 2, p. 136, 13 Jan. 1687.
[86] H.M.C., *MSS of Mrs Stopford-Sackville*, 1 (1904), p. 232, 21 Sept. 1754.
[87] *Faulkner's Dublin Journal*, 18 May 1742.
[88] P.R.O., ADM 36/898.

to Dublin, and then General John Cope and his servant to Parkgate. The ship returned to Dublin without warrant passengers, and sailed with Colonel Cornwallis, his wife and two servants to Parkgate. Whereas the captains' logs tend to mention only a single important person on a particular voyage, if one is mentioned at all, the muster rolls list them all. For example, when the duke of Devonshire as lord lieutenant embarked at Parkgate in March 1738, it was with a retinue of 38: The duke, duchess and two children, two A.D.C.s, two secretaries and a gentleman of the bedchamber, two chaplains, four pages, four gentlemen for his Grace, her Grace's four women, a steward, a cook and thirteen footmen.[89]

The average number of warrant passengers carried on each voyage was low: seven in 1738, twelve in 1753, ten in 1758. There was therefore a good deal of spare capacity on most voyages, and there were plenty of voyages when no warrant passengers were carried. The remaining passengers, and we know that there were two hundred of them on one voyage, travelled by private arrangement with the captain and cannot be traced in the ship's documents. For example, Dr Patrick Delany as dean of Down was sufficiently an establishment figure to claim official status on occasions: in 1732 [90]

> a warrant was passed last Saturday for the Yacht to be at Holyhead the 15th [October] to bring over the Rev. Dr Delany and his lady, from Chester.

The lady was his first wife. His second wife, née Mary Granville, left a record of several trips across the Irish sea, and in 1744 she sailed on R.Y. *Dublin*:[91]

> On Sunday evening we removed from Chester to Parkgate in hope of sailing next morning early, but the wind was contrary, and we were obliged to remain there all Monday. We were so lucky as to get a very clean, good lodging, and on Tuesday morning went on board the yacht.

The yacht's muster roll shows that for this voyage, eight warrant passengers were carried, and Mrs Delany was not one of them.[92] Ten

[89] *ibid.*
[90] *Dublin Journal*, 10 Oct. 1732.
[91] Mary Delany, *The Autobiography and Correspondence of Mary Granville, Mrs Delany*, ed. Lady Llanover (6 vols., 1861-2) 2, p. 365.
[92] P.R.O., ADM 36/900.

years later she sailed with her husband on R.Y. *Dorset* and clearly they were not expected:[93]

> We have good reason to think that we shall sail this evening; the wind is turning about and is very temperate and pleasant, and we have secured our passage in the yacht. She is a charming clean new ship, and reckoned the best sailor on the coast. The Dean went on board her yesterday to fix the best accommodation he could, and had we not come to Parkgate as we did, we should not have found room. People come every day, and the place is crowded.

But four years later she and her husband did have warrants, and are inscribed in R.Y. *Dorset*'s muster roll as 'Dean of Down and Mrs Delany'.[94]

There survives a long account of a voyage on R.Y. *Dublin* in 1738 by George Pakenham who met Lord and Lady Buttevant at Parkgate.[95] No passengers on this voyage had warrants.

> Our goods carried to the boat which went aboard the yacht. Came after with Lord and Lady B. and were received with kettle drums, trumpets etc. No other company of fashion . . . commanded by Captain Weller and very fine accommodation aboard.

But the yacht ran into heavy weather and could sail no further than Beaumaris:

> The passengers were all much fatigued, and the Captain telling us he could not make the passage but must go back to Parkgate to wait for a fairer wind, we chose rather to go ashore here, which we did to the number of 200 in all, in order to go overland to Holyhead, there to take the 'Pacquet'. Lord and Lady B. and I came in a boat first, and at going from the ship side were saluted with 8 guns.

So the 'no other company of fashion' turned out to be two hundred fellow passengers. The vice-regal status of the Royal Yacht made its

---

[93] Mary Delany, *Autobiography* 3, pp. 276–7, 14 June 1754.
[94] P.R.O., ADM 36/7115, 3 July 1758.
[95] George Pakenham's journal, 10–11 Oct. 1738, in *Analecta Hibernica* 15 (1944), p. 114.

captain very conscious of ceremony, and nobility were always sa-
luted by the firing of the appropriate number of guns.

There was clearly a social cachet attached to travelling in the Royal
Yacht which attracted the nobility and gentry to Parkgate, which in
turn gained a certain esteem. Not only was the yacht's accommodation good but the ship was a sound and safe sailer, with far more
crew members to attend to her than could ever be found on a
comparable merchant ship: the Navy provided forty or fifty crew
compared with about six men whom one could expect on a merchant
vessel.[96] Another powerful attraction was that the yacht, as a possession of the crown, could not be required to take the vagrants who,
as we shall see, could add considerably to the variety of one's
travelling companions. Nor was the yacht likely to take the harvest
labourers who might be found in large numbers on other ships at
certain seasons.

The considerable numbers of passengers sailing on the yacht, at
considerable prices in the case of noblemen, meant that the captaincy
carried a most valuable perquisite. As we shall see with Alexander
Schomberg, not everybody approved of a naval officer earning
money in such a way.

The R.Y. *Dorset*, built in 1753 to replace the *Dublin* after her
forty-three years' service, was to last even longer, for sixty years. At
164 tons and 78 feet long, she was the largest of the royal yachts to
use the Dee. From the paintings by Serres already referred to, she
was clearly an impressive sight, ornately carved and gilded. Here is
a description of her cabin written in 1782:[97]

> The cabin of the yacht is red velvet with silk flowers, very
> grand indeed . . . As soon as we got upon deck we went down
> a few steps into a cabbin where there was two or three nursery
> beds for the children and their nurse, there was two doors out
> of this, one of which led into a closet where the captain slept
> and the other into the state cabbin which has two beds in it,
> one for the Lord Lieutenant and Lady it is a crimson silk bed
> and the other for someone else I don't know who . . . Each man
> has a small cabbin and bed to himself. The crew is half English

---

[96] For relative manning levels, see N. A. M. Rodger, *The Wooden World*
(1988), pp. 40–1, 116.
[97] *Correspondence of Joshua Wedgwood* (1906) 3, pp. 5–7.

and half Irish, when she is at Dublin the Irish stay ashore and when she is here the English stay ashore.

She had a complement of fifty men. Her first commander was Captain John Weller junior, formerly of the *Dublin*, but he moved on after two years. His successor, Captain Hugh Bonfoy, set the precedent for the rest of the yacht's service by remaining in command until his death. It became the practice, in fact, for the captains to retire from the active navy, though still on the captains' list, when they accepted the lord lieutenant's service. Hugh Bonfoy was in command from 1755 until he died in 1762. The actor Tate Wilkinson met him in 1757:[98] From Chester

> I went with Captain Bonfoy, who was then commander of the Royal Yacht for Park-Gate, as the Captain had said he would sail that afternoon; here we were detained with several persons of fashion, who had been impatiently attending on the caprice of the wind. We all went on board but all returned as the wind continued obstinate.

The next commander, Captain William Williamson, took charge of the *Dorset* in 1762 and was in command when he died in 1771, to be succeeded by Alexander Shomberg.

Alexander Shomberg, born in 1720 about the time that his German Jewish father settled in England, founded something of a naval dynasty. While his two brothers became physicians like their father, Alexander became a captain in the royal navy, as did his nephew Isaac; one of Alexander's sons, Sir Charles, also became a naval captain, while another son, Alexander, became an admiral and had two sons who were also admirals. When Williamson died, Schomberg was offered the vacant captaincy by the lord lieutenant, Lord Townshend. Unfortunately the appointment was opposed by the first lord of the admiralty, the earl of Sandwich, who wrote,[99]

> I am persuaded when he comes to reconsider the matter he will not persevere in that pursuit, as I have informed him by letter that the person who retires to the command cannot have any claim to be employed in active service in His Majesty's Navy

[98] Tate Wilkinson, *Memoirs of his own Life* (4 vols, 1790) 1, p. 151.
[99] H.M.C., *11th Report part 4 (Townshend MSS)* p. 410, 30 Aug. 1771.

in case of war, or future desire to go to sea, in a line of battle ship.

Schomberg was furious when he heard of this and wrote to Townshend to complain of [100]

> the impropriety (I will not call it by a harsher name) of Lord Sandwich's interposition and misinterpretation when he writes to you of the determined incompatibility of my acceptance of the Dorset Yacht with my future employment in any active service . . . I mentioned Captain Weller who commanded a 74-gun ship in the last war after having been for some time commander of the Dorset Yacht . . . to which his Lordship replied that he was not then at the [Admiralty] Board . . .

Schomberg rather spoiled his case by writing intemperately,[101]

> My noble Lords at Whitehall think me weak enough to leave my cake and gnaw the streamer

for it was the thought that Schomberg was too interested in the financial aspects of the post which disturbed Sandwich:[102]

> I am sure, my dear Lord [he wrote to Townshend] you who are a military man and have the most proper notions of the sort of delicacies due to the preservation of a military character, will not think the carrying passengers for emolument is a proper school for a person that is to command a fleet.

And that was that. Townshend persisted with his offer, Schomberg accepted it and remained commander of the R.Y. *Dorset* until he died at the age of 84. He showed some signs of thwarted ambition as we have seen over the naming of the Point of Ayr lighthouse, and his reward had to be the knighthood conferred on him in 1777 by the then lord lieutenant, the earl of Buckinghamshire. This, then, was the view taken of the yacht's captains by those who looked from a

---

[100] *ibid*, 4 Sept. 1771.
[101] *ibid*, 9 Sept. 1771. The saying derives from lines by Matthew Prior:
"And he must be an idle dreamer
Who leaves the pie and gnaws the streamer."
*Alma*, canto 1, lines 387–8; see *The Literary Works of Matthew Prior*, ed. H. B. Wright and M. K. Spears (1959) 1, p. 481. A streamer was a pie decoration, perhaps a paper frill (O.E.D.).
[102] *ibid*, 2 Oct. 1771.

distance, as indeed it was of the captains of the Post Office packets at Holyhead, who were naval officers that had definitely and officially retired to a civilian appointment. As Sandwich went on to write,[103]

> if lucre is a person's object let him have it, but then do not let him aspire to honours that for the good of the Service must be pursued thro' a different channel.

Schomberg's attitude can be compared unfavourably with that of John Skinner, retired naval officer and captain of Post Office packets at Holyhead for thirty-two years. Skinner declined knighthood from George IV in 1821 on the grounds that he needed the income of a packet captain and could not afford to retire to knightly status. The king gave him a gold snuffbox instead.[104]

The usual pattern of sailing continued, for a while, much as before: the yacht normally sailed between Dublin and Parkgate with occasional visits to Holyhead. In 1764 the yacht was at Dublin on fourteen occasions, visiting Parkgate twelve times and Holyhead four times. The total number of sailings in a year varied considerably, partly because the yacht visited Plymouth for a refit every three years, partly through uncertainties of weather. In 1785 the yacht was at Dublin seven times, visiting Parkgate only three times and Holyhead four times. But for three periods (February to April, April to June, November and December,) the yacht remained in Dublin harbour because of the bad weather.[105] Two years later the Parkgate Packet Company's ships had begun sailing and the R.Y. *Dorset* had an altered sailing pattern: nine visits to Holyhead and only four to Parkgate.[106]

As the years went by the yacht was used less and less. In the ten years before the Packet Company began operations (omitting 1783 when the yacht spent six months refitting) the average number of sailings a year was 26.8 but during the following ten years the average fell to 16.3. For the ten years from 1800 the average was 13.6. There were several reasons for the decline in the yacht's usefulness. The Packet Company's ships offered respectable accommodation and much more of it. The R.Y. *Dorset* was growing old and required extensive repairs, with a four-month refit in 1802, six-month refit in

[103] *ibid.*
[104] J. Sparrow, *Biography of J. M. Skinner Esq* (1866), pp. 16–17.
[105] P.R.O., ADM 51/249.
[106] P.R.O., ADM 51/249.

1805, followed by three months of repairs the year after. The improvements in the roads to Holyhead and the increase in the number of boats there meant that there was less custom at Parkgate, and less need for a Royal Yacht at any port. After the Act of Union in 1800, Dublin ceased to be a capital city and quickly began to lose its social sparkle, while the Irish members of Parliament preferred to go to Westminster via Holyhead.

Schomberg remained as yacht commander until his death in 1804, although he was then 84 years of age. He did not always sail the vessel himself: his sailing master in the earlier years, Thomas Simmons, was quite often recorded as bringing the yacht into Parkgate.[107] Simmons became master and pilot in 1750 and did not retire until June 1784 when he was nearly 90 years old.[108] However, Schomberg was still being recorded at Parkgate as commander in 1802.[109]

Captain Lambert Brabazon, Schomberg's successor, was the senior captain in the navy (as Schomberg had been for many years) and was probably in his seventies when he died in 1811. His ship did not survive much longer.

The yacht had begun to spend very long periods at anchor in Dublin Bay: seven months in 1800, five months in 1801, four months in 1803, nine months in 1807, six months in 1811.[110]

The last commander of the R.Y. *Dorset* was Andrew Sproule. He brought her to Parkgate on her last visit in October 1812. On the 25th he anchored in Beerhouse hole, just as William Wright had anchored R.Y. *Portsmouth* 126 years earlier. On the 26th he 'came up to Parkgate, anchored and moored ship' for four days, when he landed eleven warrant passengers including the Staples family.[111] In 1813 the *Dorset* went to Deptford, spent a long time in dock and was sold in 1815. Sproule took charge of his new ship, R.Y. *William & Mary*. Built in 1807, at 200 tons she was too big for the Dee estuary and never visited Parkgate; but there was little work for her anywhere. During the year from October 1814 she was idle at Dublin for three months, as she was for six months during the following year, with a three-month refit at Plymouth in between. In the year

[107] The 'Parkgate Account' (Customs Account Book)—see bibliography.
[108] P.R.O., ADM 36/10678.
[109] Chester City R.O., *Parkgate Subsidy Book*, CAS/17.
[110] P.R.O., ADM 51/1326, 1350, 1443, 1620, 1710.
[111] P.R.O., ADM 51/2260.

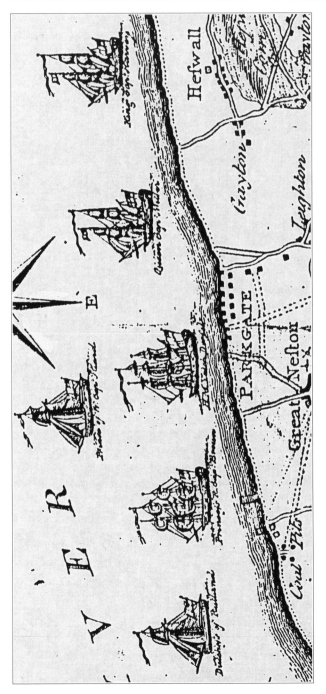

Figure 13. A section of James Hunter's *A New Map of the Hundred of Wirral with the proposed canal from the Chester Canal Bason to the River Mersey*. The captions read: at the top, Prince of W[ales], Capt. Heard; below, left to right, Dutchess of Rutland, Princess R[oyal] Capt. Brown, H.M. Yacht Dorset, Queen Capt. Miller, King Capt. Harvey. (Reproduced by permission of the County Archivist, Cheshire Record Office).

from September 1816 she spent a full nine months immobile at Dublin.[112] Not only had the long association between the Royal Yachts and Parkgate drawn to a close; the role of the yacht itself was passing away.

This lack of purpose became even more pronounced after the advent of steam ferries from Holyhead and Liverpool to Dublin in the early 1820s. When William Burnaby Green was appointed as a junior officer to R.Y. *William & Mary* in 1823, he described his full court dress of garter blue coat richly embroidered about the chest, cuffs and collar with sprigs of shamrock, white breeches with gold garters, hat and feathers, sword. His undress uniform was a brown coat with shamrock buttons, buff waistcoat and breeches; but apart from attending his Excellency as part of his suite, 'I have literally nothing in the world to do'.[113]

R.Y. *William & Mary* was withdrawn from the Dublin station in 1827. Her successor until 1832, R.Y. *Royal Charlotte*, does not seem to have been replaced.[114]

### LIST OF THE ROYAL YACHTS ON THE DUBLIN STATION

| | | |
|---|---|---|
| R.Y. *Mary* | gift to Charles II 1660<br>on station c.1661–75<br>James Sharland 1665–72<br>William Burstow 1672–5 | 92 tons |
| R.Y. *Monmouth* | built 1661<br>on station 1675–8, 1689–98<br>Morgan Kempthorne 1675–8<br>William Wright 1687–98 | 103 tons |
| R.Y. *Portsmouth* | built 1674<br>on station 1679–87<br>William Wright 1679–87 | 133 tons |

---

[112] P.R.O., ADM 51/2964.
[113] Professor Callender, 'The Lord Lieutenant of Ireland and his yacht', *Mariner's Mirror*, 14 (1928), p. 58.
[114] *Navy List*, 1820s and 1830s.

| R.Y. *Navy* | built or rebuilt 1673 | 74 tons |
| | on station 1689–93 | |
| | Phineas Pett 1689–93 | |
| R.Y. *Soesdyke* | bought 1693 | 116 tons |
| | on station 1693–1701 | |
| | Phineas Pett 1693–4 | |
| | George Breholt 1694–1701 | |
| R.Y. *Charlotte* | built 1677 | 143 tons |
| | on station 1701–9 | |
| | George Breholt 1701–9 | |
| R.Y. *Dublin* | built 1709 | 148 tons |
| | on station 1709–1752 | |
| | George Breholt 1709–11 | |
| | Henry Lawson 1711–34 | |
| | John Weller Sr 1734–51 | |
| | John Weller Jr 1751–2 | |
| R.Y. *Dorset* | built 1753 | 164 tons |
| | on station 1753–1813 | |
| | John Weller Jr 1753–5 | |
| | Hugh Bonfoy 1755–62 | |
| | William Williamson 1762–71 | |
| | Alexander Schomberg 1771–1804 | |
| | Lambert Brabazon 1804–11 | |
| | Andrew Sproule 1811–13 | |
| R.Y. *William & Mary* | built 1807 | 200 tons |
| | on station 1813–27 | |
| R.Y. *Royal Charlotte* | built 1824 | 202 tons |
| | on station 1827–32 | |

For references, see the text for each ship; also J. J. Colledge, *Ships of the Royal Navy* (1969) vol. 1.

# 4 Merchant Vessels at Parkgate

A merchant vessel typical of those using the Dee estuary in the mid-eighteenth century is illustrated overleaf: the *Minerva* of Chester (figure 14). It is a brig—a two-masted vessel with square sails on both masts. At the stern can be seen a yard projecting aft of the mainmast, and furled to it is the gaffsail or brigsail, a fore-and-aft sail which is characteristic of the brig.[1]

There were two ships of this name known to be using Parkgate in the 1750s. One was the brig *Minerva*, 100 tons, 6 guns, 11 men, John Brown master, which received an Admiralty pass to sail to Marseilles in 1753.[2] She is known to have been taking lead from Chester to Malaga and Lisbon, returning with wine, lemons and raisins.[3]

From the same source it is clear that another vessel called the *Minerva*, John Matthews master, was a different ship, and was carrying lead to Dublin, returning with linen, cowhides and coney-wool. But Matthews was carrying passengers as well. In 1751 he took vagrants from the Neston house of correction to Dublin.[4] The following year he received high praise from the dean of Down, Dr Patrick Delany:[5]

> I will send Mr Gavan's coach-and-six from Chester for you, which shall set you down safe at Parkgate, where I will appoint the best vessel upon the coast, the Minerva, with the civilest and soberest master, Captain Matthews, to meet you at your day and convey you hither [Dublin].

---

[1] Liverpool ware ship bowl, Liverpool Museum accession no. 50.60.4.
[2] P.R.O., ADM 7/86, 15 Nov. 1749.
[3] P.R.O., E 190 1427/4.
[4] Cheshire R.O., QJF 179/2.
[5] Lady Llanover, ed., *Autobiography of Mary Granville*, 3, p. 101, 14 March 1752.

Figure 14. The *Minerva* of Chester. Liverpool ware ship bowl.
Delftware (tin-glazed earthenware), painted decoration in underglaze
blue, enamelled in orange and yellow.
(Liverpool Museum accession number 50.60.4. Reproduced by permission
of the National Museums and Galleries on Merseyside.)

It has been possible to garner the names of 362 ships known to have
anchored at Parkgate, 1686–1815.[6] This total does not include the
many which may well have done, for example those vessels which
sailed from Dublin bound for 'Chester' or Chester Water. Of the
362 ships, the rig is known of about one-fifth:

[6] The principal sources have been: Chester, Dublin and Liverpool
newspapers (see bibliography); Dublin and Chester directories; *Lloyd's Lists*
and *Lloyd's Registers*; Register of Admiralty passes (P.R.O., ADM 7/75–126);
Register of ships entering or leaving the port of Chester (Cheshire R.O., QDN
1/5); Liverpool shipping registers; Parkgate Customs accounts 1776–1802.

Rig of ships at Parkgate

| 3 masts | ship | | 9 |
|---|---|---|---|
| 2 masts | brig | 35 | |
| | snow | 8 | |
| | galliot | 1 | 54 |
| | schooner | 1 | |
| 1 mast | sloop | 12 | |
| | cutter | 6 | 20 |
| | yacht | 2 | |

These descriptions should not, however, be accepted too rigidly, particularly as regards 'ship'. Technically, a ship was deemed to be a three-masted vessel with square sails. But the word was often used more loosely, for example 'the good ship or vessel called a dogger and by the name of the Judae of Dundalk'.[7] A dogger is a two-masted fishing vessel. The same source refers to 'the ship or slope Nancy',[8] a sloop having a single mast.

Vessels could also be given different descriptions at different times. For example, the *Sisters*, built in 1789 at Parkgate, was registered three times at Liverpool: in 1789 as three masts, one deck; in 1790 as two masts, two decks; in 1793 as three masts, two decks. The vessel is therefore described variously as a ship or a brig.[9] The *Princess Royal*, registered as a ship in 1787, was described as a brig in 1798 and as a snow in 1812.[10] A snow is a type of brig where the brigsail is carried on its own short mast next to the mainmast.

In theory there is a difference between a brig (with square sail on both masts) and a brigantine (with square sails on one mast, fore-and-aft sails on the other), but this difference is not evident in the sources found. Most sources refer simply to brigs, with the exception of the Liverpool Shipping Registers which prefer the term brigantine for all such two-masted vessels.

The size of the ships, indicated as capacity measured in tons, has to be taken with a large pinch of salt. The formula for calculating tonnage, originally length times breadth times the depth of hold

[7] John Glegg's account book (University of Liverpool, Sidney Jones Library, MS 25.19 — 19 Nov. 1762.
[8] *ibid*, 5 Dec. 1763.
[9] Maritime Record Centre, Liverpool, Liverpool Registers of Shipping.
[10] 1798: *Saunder's* [Dublin] *Newsletter*, 20 June; *Cheshire Sheaf* 1st series 1, p. 107 item 346 (Nov. 1878); 1812: Lloyd's Register no. 502.

divided by a hundred, was altered in 1694 and again in 1733; and because the burthen of a ship affected the tolls it paid, stated tonnage can vary widely. In their evidence to a House of Commons committee in 1732, Captains Stevens and Bell both averred that ships entered at the Chester Custom House at 50 tons were commonly 10 or 12 tons more.[11] The River Dee Company's records, using the more elaborate formula of keel length × breadth on midship beam × half breadth divided by 94, yields some suspect tonnages which vary from entry to entry for the same ship. For example, the cheese brig *Suttle*, recorded six times between 1742 and 1745, is credited with a burthen of between 80 and 100 tons.[12] Nevertheless it is possible to gain a good idea of the sizes of ships using Parkgate. Of the 362 ships, the burthen can be given of 36 per cent, as follows:

| | |
|---|---|
| under 50 tons | 22 |
| 50–100 | 68 |
| 100–130 | 23 |
| 130–170 | 15 |
| over 170 | 3 |

Most vessels using Parkgate were between 50 and 150 tons, which is small as eighteenth-century ocean-going shipping went, and is an indication of the shallowness of the river. The largest ship recorded at Parkgate was the 300-ton *Stanislaus Angus* from Danzig with timber. Despite the guidance of a pilot, the ship went aground twice and damaged the keel.[13]

Most of this information has been gathered for the years 1740 to 1800. At that time, then, an average trading vessel using Parkgate was a brig, with two masts and a single deck, between 100 and 120 tons with a draught of 10 or 12 feet, 65 to 70 feet long and 20 feet wide. Out of all these vessels known to have come to Parkgate, only about 10 per cent can be shown to have been regulars. We shall see a more exact comparison of regular traders with occasional visitors when we look at the last quarter of the eighteenth century, for which detailed figures survive.

[11] *Journal of the House of Commons*, 21, p. 812.
[12] Cheshire R.O., QDN 1/5.
[13] Glegg's account book (see note 7 above), 27 Sept. 1765.

There is an excellent record of the ships which arrived at Parkgate in the fourth quarter of the eighteenth century, preserved in the 'Parkgate Account', the customs account book of Humphrey Read, deputy controller at Parkgate.[14] These accounts are now unique, as no other eighteenth-century record of this type has survived.[15] Unfortunately the record does not overlap the surviving exchequer port books for Chester, which are missing after 1770, and the accounts for Chester do not usually specify which ships called at Parkgate.[16]

As so often with customs records, there is some difficulty in interpreting the Parkgate Account. First, it records arrivals only, so that vessels such as the cheese ships which sailed from Chester and called at Parkgate to pick up lead are not shown. Secondly, virtually all the ships recorded came from Ireland or the Isle of Man; a single vessel from North Carolina is the only exception. It may be that all other ships went up the New Cut to Chester, but one cannot be sure. Thirdly, the account naturally records imports, even when, as with livestock, no duty was payable. Therefore the type of ship which is known to have visited Parkgate in the 1760s to be repaired, is not recorded by Humphrey Read.

Of the 169 different ships which are listed in these accounts over twenty-five years, only 41 called more than twice. The very large proportion, more than 74 per cent, which called once or twice only, usually brought livestock: cows or pigs with a few sheep. D. M. Woodward has noted that in the previous century the livestock ships tended individually to be only occasional visitors to the Dee.[17]

The long-term regular users of Parkgate, defined as those which called in five or more consecutive years, number fourteen vessels. Of these, one was the R.Y. *Dorset*; five were passenger ships belonging to the Parkgate Packet Company; and the remaining eight were traders.

---

[14] This account exists in two volumes which have become separated. The first, for 1776–90, is kept on exhibition at H.M. Customs & Excise Museums & Records Unit, Room M10E, Custom House, Lower Thames Street, London. A transcript by Edward Carson is in the Cheshire R.O. (942/Z1/NES). The second, for 1790–1802, is in the Chester City R.O. (CAP/4).

[15] See Edward Carson's introduction to his transcript (note 14 above).

[16] For the eighteenth century, the Exchequer Port Books for Chester are at the P.R.O., E 190/1361–1442.

[17] D. M. Woodward, 'The overseas trade of Chester, 1600–1650', *T.H.S.L.C.* 122 (1971), p. 36.

The number of different vessels arriving at Parkgate each year averaged 18.3, making a mean total of 60.7 visits a year. The least active year was 1777, when only seven ships made thirty visits. The highest number of different ships was 31 in 1790, making 89 visits, and in only one year was there a higher number of total visits—103 in 1798. These numbers suggest that Parkgate was never a busy port, and contrived to stay in business with average arrivals of only one or two vessels a week. Of course, the traveller did not see the statistical average:[18]

> We see every day vessels coming from Dublin, with great numbers of passengers for London, from men of rank to the lowest station.

As this traveller remarked, the great majority of all vessels at Parkgate, as recorded in these accounts, came from Dublin. Other vessels, usually with livestock, came from Newry, Dundalk, Wexford and a variety of other Irish ports, in that order.

The frequency of shipping was naturally governed by the weather:[19]

> We are returned to Parkgate, where we find the wind as obstinate as ever.

From another, perhaps rather surprising source, we can learn how long vessels could expect to remain windbound at Parkgate. Although sailing ships could find themselves unable to sail from any port, they were especially vulnerable half way up an estuary, and passengers were always very conscious of the likelihood:[20]

> for consider, my Jenny, besides the tediousness of the passage, how long I may happen to wait at Parkgate.

They waited with varying degrees of calm:[21]

> here [at Parkgate] we were detained with several persons of fashion, who had been impatiently attending on the caprice of the wind.

---

[18] W. R. C[hetwood], ed., *A Tour through Ireland in several entertaining Letters* (1746), p. 34.
[19] *ibid.*
[20] B. Fitzgerald, ed., *Correspondence of Emily, Duchess of Leinster* (vol. 1, Irish MSS Commission, 1949), p. 55, 28 June 1757.
[21] Tate Wilkinson, *Memoirs of his own Life* (1790) 1, p. 151.

The accounts of the Neston house of correction for the fifty years from 1750 to 1800 reveal the length of time that vagrants, who were being returned to Ireland under the Poor Laws, had to wait for a ship.[22] As the county authorities did not wish to pay for the vagrants' maintenance for one day longer than necessary, the delays to sailing caused by adverse weather were accurately recorded. A month's wait was not uncommon. In 1775 there was a delay of eight weeks, during which the unfortunate vagrants were put on board ship four times, only to have to return to the house of correction when the wind remained contrary.[23] The longest recorded delay between sailings was 65 days, or more than nine weeks, in 1757.[24] The rival service from Holyhead saw advantage in advertising these delays:[25]

> I was informed by a person from Chester that it [the passenger service from Parkgate to Dublin] was very uncertain, and depended on the freight and wind; that perhaps we might stay a fortnight or three weeks and not get passage.

A glimpse of the easy pace of life at Parkgate can be gained from the first four issues of the *Chester Chronicle* in 1775, when for the only time it printed 'Parkgate Port News':

9 May      Arrived—Dorset Yacht, Schomberg with passengers. No vessels sailed this week. The King George, Briscoe, and the Murray, Totty, wait for a wind.

15 May      Sailed—Dorset, passengers. King George, merchandize. The Ponsonby, Harrison, horses. Arrived—Nonpareil, Samuel Davies, passengers.

22 May      Arrived—Charlotte, Thomas Guile, with dung. The Mary, Humphrey Davies, and the Molly, Peter Lash, both from Newry in ballast. The Hibernia, Edward Jefferson, with passengers.

29 May      Arrived—Success, Lawrence Revet, ballast. King George, Daniel Briscoe, passengers.

---

[22] Cheshire R.O., Quarter Sessions files, 1750–1800, QJF 178–228.
[23] Cheshire R.O., QJF 203/2.
[24] Cheshire R.O., QJF 185/2.
[25] W. K. R. Bedford, *Three Hundred Years of a Family Living* (1889), p. 75.

In the same week, three times as many ships went to Chester.[26]

If life was relatively slow-paced for Parkgate mariners, here is an advertisement which suggests the flavour of life as it was enjoyed by Thomas Guile, a regular trader between Parkgate and Dublin. He was master of the *Charlotte* between 1772 and 1776, and of the *Salisbury* between 1772 and 1790.[27]

> Strayed, stolen or otherwise conveyed, from the house of Matthew Ryan Great Neston [the Golden Lion] on 21 April [1780], where a joyous Parish Meeting was held: a dark-brown bath-rugg GREAT COAT with a velvet collar, under which is wrote—Cap: T. G. Parkgate . . . if it was not stolen, it may probably (as it is a loose coat) have strayed, being somewhat intoxicated, and have forgotten its master, who believes there was a ginger-bread cake in the pocket (if he had not eaten it) before it took its departure. Half a guinea reward offered, and no questions asked.

At any one time there were likely to be about six vessels which were trading regularly between Dublin and Parkgate, until 1785 when the advent of the Parkgate Packet Company added a second tier to the trading pattern. The traders used to carry mixed cargo, or horses, or passengers, or all three as the occasion demanded. In the first half of the eighteenth century there is not enough surviving evidence to pinpoint which the regular traders were, and one gets no more than glimpses of particular ships, such as the *Racehorse*, which was sailing between 1730 and 1762 and is mentioned in a number of autobiographies.[28] The Dublin newspapers do not give much shipping information in the earlier years, and when they begin to do so in the 1750s, they give both Parkgate and 'Chester' for the destination of the same ships. But in this company one can pick out the *Racehorse* (Norman), the *Minerva* (Matthews) and four others as carrying passengers on a regular basis.[29]

---

[26] *Chester Chronicle*, 9–29 May 1775.
[27] *Chester Chronicle*, 28 April 1780.
[28] e.g. Dudley Bradstreet in 1738 (G. S. Taylor, ed., *The Life and Uncommon Adventures of Captain Dudley Bradstreet*); Letitia Pilkington in 1748 (*Memoirs*); the anonymous authors of *A Tour through Ireland* (ed. W. R. C[hetwood]) about the 1740s.
[29] George Faulkner's *Dublin Journal* for 1753.

In 1765, when the tendency to name 'Chester' had died out, six vessels were recorded at Dublin, besides the Royal Yacht, as taking passengers to and from Parkgate regularly.[30] In 1770 there were rather more: nine or ten trading vessels were carrying passengers, whereas in 1775 there were only five regular traders.[31]

From 1782 the regular traders are listed in the Dublin directories; and although these books list them as traders with Chester, they can be identified as Parkgate ships from the customs account.[32] In 1782 and 1783, six 'constant traders' were listed, dropping to four in 1784 and 1785, probably under pressure from Liverpool. In 1785 the Parkgate Packet Company was formed, and the 'constant traders' were reduced to two. These were Thomas Guile's *Salisbury* and Henry Totty's *Hawke*, which continued until 1791 when the *Hawke*, at least, switched to Liverpool. In 1788 the masters of three trading vessels, the *Hawk*, the *Salisbury* and the *Dublin*, announced that they intended to sail in rotation every fortnight; but the *Dublin* does not seem to have stayed the pace.[33] No further 'Chester traders' were mentioned in the Dublin Directories, but they were still there: the customs account reveals that, although the regular traders lapsed in the mid-1790s, they revived at the end of the decade. From 1798 John Connell and George Norman were both calling frequently at Parkgate.[34] The surviving customs account ceases after the first quarter of 1802 and subsequent information about Parkgate shipping is hard to find.

Sometimes, as we have seen happened in 1788, the vessels based at Parkgate acted in concert. One such occasion in 1771 was prompted by unwelcome competition for passengers:[35]

> We the undersigned Masters of Vessels constantly employed in the trade between Parkgate and Dublin, beg leave to return our most sincere and hearty thanks to the nobility, gentry, merchants and traders . . . we shall make it our study to use every effort to render our vessels and accommodations as agreeable as possible.
>
> And as the owners and masters of several vessels, employed

---

[30] *Freeman's Dublin Journal*, 1765–6.
[31] *ibid*, 1770 and 1775.
[32] *Wilson's Directory of Dublin*, 1782–94.
[33] *Chester Chronicle*, 28 March 1788.
[34] Chester City R.O., CAS/17.
[35] *Chester Courant*, 12 Nov. 1772.

during the summer season, in the coal trade between Ness and Dublin, have of late assumed the title of Parkgate traders, by which device . . . many passengers have been induced to venture themselves aboard such, to their manifest hazard and our great disrepute: we find ourselves under the necessity of thus acquainting our friends and the public, that we constantly have our respective vessels well found, manned, and in right good sailing order . . .

This advertisement was signed by the masters of eleven vessels.

The outbreak of war in America in 1775 brought trade to a standstill, and the following advertisement represents an attempt by Chester merchants to revive it:[36]

Each week one of the traders is in readiness, and will sail for Dublin loaded or not loaded, so that passengers will not be detained, as at other places. The management of the trade ships is left to Robert Hincks Esq, banker, Mr James Folliott, merchant, and other gentlemen in this city, who will make a point of having one ship in good condition, ready to depart, from Parkgate to Dublin every week.

| | |
|---|---|
| The Alexander | Hugh Williams |
| The Britannia | Gwin Brown |
| Conolly | Daniel Briscoe |
| Murray | Henry Totty |
| Active | Thomas Simmons |

The venture seems to have made a bad start and had to be resumed four months later with this advertisement:[37]

The traders [listed above] who have been confined to Chester by privateers, are now sailing again.

A year later it was reported that two of these ships, the *Active* and the *Alexander*, had arrived at Parkgate with Irish linens for the Chester fair, having been convoyed from Dublin by the *Stag* sloop of war.[38]

A comparison of these merchantmen with the naval vessel underlines the relatively small size of vessel using the Dee. The *Active* and

[36] *ibid*, 1 April 1777.
[37] *ibid*, 8 Aug. 1777.
[38] *ibid*, 17 July 1778.

the *Alexander* were both 130 tons, whereas the *Stag*, no more than a 5th-rate naval warship, had a burthen of 707 tons.[39] The *Stag* would have been able to come no further than Chester Bar at the mouth of the estuary.

Until 1785, passengers between Dublin and Parkgate either travelled in the Royal Yacht or took their chance in a trading vessel. To the captains, passengers were just another kind of freight, with the advantage of being 'self loading freight'.[40] A fairly typical example of the kind of mixed cargo which passengers might find themselves sharing was carried to Dublin in 1771 by the *King George*, Daniel Briscoe master, from Parkgate with passengers, twenty-two troop horses, and merchandize.[41] Troop horses, remounts for the army in Ireland, were often carried from Parkgate: in 1748 George Wood set sail on a ship with thirty-one troop horses on board, besides a great quantity of merchants' goods and passengers.[42] A large number of horses on board could prove dangerous in bad weather. One pair of travellers sent their servant and horses from Parkgate: at Beaumaris,[43]

> he informed us that the vessel was drove into that harbour by contrary winds; that our horses broke loose in the hold, and the master of the ship was obliged to cut their throats to prevent further damage.

These travellers had earlier been warned against sailing on Holyhead packets with troop horses aboard.

The complaint we have read from 1771 that coal ships were seeking to carry passengers, reflected the period after 1760 when the nearby Ness Colliery was opened. Before that there were no specific coal ships at Parkgate but coal might be carried as a part of the cargo. In 1744 the *Union* of Dublin, Purcell master, arrived with passengers and coals.[44]

[39] Liverpool Shipping Registers, Albert Dock, Liverpool; J. J. Colledge, *Ships of the Royal Navy*, 1, p. 524.
[40] The modern R.A.F. term for passengers! See *The Daily Telegraph*, 10 Aug. 1987, p. 10.
[41] *Faulkner's Dublin Journal*, 9 March 1771.
[42] H.M.C., *15th Report*, appendix, part vii, MSS of Sir T. G. Puleston, p. 337.
[43] *A Tour through Ireland* (see note 18 above) p. 50.
[44] *Faulkner's Dublin Journal*, 19 June 1744.

When John Wesley crossed from Parkgate in 1762,[45]

> The sun shone bright, the wind was moderate, the sea smooth, and we wanted nothing but room to stir ourselves; the cabin being filled with hops, so that we could not get into it but by climbing over them on our hands and knees.

Hops were a frequent return cargo for the linen ships. When George Pakenham described Chester in 1738, he said there was [46]

> Great trade from Ireland hither with linen etc, for which they exchange hops chiefly . . .

In 1771 John Wesley sailed on two Parkgate ships: the *Kildare*, which he described as 'abundantly the best and cleanest ship which I have sailed in for many years', and the *Nonpareil*, the same ship which had been carrying hops in 1762. Yet it is known from the customs records that both the *Kildare* and the *Nonpareil* were carrying coal and lead to Dublin that year, though not on the dates that Wesley travelled. He did share the *Kildare*, though, with a cargo of merchandize and horses.[47]

We rarely get much insight into the meaning of the ubiquitous term 'merchandize'. We get a glimpse, though, when the *George* brought into Dublin a cargo of passengers, merchandize and 'a wardrobe for the Crow Street theatre'.[48] But when in the same year the two Parkgate ships *Trevor* and *Nonpareil* were lost in a storm, the lost cargo was described in some detail. The *Nonpareil* was carrying at least one hundred passengers and the only cargo mentioned was a passenger's coach and horses. The *Trevor*, on the other hand, was carrying thirty or forty passengers, and a very rich cargo of India goods which had been carried overland from London to Chester. It was said to be worth between £30,000 and £40,000, and included wrought silks, thread silk, silk lace, thread lace, millinery ware, silk and gold and silver tambour waistcoats. She also carried coals and £6,000 in money:[49]

[45] John Wesley, *Journal*, 2 April 1762.
[46] *Analecta Hibernica*, 15 (1944), p. 115.
[47] J. Wesley, *Journal*, 22 April, 22 July 1771; P.R.O., E 190/1440/10, 26 Jan., 28 March, 20 April, 24 May, 3 June, 11 and 12 July, 22 July, 2 Aug. 23 Sept. 1771.
[48] *Freeman's Dublin Journal*, 16 May 1775.
[49] *ibid*, 24, 27 Oct. 1775. See also *Chester Chronicle*, 23, 30 Oct, 6, 13 Nov. *Lloyd's List*, 27 Oct. 1775.

> The captain, all the rest being dead, was entreated by this man [the sole survivor] to attempt his escape but would not, which is imagined here was owing to a great charge of money he has on board, and that he supposed he would be accountable for it.

Parkgate was able to establish itself as a port and packet station because it could provide the services which both shipmasters and travellers required, and which were not available at Dawpool, for example. One of the important services was ship repairing, which sometimes turned to ship building as well. The proximity of Neston, which had been more than a mere village since the mid sixteenth century when the New Quay was established, and which already had carpenters and blacksmiths, must have helped Parkgate develop its ship-repair capabilities. There is a reference to a ship-carpenter at Neston, William Harrison, in 1680.[50]

We have already seen that Captain Wright brought the Royal Yachts *Portsmouth* and *Monmouth* to Parkgate in the 1680s to clean their sides. The first ship known to have been built at Parkgate is the *Exchange*, 90 tons, built in 1701.[51] At about that time two ship-wrights are known by name in the area: Thomas Barber who took a lease at the Leighton end of Parkgate, and Edward Richardson who leased a house in Neston.[52] From then on, many names of ship-carpenters, shipwrights, ship-painters, ropemakers, sailmakers, and anchor smiths can be found in the Neston parish registers. A few ships only can be named as Parkgate-built before 1780: the *Frances* in 1711, the *Maxwell* in 1714, the *Duke* in 1737.[53] During this period we know of two ship builders. One was Robert Prenton, who had a house at the north end of Parkgate.[54] The other was Samuel Ansdell, who bought a considerable amount of land on Moorside Lane, to the south of Parkgate, in 1729.[55] In 1737 and 1738 he led teams of fifteen

---

[50] Harrison's lease, Mostyn (Bangor) MS 4564.
[51] P.R.O., CO 5/1441; see R. Craig, 'Shipping and shipbuilding in the port of Chester', *T.H.S.L.C.* 116 (1964), p. 62.
[52] Mostyn MSS (Bangor) 4410, 4617.
[53] For *Frances*, P.R.O., CO 33/17; for *Maxwell*, P.R.O., CO 5/1443; for *Duke*, A. C. Wardle, 'The Early Liverpool Privateers', *T.H.S.L.C.* 93 (1942), p. 96.
[54] Mostyn MSS (Bangor) 4449.
[55] Deeds in the possession of Mr R. Lowry of Neston.

ship-carpenters who worked on the R.Y. *Dublin*.[56] In 1741 he bought some standing trees from Sir Thomas Mostyn and agreed to pay for them by instalments, one instalment to be in the form of a 30-ton flatt, or river barge, to be used at a salt-works at Mostyn in Flintshire. But Ansdell paid only the first instalment, did not finish the flatt, and 'absconded himself for fear of his creditors'.[57] He surrendered himself and was declared bankrupt.[58] Ansdell later signed on as a carpenter on the R.Y. *Dublin*, and served on her and her successor the R.Y. *Dorset* until he died in 1755.[59]

A different glimpse of the Parkgate ship-repairers is given by a set of sixty-two Acts of Protest, sworn statements before a magistrate, which were recorded by John Glegg for the years 1762 to 1768.[60] Many of these statements concern damage to ships, and four of them mention the ship-repairers. The dogger *Judae* was loaded with coal at Bagillt and crossed the river to Parkgate 'to get this said vessels lecks stopt'.[61] Richard Williams brought his brigantine the *Robert* of Dublin to Parkgate to get a new anchor and cable.[62] The *William and Agatha*, loaded with lead for Bordeaux, went ashore, 'and as there was no shiprepairers at Dawpool, has got a pilott and brought the vessel to Parkgate'. The repairs and pilotage cost £41.[63] The *Henry & Providence*, bound for Dieppe with lead, came to Parkgate so that carpenters could stop her leaks.[64]

The high point of Parkgate as the cradle of new ships was between 1785 and 1790, when a dozen ships were built by Thomas Makin, whose business partner was John Washington. Washington was a Liverpool businessman: from 1769 a Captain John Washington was living in Liverpool, described in 1774 as a merchant. In 1772 'John Washington & Co, timber yard' was recorded in Liverpool.[65] This

---

[56] P.R.O., ADM 36/902.

[57] Mostyn MSS (Bangor) 6913.

[58] A. C. Wardle, 'Some glimpses of Liverpool in the first half of the 18th century', *T.H.S.L.C.* 97 (1946), p. 149, quoting *Birmingham Gazette* 16 Aug. 1741.

[59] P.R.O., ADM 36/902.

[60] Account book of John Glegg, University of Liverpool, Sidney Jones Library, MS 25.19.

[61] *ibid*, 19 Nov. 1762.

[62] *ibid*, 11 Sept. 1763.

[63] *ibid*, 27 Feb. and 11 March 1767.

[64] *ibid*, 1 Nov. 1767.

[65] *Gore's Directory of Liverpool*, 1769, 1772, 1774.

may possibly have been the same man who captained the ship on which William Hughes tried to escape justice in 1757, as we shall see in Chapter Eight.

Makin's ship building was probably done at the north end of Parkgate, for Washington leased a piece of waste ground 'to be used as a ship and timber yard, near the road leading from the dwelling house of John Wright towards Gayton, in Leighton'.[66]

It would seem that Washington used his experience as both shipmaster and merchant to help launch the Parkgate Packet Company, the first attempt at Parkgate to provide ships specifically intended for passengers, other than the Royal Yacht. Of course the Packet Company also stimulated the shipyard: the first three ships known to have been built there were the packet ships the *King*, the *Queen* and the *Princess Royal*. However, disaster struck when John Washington, 'of Makin and Washington, shipbuilders of Parkgate', died in 1789.[67] Makin became bankrupt and the 'shipbuilder's stock-in-trade, timber, shed and mould room, smithy, anvil and smith's tools, a vessel on the stocks of 130 tons' were put up for sale.[68] At the time there were eight apprentices bound by indenture to the partnership, 'deserted by Thomas Makin and left at Leighton without employment' and the court of Quarter Sessions discharged them from their apprenticeships.[69]

### Ships known to have been built at Parkgate

| Date | Name | Tonnage | Description | Source |
|------|------|---------|-------------|--------|
| 1701 | *Exchange* | 90 | | P.R.O., CO 5/1441 |
| 1711 | *Frances* | 78 | ship | P.R.O., CO 33/17 (Craig) |
| 1714 | *Maxwell* | 90 | | P.R.O., CO 5/1443 |
| 1737 | *Duke* | 120 | snow | *Wardle* |
| 1785 | *King* | 100 | brig | *Chronicle* |
| 1786 | *Queen* | 100 | | *Chronicle* |
| 1787 | *Dublin* | 66 | brig | Liverpool Register, 1792 |

---

[66] Mostyn MSS (Bangor) 4491.
[67] *Chester Chronicle*, 15 April 1789.
[68] *Chester Chronicle*, 14 Aug. 1789, 19 March 1790.
[69] Cheshire R.O., QJB/3, 12 Jan. 1790.

| Date | Name | Tonnage | Description | Source |
|------|------|---------|-------------|--------|
|  | *Ferret* | 24 | schooner | *Lloyd's Register,* 1790 |
|  | *Princess Royal* | 134 | ship/brig/ snow | *Chronicle* |
| 1788 | *Active* | 101 | galliot/hoy | *Lloyd's Register* |
|  | *Charlotte* | 168 | brig | *Lloyd's Register* |
| 1789 | *Elizabeth* | 156 | brig | *Lloyd's Register* |
|  | *Sisters* | 158 | ship | *Lloyd's Register* |
| 1790 | *Oporto* | 147 | brig/snow | *Lloyd's Register* |
| 1791 | *Dreadnought* | 11 | cutter | Craig |

Sources:

*Wardle.* A. C. Wardle, 'The early Liverpool privateers', *T.H.S.L.C.* 93 (1942), p. 96.

*Chronicle.* *Chester Chronicle* (see the preceeding chapter).

Craig. Personal communication from Robert Craig, author of 'Shipping and shipbuilding in the port of Chester', *T.H.S.L.C.* 116 (1964), p. 53.

As has been seen, the onset of the War of American Independence caused a paralysis of trade. At Liverpool in 1775,[70]

> Our once extensive trade to Africa is at a stand: all commerce with America is at an end. Peace, harmony and mutual confidence must constitute the balm that can again restore to health the body politic. Survey our docks; count there the gallant ships laid up and useless. When will they again be refitted?

Nevertheless, trade continued and the customs accounts show that the traffic between Parkgate and Dublin did not come to a halt. The loss of the *Trevor* and the *Nonpareil*, combined with the dangers from privateers, together put a damper on the passenger traffic. We have seen that in 1777 a concerted attempt had been made to organize regular merchant ships for the benefit of passengers.[71] This attempt may be seen as foreshadowing the formation of the Parkgate Packet Company. But the war made any such move seem precarious, and in 1779 it even seemed to Joseph Hayes, beer brewer of Neston and

[70] *Gore's General Advertiser,* 29 Sept. 1775.
[71] See note 36 above.

the landlord of the Old Quay house of correction, that the shipping might cease altogether:[72]

> Should the trade from Parkgate be reduced so as not to employ the ships to pass as usual (which is too likely to happen) the vagrants will certainly be sent to the port from whence the passage to Ireland is most frequent.

Four years later the Cheshire Quarter Sessions declared that 'vessels very rarely sail from [Parkgate] to the north of Ireland'.[73] The magistrates also were worried about transporting vagrants but the number of sailings recorded in the house of correction accounts show that they need not have been, as much the usual number of vessels continued to sail.[74]

The resumption of peace caused a boom in trade, great waves of travellers and in a new initiative at Parkgate, where the Parkgate Packet Company was formed. The new venture was announced by the local newspaper in September 1785:[75]

> On Wednesday 23rd was launched at Parkgate a new vessel called the King, Richard Hammond commander, burthen about 100 tons, fitted up with very elegant accommodations for the reception of nobility, gentry and others: for their conveyance between Dublin and Parkgate; at which place another packet of like burthen, to be called the Queen, is now building . . . these two packets called the King and Queen, we hear, are to be in joint concern with a packet called the Prince of Wales . . . It is not doubted that the passage trade will regain what it has for some years back (for want of such packets) been deprived of by a neighbouring port.

The rival port was Liverpool, whose belated entry into the passenger trade will be examined presently.

The *Queen* was duly launched in March 1786, and a fourth vessel, the *Princess Royal*, was launched in August 1787. The new venture proved very popular:[76]

[72] Cheshire R.O., DHL 64/30, 31.
[73] *Chester Chronicle*, 9 May 1783.
[74] Cheshire R.O., QJF 211/1–4.
[75] *Chester Chronicle*, 2 Sept. 1785.
[76] *Directory of Chester*, 1787.

The interest and reputation of [Neston and Parkgate] have of late been not a little increased by the extensive and brilliant patronage shewn to the Parkgate packets; which, from the regularity of their sailing, the excellence of their accommodations, and every other advantage, seem to have decided ascendancy over all others; and in consequence, Parkgate is become the resort of elegance and fashion. These packets sail regularly at least four times a week.

It was not long before the success of the Parkgate packets began to excite the envy of the Holyhead mail packet interests. Just as the reputation of Parkgate had been depressed by the shipwrecks of 1775, so had the Holyhead route been affected by the drowning of sixty passengers on the Menai Straits ferry in 1785.[77] It was noted that the new *King* packet had left Dublin two hours after the Holyhead packet *Duchess of Rutland*, and was off the Head two hours before her. A year later the *Duchess of Rutland* was to join the Parkgate fleet.[78]

Towards the end of 1787 the *Princess Royal* met a contrary gale and was driven all the way to Milford. A letter was published in some London papers which said that the ship was liable to disaster, and its captain, James Brown, wrote in reply. He deplored this attempt to damage the reputation of the Parkgate packet service. He explained in detail why he had gone to Milford, and how he came to run aground at the Point of Ayr on his return (because the light in the lighthouse had been allowed to go out). The proprietors supported him and said how safe their ships had been.[79] Later in the same year, two other packet captains offered £50 for the prosecution of people who were spreading malicious rumours of wrecks:[80]

These reports originate with persons interested to prejudice the Parkgate packets.

Assertions of the dangers of travelling from Parkgate continued to be published in Wales. In describing Holyhead, Bingley wrote,[81]

[77] *Chester Chronicle*, 9 Dec. 1785.
[78] *Chester Chronicle*, 17 Nov. 1786, 23 Nov. 1787.
[79] *ibid*, 11 Jan. 1788; Chester City R.O., QAP/1.
[80] *Chester Chronicle*, 17 Oct. 1788.
[81] William Bingley, *North Wales* (1804), p. 306.

The passage, both from Parkgate and Liverpool, has been found extremely dangerous, on account of the Welsh coast, along which the packets have to run more than half way. On this coast, in heavy gales of wind from north-east they have often been wrecked.

This statement cannot be supported by any evidence at all. George Nicholson actually quoted some evidence which turns out to be spurious:[82]

This passage from Holyhead is considered much safer than those from Liverpool or Parkgate.

To which he added, in the slightly different context that Holyhead harbour was unsafe,

On 18th December 1790 the Charlemont packet belonging to Parkgate was lost, on the north point of Salt Island, when 110 people perished . . .

But the *Charlemont* did not belong to Parkgate and was never recorded there. Rather, it came from Liverpool.[83]

The *Chester Chronicle* sprang to the defence of the local interests. It praised [84]

the regularity with which the official messengers, with government despatches, have arrived in Dublin during the present most important national concerns. In this interesting particular the Irish papers are very flattering in their plaudits; one and all declaring that without the aid of the Parkgate packets, there would have been a chasm in the train of political events, as also in the commercial intercourse between this and the sister kingdom.

A year later, the same paper had this to say: [85]

Parkgate seems at this moment to out-flourish its former outflourishings; the packets, for a considerable time past, have been filled with the richest freights of fashion, and the

---

[82] George Nicholson, *The Cambrian Traveller's Guide* (1813), p. 647.
[83] *Wilson's Directory of Dublin*, 1786–90; *Annual Register* (1790), p. 228.
[84] *Chester Chronicle*, 30 Jan. 1789.
[85] *ibid*, 11 June 1790.

excellence of their accommodations are subjects of praise among the first circles of the two kingdoms.

It must have been about this time, 1790 or a little after, that a commemorative jug and bowl were made to celebrate the Packet Company. They are printed with the handsome likenesses of five packet ships, and beneath them is the legend, 'Success to the Parkgate Packets'. The jug is exhibited in the Liverpool Museum.[85] The bowl, in private hands (figures 15, 16), has the same scene as the jug inside the bowl, and a different view of the ships on the outside. The ships are probably the same as the five packet ships sketched and named on James Hunter's map of Wirral, which is also illustrated here.[86]

Two years later, in 1792, the Parkgate packet fleet was increased to six vessels, travelling in 'regular rotation'.[87] This was the peak of their success; but as the road communications were improved, the Holyhead route was soon to become the more attractive prospect. In 1796 disaster struck the Parkgate fleet when the *Queen* was totally lost on Birkdale Strand. All the passengers were saved, and they paid a high compliment to Captain Thomas Miller 'for his abilities and humane attention'.[88]

In 1804 the crews of the Parkgate packets were acting together for an unusual reason. Fifty guineas reward was offered by the Admiralty for information about [89]

A most violent outrage committed on 9th October at Parkgate on Lt Thomas Jennings, commander of H.M. hired tender Favorite and his crew, by the crews of the several packets called the King, Prince of Wales, Duke of York and Princess Royal, who assisted by others (in all about 30) armed with cutlasses and other offensive weapons, went on board the Favorite, and after assaulting Lt Jennings and crew, rescued from them a seaman who had been impressed by the Lieutenant.

Shortly after this incident there is evidence that something was wrong with the packet service, for in 1806 Captain James Brown, who had served the Parkgate Packet Company for twenty years as

---

[85] Liverpool Museum, ref. 54.10.
[86] James Hunter, *A new map of the Hundred of Wirral*, c.1790.
[87] *Chester Chronicle*, 13 July 1792.
[88] *ibid*, 9, 30 Dec. 1796.
[89] *ibid*, 9 Nov. 1804.

Figure 15. 'Parkgate Packet' Bowl, *c.*1790.
The legend inside the bowl reads 'Success to the Parkgate Packets'. This
bowl (in private hands) portrays five Parkgate packets. A companion jug,
showing the same scene as the inside of the bowl, is in the Liverpool
Museum (accession number 54.10.)

master of the *Princess Royal,* left them to set up on his own. He
bought two packets: the *Bessborough,* which he captained himself,
and the *Loftus,* with Captain Clements. Both these vessels were
discarded mail packets from Holyhead: the *Bessborough* had begun
sailing as far back as 1759, and the *Loftus* in 1790.[91] Yet the local
newspaper welcomed them:[92]

> We are happy to see the spirited exertions of Captain Brown
> meet with such success, for which the inhabitants of Parkgate
> are much indebted; the packet trade at that place had fallen into

[91] For *Bessborough,* POST 59/10; for *Loftus,* see *Wilson's Directory of Dublin,*
1790.
[92] *Chester Chronicle,* 20 June 1806.

Figure 16. The external surface of the commemorative bowl,
'Success to the Parkgate Packets'.


a kind of disrepute, but it has renovated astonishingly in a few
weeks.

The Packet Company, which at that time was controlling three ships,
decided to remedy its fortunes by buying a fourth:[93]

> The public is respectfully informed that the King, Prince of
> Wales and Duke of York packets, sail from Parkgate to Dublin:
> there is also a new packet, called the King George, Thomas
> Walker master, built at Gravesend . . . supposed to be one of
> the fastest sailing vessels in the Channel. They sail regularly
> every day.

Unfortunately, by buying a vessel that was not built for the conditions of the North-west, the Company made the mistake which
Samuel Pepys had managed to avoid in 1675, as she was 'considered
too sharp built for the sands'.[94] On only her second voyage to
Dublin, the ship ran aground on Dawpool Bank. At that stage she

[93] *ibid*, 22 Aug. 1806.
[94] *Faulkner's Dublin Journal*, 23 Sept. 1806.

was not injured, but the returning tide threw her against the sandbank and water began to enter the hold. There was a large number of passengers on board – estimates varied from 100 to 170 – and all were drowned save four or five.[95] The captain, Thomas Walker, was buried at Neston where his infant son was baptised the next day.[96]

This grievous loss seems to have been the end of the Parkgate Packet Company, and the following year their original ship, the *King*, was offered for sale.[97] The *Duke of York* continued to sail for a year or two, and the field was then left to Captains Brown and Clements in the *Bessborough* and the *Loftus*. The *Loftus* is last recorded at Dublin in 1814, the *Bessborough* in 1815.[98]

A clue to the management of the Parkgate packets can be gleaned from an account book belonging to Joseph Hayes, already mentioned as a Neston brewer.[99] When the *King* and *Queen* were launched, Hayes bought five shares in the two ships for £250. In 1788 he noted that he paid £10 insurance on the ships for the first three months of the year, but there is no further mention of insurance. Between 1788 and 1807 he received varying dividends amounting in all to £326. After the *King* was sold, 'the *Queen* having been wrecked', he was paid a final dividend of £13 7s. 6d. on each share, totalling £66 17s. 6d.

It has already been suggested that John Washington, the partner of Thomas Makin the shipwright, was likely to have been a moving spirit behind the formation of the Packet Company. When the proprietors endorsed Captain Brown's letter to the press in 1788, it was signed by John Washington. When he died in 1789, the partnership was shown to have held four shares in the King and *Queen*, and two shares in the *Princess Royal*, which latter ship had twenty-two part-owners.[100]

Some of the packet advertisements were signed 'Matthews, agent'. John Matthews lived at Moorside and died in 1797.[101] There are

[95] *ibid*; *Chester Chronicle* 19 Sept., 3, 17, 24 Oct. 1806; *Lloyd's List*, 19 Sept. 1806; *Annual Register* 1806, p. 444.
[96] Neston parish register, 1806.
[97] *Chester Chronicle*, 17 April 1807.
[98] *Wilson's Directory of Dublin*, 1814, 1815.
[99] Cheshire R.O., DHL 52/4.
[100] *Chester Chronicle*, 15 April, 14 Aug. 1789; R. Craig, 'Shipping and shipbuilding in the port of Chester', *T.H.S.L.C.* (1964) 116, p. 53.
[101] *Chester Chronicle*, 13 July 1792; 21 April 1797.

scattered reports of meetings of the proprietors: they met at Mrs Edwards' at the Two-Mills (probably the *Yacht Inn*) to agree the accounts for 1789 and make a dividend; and before the fateful decision to acquire the *King George*, 'a meeting of the owners of the King and Princess Royal Parkgate Packets' was announced.[102]

The Company maintained a storehouse at Parkgate. In 1804 'Mr Thomas Peacock and the Parkgate Packet Company' rented the former herring curing and drying house, 'sheds, spacious yards and premises' as a packet store house, and the rent was paid until 1809.[103]

## PARKGATE PACKET SHIPS 1785–1815

Vessels associated with the Parkgate Packet Company

| Name | Years recorded at Parkgate | Type and size | Master |
|------|------|------|------|
| *King* | 1785–1807 | brig, 100 tons | Richard Hammond 1785–9 Philip Hervey 1790–5 Joseph Grumley 1796–1807 |
| *Queen* | 1786–96 | brig, 100 tons | John Miller 1786–9 Thomas Miller 1790–7 |
| *Prince of Wales* | 1785–1807 | cutter | John Heird 1785–97 Edward Edwards 1798–1807 |
| *Princess Royal* | 1787–1809 | ship/snow, 132 tons | James Brown 1788–1809 |
| *Duchess of Rutland* | 1787–91 | sloop | Ben Hartwell 1787–8 Matthew Hewitt 1789–91 |
| *Favourite* | 1792 | | Matthew Hewitt |
| *Lady Fitzgibbon* | 1792–9 | brig | Matt Harrington 1793 James Scallion 1794–6 Robert Norris 1797–8 J. Toole 1798 |

---

[102] *ibid*, 26 March 1790; 11 July 1806.
[103] Cheshire R.O., DHL 52/5, p. 18.

| Name | Years recorded at Parkgate | Type and size | Master |
|------|------|------|------|
| *Dartmouth* | 1798–9 | cutter, 73 tons | John Connell |
| *Duke of York* | 1802–8 | | John Connell |
| *King George* | 1806 | | Thomas Walker |

### Other vessels described as passenger packets

| Name | Years recorded at Parkgate | Type and size | Master |
|------|------|------|------|
| *Dublin* | 1800–4 | | George Norris |
| *Venus* | 1802–5 | | Richard Guile 1802 Edward Brown 1803–5 |
| *Queen* | 1801–4 | | Thomas Miller |
| *Bessborough* | 1806–15 | 70 tons | James Brown |
| *Loftus* | 1806–14 | | Clements |

Sources:
*Wilson's Directories of Dublin*, augmented by the *Chester Chronicle*.

# 5 *The Alternative Routes*

To understand the place of Parkgate in the passenger traffic to Dublin, we must look at the other ports from which passengers could sail. Chief amongst these was Holyhead, where the boats provided for the Post Office mails took increasing numbers of passengers as its approach by land was improved. Portpatrick, Whitehaven and Bristol were sometimes ports of embarkation for Dublin, and eventually Liverpool also turned its attention to the passenger trade.

Holyhead is sixty miles by sea from Dublin, the nearest harbour to Ireland south of Scotland. The English government sent its Irish letters through Holyhead from the latter half of the sixteenth century and there were instructions for the post couriers dated 1574.[1] In 1598 the mayor of Chester was instructed that he must not delay Irish despatches while waiting for a favourable wind, but must send them to Holyhead:[2]

> there shalbe a boate ready attending to bringe them over by tydinge and other paynes of rowing although the wyndes should contynue contrarye.

It was not until the Civil War that a contractor for the Holyhead packet boats is named in the surviving records. He was Captain Stephen Rich, who had brought his ship, the *Rebecca*, into the Dee in 1645 to prevent any help reaching the besieged city of Chester.[3] Rich must then have been moved by parliament to Holyhead: he employed two boats for the packet service from November 1646, and the following year the commissioners of the Navy were instructed to make a contract with him, 'one to be constantly attending at Dublin and the other at Holyhead'.[4] One of Rich's ships, the *Patrick*

---

[1] *Cal. S.P. Dom., Elizabeth 96*, pp. 191–8 (May 1574).
[2] H.M.C., *8th Report, Appendix 1* (1881) MSS of Chester, p. 397.
[3] R. N. Dore, 'The sea approaches: the importance of the Dee and the Mersey in the Civil War in the North-west', *T.H.S.L.C.* 136 (1986), p. 14.
[4] *Cal. S.P. Dom., 1645–47* (1891), p. 612.

of Ireland, was captured in 1649 by the Irish but was recaptured and the government agreed to pay the salvage charges.[5]

There is little surviving mention of passengers in these years, but in 1649 Colonel Reynolds' regiment was marched to Anglesey for shipment to Ireland: they were ordered to pay for everything and not antagonise a poor country.[6] The soldiers, or some of them, may have travelled on a post bark but are more likely to have been picked up by a naval vessel. Rich did not receive regular payments, and he had to lay up one bark for lack of funds. The Navy Committee was urged to make speedy payment, but in the same year Rich was charged with neglecting his duty as postmaster.[7]

In 1650 a new postmaster at Holyhead was employed, Major Thomas Swift, governor of the Holyhead garrison. Two years later his ship was seized by the admiralty which had to be asked to release it.[8] An agreement had been made in 1651 that he was to be paid for eight men 'on the packet boate between Holyhead and Dublin', four being paid at Dublin and four in England. In 1656 this payment was made [9]

> for the management of the new Pacquet Boat named the Grace of Hollyhead being the Pickaroon vessel lately taken from the Enemy.

A pickaroon was a small pirate ship.

There were dangers on the seas for both passengers and the mail during these years. In October 1651,[10]

> Two pirates riding in this Bay, near the mouth of this harbour, for the space of sixteen days last past . . . On Saturday last took a vessel coming to this harbour from Chester Water, wherein were many passengers, who disputed with the pirates until by grenados thrown aboard them by the enemy their powder was fired and many of the passengers destroyed; and the same morning took the packet-boat coming from Holyhead.

---

[5] *Cal. S.P. Dom., 1649–50* (1875), p. 147.
[6] *ibid*, p. 98 (17 April 1649).
[7] *ibid*, pp. 109, 212.
[8] *Cal. S.P. Dom., 1651–52* (1877), p. 121.
[9] 'Commonwealth state accounts, Ireland, 1650–56' in *Analecta Hibernica* 15 (1944) pp. 233, 308.
[10] Robert Dunlop, *Ireland under the Commonwealth* (1913) 1, pp. 67–8.

The Restoration not only brought reform of the Post Office,[11] but it brought criticism of Major Swift. Two applications were made for his job on the grounds that he was 'a rebel against the late king'. One of his captains, Bartlett, complained that the two post barks had long been in the charge of a fanatic. In this same year, 1660, the two packet boats were named as *Swallow* and *Rose*.[12]

The word 'packet', originally used in the seventeenth century for ships carrying Post Office packets and letters, became more loosely applied in the eighteenth century to include ships which carried passengers. The Parkgate Packet Company, founded in 1785, never carried mail for the Post Office. The Holyhead mail packet captains, anxious to draw the distinction, sometimes referred to the Parkgate 'packets' as 'passage boats'.[13]

In the early 1660s it was not the packet boats that were recorded as carrying government officials on the Irish crossing but the naval ships *Harp* and *Dartmouth*.[14] In 1667 John Swift was confirmed as postmaster at Holyhead; he was being paid £400 to operate three packet boats. Three boats seems to have remained the number in use until 1768.[15] It now becomes more evident that passengers were frequenting Holyhead: in 1669,[16]

> We await a passage, but the weather is so bad that the packet which started yesterday was forced back.

A year later, in 1670,[17]

> The loss of the packet boate called the Guift in her passage from Holyhead . . . and 22 passengers in her drowned amongst whom Captain Bulkeley a brother of Lord Bulkeley's is said to bee one.

But the service was certainly not reliable. In 1673 the deputy post-master of Ireland was being urged,[18]

---

[11]  12 Charles II c.35.
[12]  *Cal. S.P. Dom., 1660–61* (1860), pp. 96–7, 126, 264.
[13]  B.L., Add. mss 39, 769.
[14]  *Cal. S.P. Dom., 1662–64*, p. 264; *1664–65*, p. 415.
[15]  *Cal. S.P. Dom., 1667* (1860), p. 200.
[16]  *Cal. S.P. Ireland, 1669–70*, pp. 23–4.
[17]  *Cal. S.P. Dom., 1670* (1895),p. 566.
[18]  POST 94, R. Whiteley to G. Warburton, Feb. 1672/3.

You must forthwith provide better boats, those being so bad that (as we are informed) your mariners will not venture to sea in them except in fair weather.

James Vickers, whom we have already met in connection with his opposition to the Royal Yachts, contracted in 1689 to maintain three packet boats for £450 a year.[19] However, the Post Office stopped sending letters to Ireland in May 1689 when James II was in that country, and alternative routes had to be found.[20] One was from Carrickfergus to Portpatrick in Scotland, but arrangements more local to the Dee were sought:[21]

The Committee for Ireland direct that you immediately secure a packet boat for carrying letters and passengers between Carrickfergus in Ireland, and Liverpool, Neston and Mostyn as you shall find most convenient.

Normal service was resumed in 1692,[22] but the dangers were not yet over. That same year, Vickers' 70-ton dogger, the *Grace*, was captured by two French privateers, the *Swift* and the *Martin*, commanded by two commissioners for James Stuart, and held her to ransom. The Crown repaid Vickers £50 for the ransom and £100 to re-equip her.[23]

When Vickers' contract came up for renewal in 1705, he was to be paid £600 a year for furnishing three vessels. These were called the *James*, the *Anne* and the *Expedition*. All three were damaged in storms the following year and the *Expedition* was lost. A year later, in 1707, James Vickers died, leaving a widow and eleven children.[24]

Until 1742, the date of the earliest surviving Post Office establishment book, information about the Holyhead packets is scattered and scanty. There was an embarrassment in 1716 with the contractor, Viccars, who oddly enough was a successor to James Vickers (a third Vickers was agent in 1773). Viccars was suspended in 1715 as a

[19] *Cal. Treasury Books* 10 part 1, p. 271, 5 July 1693.
[20] T. V. Jackson, 'The Irish Post Office, 1638–1703', *Bulletin of the Postal History Society*, 100 (March–April 1959), p. 3.
[21] *Cal. S.P. Dom., 1689–90* (1895), p. 225, 21 Aug. 1689.
[22] *Cal. S.P. Dom., 1691–92* (1900), p. 299, 26 May 1692.
[23] Edward Watson, *Royal Mail to Ireland* (1916), p. 63; *Cal. Treasury Books* 9 part 4 (1931), p. 1491, p. 1806; *ibid*, 10 part 1 (1935), p. 332.
[24] *Cal. Treasury Books* 21 part 2, 1706–7 (1952), p. 35; POST 1, Treasury Letter Book 4, p. 53.

suspected Jacobite, thought to have encouraged correspondence between the disaffected; and John Mackey was brought in from Dover. But the owners of the boats would neither sell nor hire them to Mackey, because Viccars was trying to run a private, rival service.[25]

In 1723 William Wilson became the contractor, and he encountered the same difficulty that James Vickers had once complained of. Up to 1726 he made little profit:[26]

> most people finding it more convenient to pass the sea either on the yacht that attends the Government of Ireland's service, or else go in merchant ships.

Wilson's contract was renewed in 1730 for seven years at £900 a year.

Two passengers in these years give us fleeting information about the packet ships. Jonathan Swift in 1727 mentioned the *Grafton* packet and Captain Jones who 'has not treated me with the least civility'.[27] Ten years later George Pakenham mentioned the *Carteret* and *Lovell* packet boats and actually sketched the *Lovell*, showing that it had two masts and square sails, like a brig.[28] The service, according to a Dublin newspaper, had become more reliable by the 1730s:[29]

> It is very remarkable that seventy-five packets have arrived here regularly from Holyhead, without two being due at any one time, which is a proof that it is an easy passage by sea to this place.

John Power was the contractor in 1742, and from this year onwards an almost complete record of the sailing packets can be assembled. He contracted to provide three packets of 60 to 70 tons each, with eleven men and two boys, for £900 a year.[30] Three years later an increase in traffic led to speculation that the number of ships might be increased from three to five, although this did not actually happen until 1768.[31] There survives from 1748 the actual contract of Power's successors. By articles of agreement dated 15 December

[25] *Cal. Treasury Books* 30, 1716 part 2 (1957), pp. 348–9, 423.
[26] *Cal. Treasury Books & Papers* 1729–30 (1897), pp. 396–7.
[27] Herbert Davis, ed., *Jonathan Swift, Works* (1969) 5, p. 205.
[28] George Pakenham's journal, in *Analecta Hibernica* 15 (1944), pp. 117–18.
[29] *Faulkner's Dublin Journal*, 4 Aug. 1733.
[30] POST 59/3.
[31] *Faulkner's Dublin Journal*, 5 Oct. 1745.

1748, between the postmasters-general and John Bertrand, Theophilus Thompson and Thomas Blair, they agreed to furnish for ten years, three vessels for the conveyance of His Majesty's Mails of Letters between Holyhead or Chester Water and Dublin, for £900 a year.[32] The alternative of sending mails via Chester Water is interesting, in view of the fact that this option was never used, except possibly during the years 1689–90 when Dublin was not under the control of the English crown. The wording of the contract may well date from those years, in case the difficult access to Holyhead broke down: but the only serious alternative to Holyhead that was considered for the Dublin mail was Porthdinllaen, a nearby harbour on the west coast of Wales.[33] The ships then in use were named in the contract (see the list at the end of this section); they were to carry one commander, one mate, one able seaman and two boys, and sail three times a week. The commanders were appointed by the postmasters-general and paid by the contractor £36 a year. The contractors agreed to build three new packet boats over the next eighteen months, but this does not seem to have happened, as the same three ships were still being listed in 1757.[34]

The proposal to increase the number of ships was revived in 1767 when the deputy postmaster-general for Ireland, Mr Fortescue, urged that three extra packet boats should be employed. In support, the resident surveyor, Atkinson Robinson, reported that

the wants of Government . . . frequently require a Packet Boat to be sent by express, without a mail

so that three or four mails had to be sent together. In January 1768 the Treasury approved the plan, so long as 'the utmost Oeconomy be observed'.[35]

For four years there were six packet boats sailing, but not enough funding had been allowed for an efficient service. The contract for 1759 had provided three boats for £350 each, whereas the three new boats in 1768 were allowed only £700 between the three: 'The terms of the last are greatly too low and the service has suffered

[32] POST 12/1. This document is wrongly dated in the catalogue of the Post Office Archives as 1764.

[33] M. Elis–Williams, *Packet to Ireland, Porthdinllaen's Challenge to Holyhead* (1984), p. 11.

[34] *Faulkner's Dublin Journal*, shipping arrivals, 1757.

[35] POST 1/9, Treasury Letter Book, 14, 21 Dec. 1767, 11 Jan. 1768.

by it'.[36] Both contracts were due to expire in 1773, and it was proposed that this opportunity should be taken to make two reforms: to end the system of using a private contractor to find the packet boats, and for the post office to contract directly with the masters of the vessels; and to use five vessels of 70 tons and eleven men each, thus achieving greater efficiency at no greater cost, £350 for each vessel.[37] From 1773, therefore, there exist records of the commissions of the individual packet captains.[38]

We have already noticed that the command of the Royal Yacht could make a lot of money for its captain, and the same applied to the commands of the post office packets. As Thomas De Quincey wrote,[39]

> The packets on this station were at that time [1800] lucrative commands; and they were given to post-captains in the navy.

One of the most celebrated and longest-serving captains, John Skinner, had lost an arm and an eye as a naval officer before retiring as a lieutenant in 1793 to become commander of a post office packet between Falmouth and Lisbon. In 1798, while carrying the mail to America, he had to fight off a French brig, for which he was awarded 50 guineas, with another 50 guineas for his crew. He joined the Holyhead station in 1799 and remained there for thirty-two years, eventually being swept off the deck of his vessel, by then a steam packet, and was drowned in 1832, aged 71. He had been promoted to commander by George IV when the king travelled on his ship in 1821.[40]

The captains seem to have owned their own ships and in some cases had them built themselves. William Rogers, captain of the *Countess of Chichester* from 1813, gave evidence that she was constructed at his orders.[41] Rogers said that when he joined the station in 1810, the profits of each packet went to the owner; but in 1813 'a joint stock' was created so that all receipts were shared amongst

[36] POST 1/10, 11 Dec. 1772.
[37] *ibid*, 29 Dec. 1772.
[38] POST 58/33.
[39] Thomas De Quincey's autobiography, in *Collected Works* ed. D. Masson (1896), p. 205.
[40] James Sparrow, *Biography of John Macgregor Skinner Esq.* (1866).
[41] 5th Report from the Select Committee on the road from London to Holyhead etc: Holyhead mails and packets, in *House of Commons Sessional Papers* 1819, 5.

the captains. Several of the captains had, like Skinner, been employed on the packets out of Falmouth, often to the West Indies, before being posted to Holyhead, and this move was regarded as a promotion, perhaps because of the rewards involved.[42] Because the captains owned their ships, they were not always easily controlled by the agent who was responsible for their work.[43] There were complaints in 1806 and again in 1810 at the number of voyages where the captains stayed ashore and the ship was left to his mate.[44]

The number of packets remained at five until 1809 when a sixth was introduced, and in 1813 a seventh was employed.[45] The seven packet boats were still sailing in 1819 when a House of Commons committee suggested that a steam vessel should be employed to tow the packets in and out of Holyhead harbour.[46] But events were moving fast: in 1820 two privately owned steamships, the *Ivanhoe* and the *Talbot*, demonstrated that they could cut the time taken for the passage by the sailing packets in half. In 1821 the Post Office introduced two steam packets of their own, the *Lightning* and the *Meteor*, and the next year steamships took over the route entirely.[47]

There were of course other ships sailing between Holyhead and Dublin, recorded in the Dublin newspapers as carrying passengers, but they were not regulars. An exception was the *Sandwich*, which was sailing regularly in 1770 and which may have been adopted as a temporary packet in place of the *Clermont* which did not sail regularly in that year.[48] Occasionally unofficial ships, such as the *Mary*, a sloop belonging to Holyhead in 1766, brought the mail over.[49] Between 1788 and 1793 there was a ship, the *Duchess of Rutland*, replaced in 1791 by the *Favourite*, which was sailing between Dublin and both Holyhead and Parkgate.[50] The *Duchess of Rutland* returned to this split sailing pattern in 1795, for which period her log book survives.[51] She carried the mail from Holyhead for short periods in

---

[42] Colin Jones was 'promoted' to Holyhead in 1798—POST 58/33.
[43] See dispute between Captain Skinner and his agent in 1812, in POST 29 packet 4B.
[44] POST 42/97 (1806); POST 41/1 (1810).
[45] POST 58/33.
[46] 5th Report etc. (1819) see note 41, above.
[47] Edward Watson, *The Royal Mail to Ireland*, pp. 113–28.
[48] *Freeman's Dublin Journal*, shipping news 1770.
[49] *ibid*, 16 Jan. 1766.
[50] *Wilson's Directories of Dublin*, 1788–93.
[51] B.L., Add. MSS 39, 769; 39, 770; 39, 771.

1795, 1796 and 1797, but between times was carrying passengers, mainly to Parkgate. Other ships' logs which survive (at the same location) are those for the *Bessborough* (1797), *Clermont* (1799–1801), and *Uxbridge* (1801–2).

From 1802 until about 1816 there were three wherries empowered by the Irish Post Office to carry both mails and passengers in competition with the British service, much to the annoyance of the London authorities who were paying the Irish Post Office £9,000 a year for the monopoly.[52]

The eighteenth-century Post Office packets seem all to have been fairly small at about 70 tons. We have seen that John Power agreed in 1742 to provide boats of between 60 and 70 tons, and those in the 1759 contract were said to be of 70 tons.[53] The actual tonnage of the ships named in the 1748 contract were given: the *Earl of Leicester*, 70 tons; the *Fawkener*, 65 tons; the *Wyvill*, 60 tons.[54] The packet ships in use during the nineteenth century were rather larger. The *Uxbridge*, which joined the station in 1801, was said to be 98 tons.[55] An account of Holyhead published in 1783 states that the packets then were 100 tons each, but inaccuracies in the account make this detail suspect.[56]

In 1819 John Skinner gave evidence that his ship the *Union* was 105 tons:[57]

> She is cutter-rigged and what is termed cutter-built, but not very fine; we are obliged to take the ground and the consequence is we are obliged to build them much fuller.

By this he meant that the ships were relatively flat-bottomed so that they would not roll over when beached.

---

[52] POST 12/10.

[53] POST 1/10, p. 44.

[54] POST 12/1.

[55] M. Elis–Williams, *Packet to Ireland*, p. 20.

[56] 'A short account of Holyhead in the isle of Anglesey' in *Bibliotheca Topographica Britannica* 10 (1783). It states that the contractor then was Thomas Blair, who had actually operated 20 years earlier.

[57] 5th Report etc. (1819), p. 56.

Post Office Packets at Holyhead, 1646–1768

| Contractor | | Ships | Captains |
|---|---|---|---|
| 1646–9 Stephen Rich | 2 ships | | |
| | 1649 | *Patrick* | |
| 1650–60 Thomas Swift | 1656 | *Grace* | |
| | 1660 | *Swallow* } { | Bartley |
| | | *Rose* } { | Carpenter |
| 1667 John Swift | 3 ships | | |
| | 1670 | *Guift* | |
| 1689–1707 James Vickers | 1692 | *Grace* | |
| | 1706 | *Ann* | |
| | | *James* | |
| | | *Expedition* | |
| | 1711 | *Ann* | |
| | | *James* | |
| 1715  Viccars | | | |
| 1716  John Mackey | | | |
| 1723  William Wilson | 1727 | *Grafton* | Jones |
| | 1737 | *Carteret* | |
| | | *Lovell* | |
| 1742  John Power | 1742 | *Carteret* | Bowser |
| | | *Lovell* | Jones |
| | | *Windham* | Jones |
| | 1743 | *Windham* | Owens |
| 1747  John Bertrand<br>Theophilus<br>Thompson<br>Thomas Blair | 1748 | *Leicester*<br>*Fawkener*<br>*Wyvill* | Pierce Taylor<br>Alexander Matthewson<br>John Bowser |
| " | 1753 | *Leicester*<br>*Fawkener*<br>*Wyvill* | Taylor<br>Hughes<br>Taylor, Edwards |
| " | 1757 | *Leicester*<br>*Fawkener*<br>*Wyvill* | Pierce Taylor<br>Matthewson<br>Owen Taylor |
| 1759  Thomas Blair | 1759 | *Bessborough*<br>*Hampden*<br>*Prendergast* | Pierce Taylor<br>Alexander Matthewson<br>Owen Taylor |

| Contractor | | Ships | Captains |
|---|---|---|---|
| 1759 Thomas Blair | 1760 | *Bessborough* | Pierce Taylor |
| | | *Lord Trevor* | Matthewson |
| | | *Fortescue* | Owen Taylor |
| 1768 James Blair | 1768 | (same ships) | |

1768  3 new packets were employed, making 6 in all: the new ships were:

*Hillsborough*
*Clermont*
*Le Despencer*

## Post Office Sailing Packets at Holyhead, 1773–1819

| Date | Ships | Captains |
|---|---|---|
| 1773 | *Bessborough* | William Forster |
| | *Dartmouth* | Joseph Hartwell |
| | *Hillsborough* | William Parry |
| | *Clermont* | Richard Taylor |
| | *Le Despencer* | John Boyde |
| 1774 | (*Bessborough*) | Charles Flynn (for Forster) |
| 1775 | (*Bessborough*) | William Goddard (for Flynn) |
| 1778 | (*Le Despencer*) | James Furness (for Boyde) |
| 1782 | (*Hillsborough*) | John Robert Shaw (for Parry) |
| c.1785 | (Dartmouth) | Edward Hartwell (for Joseph Hartwell) |
| c.1789 | Loftus (for Le Despencer) | James Furness |
| 1795 | (*Dartmouth*) | Edward d'Auvergne (for Hartwell) |
| 1795 | *Leicester* (for *Dartmouth*) | d'Auvergne |
| 1798 | (*Clermont*) | Colin Jones (for Taylor) |
| 1799 | (*Leicester*) | John Skinner (for d'Auvergne) |
| 1801 | *Auckland* (for *Hillsborough*) | R. J. Shaw |
| 1801 | *Uxbridge* (for *Clermont*) | Colin Jones |

| Date | Ships | Captains |
|---|---|---|
| 1803 | (*Loftus*) | William Fellowes (for Furness) |
| 1804 | *Duke of Montrose* (for *Bessborough*) | Norris Goddard |
| 1804 | *Dublin* (for *Leicester*) | John Skinner |
| 1804 | *Union* (for *Dublin*) | John Skinner |
| 1805 | *Lord Charles Spencer* (for *Loftus*) | William Fellowes |
| 1809 | *Sussex* (6th packet) | Robert Judd |
| 1810 | (*Auckland*) | Richard Davies (for Shaw) |
| 1810 | (*Lord Charles Spencer*) | Roger Western (for Fellowes) |
| 1811 | *Pelham* (for *Sussex*) | Robert Judd |
| c.1813 | (*Uxbridge*) | J. Agnew Stephens (for Jones) |
| 1813 | *Countess of Chichester* (7th packet) | William Rogers |
| 1814 | *Countess of Liverpool* (for *Auckland*) | Richard Davies |
| 1819 | The packets were: | |
| | *Uxbridge* | J. Agnew Stephens |
| | *Lord Charles Spencer* | Roger Western |
| | *Duke of Montrose* | Norris Goddard |
| | *Union* | John Skinner |
| | *Pelham* | Robert Judd |
| | *Countess of Chichester* | William Rogers |
| | *Countess of Liverpool* | Richard Davies |

We shall presently examine the choices which travellers to Dublin had to make, whether to board ship in Chester Water or at Holyhead. But some passengers, particularly in the years before 1700, discovered that a sea journey from the Dee involved a call at Holyhead in any case. According to Jorevin de Rochford, writing of the Beerhouse at Parkgate in the 1660s,[58]

---

[58] de Rochford, 'Description of England and Ireland', *Antiquarian Repository* (1809), pp. 586–7.

Here are some large storehouses for the keeping of merchandize to be embarked for Ireland . . . from whence all the letters,
the messengers, and vessels that are to pass, go first to the
village of Holeyd, which is in the island of Mone or Anglesey,
as a place of rendez-vous, there being a very good harbour,
from whence a boat commonly sets out for Dublin.

De Rochford did then sail to Holyhead and in due course on to
Dublin.

In 1738 Dudley Bradstreet, an Irish adventurer, also had a broken
journey:[59]

my friend and I went on board Captain Davis' sloop called the
Race-Horse and in ten hours we sailed from Parkgate. There
blew a most dreadful storm, which kept us two days at sea, and
it was with great danger and difficulty we got into Beaumaris,
in the Isle of Anglesea in Wales. We stay'd here a good many
days, saw several venerable remains of antiquity and were kindly
used by the inhabitants. From hence we sailed to Dublin, and
after a most troublesome passage, landed there late at night.

In 1748 George Wood embarked at Parkgate but the weather was
so bad that his ship could not leave the estuary, and he went overland
through North Wales. In Anglesey he found some ships from the
Dee that could get no further:[60]

New passengers are coming in every day from Chester and
Beaumaris which has enhanced the price of food very much.

Until the middle of the eighteenth century, the problem with
Holyhead was its difficult access. For those who feared the sea, sixty
miles from Holyhead seemed preferable to twice that distance from
Parkgate; but the overland journey of ninety miles from Chester
could be difficult, and for wheeled traffic scarcely possible. Therefore
travellers would often ship their baggage in Chester Water and travel
overland to Holyhead themselves, as the earl of Clarendon did in
December 1685:[61]

---

[59] G. S. Taylor, ed., *The Life and Uncommon Adventures of Captain Dudley Bradstreet*, p. 32.
[60] H.M.C., *15th Report, Appendix part 7*, Puleston MSS, p. 338.
[61] S. Singer, ed., *The Correspondence of Edward Hyde, Earl of Clarendon*, vol. 1, p. 196.

I am this morning going for Wales, with a light train, having shipped most of my servants and horses from hence [Chester] as they tell me my Lord of Ormonde used to do.

He then met the problem of passing over the mountain of Penmaenmawr:[62]

my wife in a litter, and the rest of us on horseback (though I confess, for my own particular, I went on foot) passed over Penman Mawr, at the foot of which, on this side, I met my Lord Bulkeley's coach and servants, but they told us they had escaped very narrowly being cast away in coming over the ferry, and that the winds were so very high that it was not fit for us to attempt going that way; so the coach carried us to Bangor, where we ferried over into Anglesey, and then put my wife into the litter again; for never was, or can come a coach into that part of the country.

He arranged for his own coach to be taken to pieces and carried 'by strength of hands', but to everyone's surprise it was pulled and pushed over the mountain in one piece. John Ogilby said in 1675 that the route over Penmaenmawr was,[63]

a path not only difficult but dangerous, the ascent being rough and steep.

Collins' chart of 1693 shows that part or all of the journey between Conway and Beaumaris could be made on the Lavan sands to avoid the inland tracks. But a sand road could be treacherous, especially to wheeled traffic.[64] Lord O'Brian found the journey a trial in 1668:[65]

I came to Chester on Wednesday and shipped my goods on Thursday, resolving to put out the next tide; but the wind came about the south-west so violently, with most terrible storms of rain, that despairing of a passage, I came to Holyhead through the most heathenish country ever any man travelled.

---

[62] *ibid.*
[63] John Ogilby, *Britannia* (1675), p. 48.
[64] Greenvile Collins, *Great Britain's Coasting Pilot* (1693), plate 28.
[65] *Cal. S.P. Dom., 1668–69* (1894), p. 5, 5 Oct. 1668.

The actress George Anne Bellamy recorded that, in about 1746, the road over Penmaenmawr was too narrow to admit two horses abreast.[66] As her fellow actor Tate Wilkinson later wrote,[67]

> It [Penmaenmawr] is not so tremendous now, for though that mountain still maintains its lofty head above the clouds, yet a tolerable road is at present cut for a carriage which in 1757 was not; and instead of falling from the precipice into the deep, if your horse stumbled, there is a friendly wall to secure you from such imminent danger.

The road at Penmaenmawr was apparently completed by 1772,[68] but it was in the 1750s that wheeled traffic had begun to appear more frequently:[69]

> In August 1753, We had about a month or six weeks ago eight coaches, chariots and postchaises in the compass of 48 hours from Chester.

> In September 1759, Common these days to see two or three postchaises arriving at Holyhead at the same time.

Turnpike Acts gradually began to improve the Welsh roads. In 1757 and 1759 two routes from Mold to Conway, and in 1765 the road across Anglesey, were the subject of such Acts.[70]

In 1769 parliament voted money to build a road over Penmaen-mawr,[71] and in 1776 a daily coach service was started from the *White Lion* in Chester. Four years later a coach service on a different route, which cut out the Conway ferry, started from Shrewsbury; but when John Palmer initiated his plan for sending mail on stage coaches rather than by mounted post-boys, the London to Holyhead coach in September 1785 went through Chester.[72] However, the road from Shrewsbury was made more attractive when the route through Capel

---

[66] G. A. Bellamy, *An Apology for the Life of George Anne Bellamy* (2nd edn, 1785), vol. 1, p. 105.

[67] Tate Wilkinson, *Memoirs of his own Life* (1790), 1, p. 153.

[68] H. R. Davies, *A Review of the Records of the Conway and Menai Ferries* (1942), p. 203.

[69] J. H. Davies, ed., *Letters of Lewis, Richard, William and John Morris*, vol. 1 (1907), p. 107.

[70] 30 George II c.69; 32 George II c.55; 5 George III c.56.

[71] *Journals of the House of Commons*, 1769, vol. 32, pp. 159, 390.

[72] Howard Robinson, *The British Post Office, a History* (1948), pp. 126–40.

Curig and Betws-y-Coed was turnpiked in 1802–5; in 1808 the mail
coach from London was rerouted through Shrewsbury, much to the
alarm of Chester, although a coach from Chester continued to take
the letters for North Wales as far as Holyhead.[73] By 1810 even the
*Chester Chronicle* could publish a letter praising the passage from
Holyhead, and the easy roads to reach it, in opposition to the plan
to create a packet harbour at Porthdinllaen.[74]

Although the steady improvement in the road during the later
eighteenth century turned a difficult journey to Holyhead into a
straightforward one, to the eventual disadvantage of Parkgate, there
were other hazards besides the roads. A letter of the 1770s said,[75]

> The road from Chester to Holyhead is in general a fine turn-
> pike road, but at the ferries and on the road you meet with
> great imposition. They charge the travellers in carriages 1s.
> apiece at each ferry, whereas they ought to demand no more
> than 1d. or 2d. for a horse.
>
> You will avoid Conway Ferry, which is very disagreeable to
> strangers and sometimes dangerous.

There were many complaints about the conduct of the ferries, both
at Conway and over the Menai Straits. This was a traveller at
Conway in 1780:[76]

> We had the misery of embarking on board another ferry boat,
> the danger and destruction of horses; and hereabouts they are
> all ill-contrived and dirty, and to strange horses a service of
> great hazard, for they are obliged to leap out of, and into, deep
> water.

Nor did things improve, despite many complaints. In 1813,[77]

> It is a pity that a ferry of so much public importance should be
> regulated so very badly, and that passengers should be sub-
> jected to the insolence and imposition of such men as are here
> employed.

[73] H. R. Davies, *Conway and Menai Ferries*, p. 212.
[74] *Chester Chronicle*, 7 Sept. 1810.
[75] Quoted by H. R. Davies, *Conway and Menai Ferries*, p. 205.
[76] C. B. Andrews, ed., *The Torrington Diaries* (1936), 1, p. 169.
[77] Hamilton Fulton's report, quoted by H. R. Davies, *Ferries*, pp. 215–16.

It was not merely that the ferries were badly managed; they could also be dangerous. In 1726 the Bangor ferry sank when crowded with people returning from a fair, and all but two were drowned.[78] In 1785 the ferry boat left Abermenai in a gale which drove it on to a sandbank where it filled with water. Some sixty passengers were drowned and only one man, who lashed himself to the mast, survived.[79] Thirteen people were drowned on the Conway in 1806 when the boat carrying the Irish mail upset, and in 1808 the Conway boatmen actually deserted their own passengers when the boat was stranded:[80]

> No comments are necessary on the conduct of the boatmen, it being universally allowed that the Conway boatmen are in general far more disagreeable to passengers than the ferry itself.

A final problem with the ferries, which applied equally to the mail coaches and the packet boats, was that the conveyance of passengers came a long way second to the speeding of the mail:[81]

> We were tumbled by rugged Welsh ferrymen, without ceremony, bag and baggage, mail bags and mail baggage, into a large boat; with the accustomed delicacy and attention of mail coach travelling . . . so that the letterbags and guard are safe, the passengers and their effects may go to the devil.

The problem of the ferries was not solved until 1826 when the Conway and Menai bridges were opened.

Travellers are often irritable, and we shall see that they were often dissatisfied at Parkgate. But whereas Parkgate was agreeably close to Chester, Holyhead was a long way from anywhere, and a traveller who was detained by the weather could find it a very tedious place. In 1669,[82]

> We await a passage, but the weather is so bad that the packet which started yesterday was forced back. If I stay any time in

---

[78] W. Bingley, *North Wales*, vol. 1, p. 280.
[79] *Chester Chronicle*, 9 Dec. 1785.
[80] G. Nicholson, *The Cambrian Traveller's Guide* and the *North Wales Gazette*, 25 Feb. 1808, both quoted by H. R. Davies, *op. cit.*, pp. 212, 214.
[81] T. J. Hogg, *Life of Shelley* (1858), vol. 1, p. 395.
[82] *Cal. S.P. Ireland, 1669–70*, pp. 23–4.

this miserable place I shall not know what to do for contentment. The country about is much infected with a kind of pestilential fever and we are practically in prison.

[Three days later] I am still at this comfortless place . . . No passage has been made for three weeks.

The town of Holyhead was very largely the creation of the postal service, at the point where the small fishing community of Caergybi clustered round the church of St Cybi:[83]

It is little more than a fishing town, rendered considerable by being the place of general passage to Ireland.

Because of its isolation, even simple provisions could be in short supply:[84]

All the bread used here comes from Dublin, 13 six-penny loaves to the dozen and a supply has frequently been wanting for a week in bad weather. Here is no fresh water in the village, except from rain.

This difficulty with the food supply could be made worse when larger numbers of travellers than usual were detained in the town. When George Wood travelled to Ireland in 1748 the adverse winds that caused him to leave his ship in the Dee and travel overland to Holyhead, also caused the ships trying to make the passage to call in there for shelter:[85]

The place swarms with labouring men from Ireland who are returning from harvest, and among them their wives and children, and many other poor passengers, computed at above 700 souls, who would starve but for a collection we are obliged to make and thereout buy provisions to distribute amongst them. New passengers are coming in every day from Chester and Beaumaris which has enhanced the price of food very much.

The most celebrated dissatisfied customer at Holyhead was Jonathan Swift, who was kept there for little more than a week in 1727, but

---

[83] *Bibliotheca Topographica Britannia*, 10, p. 16—'notes communicated by a correspondent who visited Holyhead in 1770'. See also D. Lloyd Jones and D. M. Williams, *Holyhead, the Story of a Port* (1967), p. 61.
[84] *ibid.*
[85] H.M.C., *15th Report, Appendix part 7* (1898), p. 378.

who spent that week in penning savage comments on his predicament. He had intended to sail from Parkgate on R.Y. *Dublin*, but had impatiently decided that he would be delayed there and so pushed on to Holyhead. His friends in Dublin reproached him, and said:[86]

> Our advices from Chester tell us, that you met Captain Lawson; the captain was a man of veracity, and set sail at the time he told you; I really wish'd you had laid hold of that opportunity, for you had then been in Ireland the next day: besides, as it is credibly reported, the Captain had a bottle or two of excellent claret in his Cabbin. You would not then have had the plague of that little smoky room at Holyhead.

One of Swift's difficulties was that the local people spoke Welsh:[87]

> I should be glad to converse with Farmers or shopkeepers, but none of them speak English.

Or as John Wesley was to say in similar circumstances,[88]

> O what a heavy curse was the confusion of tongues!

Swift described himself as [89]

> a passenger who is in a scurvy unprovided comfortless place without one companion, and who therefore wants to be at home, where he hath all conveniences there proper for a Gentleman of quality.

He wrote, on 25 September 1727, a savage little rhyme of thirty-five lines called 'Holyhead', which starts,[90]

> Lo here I sit at holy head
> With muddy ale and mouldy bread
> All Christian vittals stink of fish
> I'm where my enemies would wish
> Convict of lyes is every sign
> The Inn has not one drop of wine.

[86] Harold Williams, ed., *Correspondence of Jonathan Swift* (1963), p. 245, Gay and Pope to Swift, 22 Oct. 1727.
[87] Herbert Davis, ed., *Jonathan Swift, Works* 5 (1969), p. 204—Holyhead Journal.
[88] John Wesley, *Journal*, 6 March 1748.
[89] Holyhead Journal, in H. Davis, *Works*, p. 204.
[90] Harold Williams, ed., *Poems of Jonathan Swift* 2 (1937), p. 420.

During the period up to the 1760s, when the journey through North Wales was difficult for wheeled traffic, the prospect of riding on horseback for over ninety miles, or even for part of that distance, could be daunting. While John Wesley could say, 'I must be on horseback for life if I would be healthy,'[91] there were plenty of people who were not at all confident in that position. Jonathan Swift was one: in 1710 [92]

> I got a fall off my Horse, riding here [Chester] from Parkgate, but no Hurt, the Horse understanding Falls very well, and lying quietly till I got up.

In 1713 he rode from London to Chester in six days, just missing the ships at Parkgate:[93]

> Having not used riding these three years, made me terribly weary; yet I resolved on Monday to set out for Holyhead, as weary as I am . . . I will be three days going to Holyhead; I cannot ride faster, say hat oo will [sic].

In 1727 Swift 'went to bed and dreamt I had got 20 falls from my Horse.'[94] Tate Wilkinson, engaged to perform with Samuel Foote's company of actors, was worried in 1757:[95]

> Our patience [at Parkgate] being exhausted, it was unanimously agreed that we should proceed to Holyhead; horses were hired—this was early in November, and was not pleasing to me, who had never rode twenty miles on horseback in my life.

At least he had more experience than the actress George Anne Bellamy:[96]

> As I had never been on horseback before, I was not sensible of the task I had undertaken.

Even those who were not obliged to ride on horseback could find the long journey through Wales very daunting:[97]

---

[91] Stanley Ayling, *John Wesley* (1979), p. 252.
[92] J. Swift, *Journal to Stella*, Letter 1, 2 Sept. 1710.
[93] *ibid*, Letter LXV, 6 June 1713.
[94] Holyhead Journal, in H. Davis, *Works*, p. 203.
[95] Tate Wilkinson, *Memoirs of his own Life*, 1, p. 151.
[96] G. A. Bellamy, *An Apology for the Life of George Anne Bellamy*, 1, p. 104.
[97] W. S. Dowden, ed., *Letters of Thomas Moore*, 1, p. 13, 28 Oct. 1799.

Poor Hobart was almost shaken to death, during ninety-seven miles, on the outside of the coach.

The harbour at Holyhead could still be described, even as late as 1813, as 'one of the rude accommodations of nature, in which the helping hand of man has not interfered.'[98] The Act of Union of 1800 which required Irish members to attend parliament at Westminster, drew the attention of these members, and hence of the legislature, to the need to improve the road from Shrewsbury as well as the anchorages both at Holyhead and Dublin. The result, eventually, was Telford's 'Great Irish Road, not completed until the early 1830s; a pier at Holyhead, started in 1811 but not finished for ten years; and a new anchorage for Dublin at Howth, in use from 1818.[99] These improvements ensured that Holyhead was fit to face the future, but came too late to have much material effect on the traffic from Parkgate.

The rivalry between the passenger interests at Holyhead and Parkgate has already been described; in fact, despite some claims to the contrary, the crossing to Ireland was usually remarkably safe from either place, even if it could sometimes be alarming. As a tailpiece to this account of Holyhead it may be worth mentioning two occurrences calculated to frighten any sea-traveller. The first happened on 8 March 1780 during the American War of Independence, when two post office packets from Holyhead, the *Bessborough* and the *Hillsborough*, were captured by the privateer *Black Prince*, sailing out of Dunkirk under American colours, with an Irish captain, Patrick Dowling. The *Black Prince* had formerly been commanded by Luke Ryan, Irish smuggler turned privateer, who was captured by the British in 1781.[100] Just after the capture of the Holyhead packets, Luke Ryan was recommended for the freedom of the Dublin merchants' guild.[101]

Perhaps this well-judged act of respect may ensure them a safety from piratical depredations which they have long looked for in vain from the victorious navy of England.

[98] G. Nicholson, *The Cambrian Traveller's Guide* (1813), p. 647.
[99] See Mervyn Hughes, 'Telford, Parnell and the Great Irish Road', *Journal of Transport History*, 4 (1963–4), pp. 199–209.
[100] G. Rutherford, 'The King against Luke Ryan', *Mariners' Mirror* 43 (1957), p. 28.
[101] *Freeman's Dublin Journal*, 20 April 1780.

The post office had to pay £453 and £614 to ransom its two ships.[102] The other occurrence was the wreck of the *Charming Jenny* in 1773, because it must have made all passengers fear what might happen to them if they were wrecked on the shores of Anglesey. The *Charming Jenny*, a cargo vessel sailing from Dublin to Waterford, was driven on to the north Anglesey shore at Llanfihangel. As Captain Chilcot lay on the beach, 'exhausted and speechless', a looter cut off his shoe buckles with a knife. The corpse of Mrs Chilcot was stripped of most of its clothing and her pockets were cut off. For six hours he was left, 'unable to move, disregarded and unpitied', while his cargo was plundered. Three men were tried for plunder and one was executed.[103] No wonder a passenger on an earlier voyage from Dublin to Parkgate, whose ship the *Pretty Peggy* was driven ashore at Abergele, said [104]

We were alarmed with an account of the country people coming down to plunder us.

The shortest distance between Great Britain and Ireland was between Portpatrick in Scotland and Donaghadee near Belfast, something over twenty miles. Direct sailings between Donaghadee and Chester Water were uncommon, but did occur: in 1667 'Mr Ellis . . . brought his chest to Donaghadee in a direct passage from Nesson.'[105] When the Holyhead to Dublin mail route was temporarily out of action in 1689, the contractor at Holyhead, James Vickers, arranged a service by two boats from Portpatrick, but it was discontinued, probably in 1690, as soon as William III had won control of Dublin.[106] But the route was re-opened in 1713 at the suggestion of Mr Manley, the deputy postmaster-general of Ireland, with two packet boats costing no more than £50 a year.[107] This continued to be a mail route until 1849, when Portpatrick harbour was declared

---

[102] POST 1/11, p. 161ff. See also E. Watson, *Royal Mail to Ireland*, p. 80.
[103] *Shrewsbury Chronicle*, 25 June, 30 July 1774, 1 April 1775; Geoffrey W. Place, 'Wreckers: the fate of the *Charming Jenny*', *Mariners' Mirror* 76, no. 2 (May 1990), pp. 167–9.
[104] *Dublin Weekly Journal*, 4 Sept. 1751.
[105] *Cal. S.P. Ireland, 1666–69* (1908), p. 340. 6 April 1667.
[106] *Cal. Treasury Books*, 10 part 1 (1935) 5 July 1693, p. 271; 18 Sept. 1693, p. 332.
[107] *Cal. Treasury Books*, 26 part 2 (1954) 15 Sept. 1712, p. 449.

unsuitable and the route between Larne and Stranraer was substituted.[108] In the 1770s the mail service from Portpatrick was provided by four vessels of forty tons each, with a crew of five including the commander. The post office did not hire the boats but paid half a guinea for each trip to individual captains. The passage could vary from two and a half hours to twenty-five hours, but the service was said to be so uncertain that its mails often had to go via Holyhead.[109]

John Wesley went to Portpatrick in 1765 because he had failed to get a ship at Parkgate or at Liverpool:[110]

> It seemed strange to cross the sea in an open boat, especially when the waves ran high. I was a little sick, till I fell asleep. In five hours and a half we reached Donaghadee; but my mare could not land till five hours after.

A year earlier the actor Tate Wilkinson had a rather hair-raising journey in the opposite direction:[111]

> When I unluckily ventured over in the depths of winter, it was in a storm, accompanied by snow with all its horrid attendants, and in an open wherry; no shelter whatever from the inclemency of the weather; the sailors all drunk; twenty pigs and sows, and horses, and a methodist preacher: whether he or the possessed swine raised the tempest I cannot determine—I rather suppose the Fates. However, we rushed on the rocks on the opposite shore, which is remarkably rugged, with a force that seemed to me astonishing: they said it was the usual manner of landing at Port Patrick.

Wilkinson's suspicion of clergymen at sea was shared by the crews of the Holyhead packets. In about 1805 the *Union* packet was delayed[112]

> by a dead calm, for two tedious days and nights, which was solely attributed by the sailors to our having a mitred prelate on board.

[108] L. R. Muirhead, ed., *Ireland* (1949), p. 107.
[109] POST 12/10.
[110] John Wesley, *Journal*, 1 May 1765.
[111] Tate Wilkinson, *Memoirs*, 3, p. 210.
[112] Sir John Carr, *The Stranger in Ireland*, p. 25.

In 1767 John Wesley twice travelled through Portpatrick. On the first occasion he found that, as complained of at Holyhead, the mail was all important:[113]

> The packet boat was ready in the morning, but we waited for the mail, hour after hour, until past three in the afternoon.

On the second occasion he found that all the mail packets were on the other side, 'so I agreed with the Captain of a small vessel'.

Apart from unusually restless travellers like Wesley, Portpatrick was not really a rival to Parkgate, Liverpool or Holyhead. If it was used, the only possible advantage was the short sea journey. When William Macready arrived there in 1815 on his way from Glasgow to Dublin, he was 'detained in a miserable inn' and the packet had to be warped out of the harbour.[114]

Whithaven was chiefly noted for the export of coal to Ireland. In the late seventeenth century Greenvile Collins wrote that there was 'a good dry Peer, where great ships take in Sea-Coles and carry them to Dublin in Ireland.'[115] During the eighteenth century it became a very busy port, with a tonnage of ships clearing outwards exceeded only by London between 1750 and 1772. Apart from coal to Ireland with flax and linen by return, there was a considerable tobacco import until about 1750. In the 1790s there was a regular packet service between Whitehaven and the Isle of Man.[116]

Although there was no regular passenger traffic to Dublin, nor even the frequent carriage of passengers in the coal ships, some travellers nevertheless chose that route. In 1720 Lord Kenmare's sister, who had advised a correspondent three months earlier to travel via Holyhead, recommended that her nephew should return to Dublin through Whitehaven.[117]

---

[113] John Wesley, *Journal*, 29 March, 29 Aug. 1767.
[114] Sir F. Pollock, ed., *Macready's Reminscences*, 1, p. 99.
[115] Greenvile Collins, *Great Britain's Coasting Pilot*, p. 14.
[116] James E. Williams, 'Growth and Decline of the port of Whitehaven, 1650–1900', (MA thesis, Leeds, 1951); see also J. V. Beckett, *Coal and Tobacco: the Lowthers and the Economic Development of West Cumberland 1660–1760* (Cambridge, 1981), pp. 39–40, 85.
[117] E. MacLysaght, ed., *Kenmare MSS* (1942), p. 101 (19 Oct. 1717), p. 121 (20 Oct. 1720).

There are daily ships that go from that port to Dublin, and that's a much better and cheaper way both for you and the horses than to make them go to Holyhead by land.

John Wesley twice crossed the Irish Sea through Whitehaven. In 1752, finding no ship ready to sail when he was in Chester, he rode to Manchester and thence to Whitehaven. In 1765 he returned from Dublin to Whitehaven, on the Felicity, because he wished to go to Carlisle.[118]

The author of *Hibernia Curiosa* said in 1764 that [119]

The passage to Ireland is frequently made from Bristol by those who are not fearful of the sea. And this is generally taken, I believe, by the quality and gentry from Ireland that visit Bath. The distance from Bristol to the nearest point in Ireland is about 200 miles.

As our present concern is chiefly with the passage to Dublin, and the Bristol traffic was mainly, so far as passengers went, with Cork and Waterford, we shall here mention Bristol only as it appeared to passengers to and from Dublin. Oliver Cromwell sailed from Bristol to Dublin in August 1649, but he had with him at least 17,000 men and 95 ships.[120]

There does not seem to have been any regular movement of passengers between Bristol and Dublin. The Dublin newspapers, which regularly named the ships that carried passengers to or from Holyhead, Parkgate and Liverpool, hardly ever mention Bristol: an exception is the *True Briton*, which Captain Blair sailed from Dublin to Bristol with passengers in 1770.[121] It seems more likely that occasional passengers would make the crossing on trading vessels, and there were always a few of these on the route. The directories of Dublin, which list this kind of information from 1782, show that there were usually three or four constant traders with Bristol; but at no time do they mention passenger packets.[122]

[118] John Wesley, *Journals*, 13 July 1752, 2 Aug. 1765.
[119] John Bush, ed., *Hibernia Curiosa* (1764), p. 2.
[120] Denis Murphy, *Cromwell in Ireland* (Dublin, 1883), pp. 73–5.
[121] *Freeman's Dublin Journal*, 8 Sept. 1770.
[122] *Wilson's Directories of Dublin*, 1782–1816.

Those Dubliners who wished to go to Bath seem often to have gone through Parkgate. In 1754, for example,[123]

> The Bishop of Kildare, Dr Fletcher, and the Bishop of Clonfert, Dr Carmichael, sailed for Parkgate on the *Draper*, Captain Forshall, to take the Bristol waters.

And a year later,[124]

> The Master of the Rolls sent a message yesterday to the Lords Justices to desire that he might have the use of the yacht to carry him to Parkgate . . . for that he found himself strong enough to venture to undertake a journey to Bath.

> [Three days later] The yacht is returned and the Master of the Rolls purposed sailing for Parkgate tomorrow morning. He is so very weak and broken that we expect the journey by land from Chester to Bath will put an end to him.

In 1789 the Marquess of Buckingham also travelled to Bath through Parkgate.[125]

John Wesley had a special interest in Bristol because he often visited the city to see the school he had established at Kingswood nearby. He never sailed out of Bristol although he once looked for a ship there; in 1767, 'finding no ship which could take over me and my horses,' he set out for Liverpool, where there was again no ship, and he ended by sailing from Portpatrick.[126] On another occasion he sailed from Fishguard on the south-west point of Wales.[127] Usually, though, if he was at Bristol he travelled through Wales to Holyhead or due north to Chester or Liverpool. On two occasions he sailed from Dublin directly to Bristol; on neither voyage did he make any mention of passengers other than his own company.[128] Both voyages ran into stormy weather.

We know of one traveller, John Ferrar, in 1795, who intended to sail from Dublin to Bristol,[129]

---

[123] *Faulkner's Dublin Journal*, 19 May 1753.
[124] H.M.C., *MSS of Mrs Stopford-Sackfield*, 1 (1904), p. 232 (21 Sept. 1754); H.M.C., *8th Report Appendix 3*, p. 55 (24 Sept. 1754).
[125] H.M.C., *Fortescue MSS*, 1 (1892), p. 481 (21, 27 June 1789).
[126] John Wesley, *Journal*, 16 May 1767.
[127] *ibid*, 1 Oct. 1777.
[128] *ibid*, 20 July 1749, 23 July 1750.
[129] John Ferrar, *A Tour from Dublin to London in 1795*, p. 2.

Having engaged our passage on board a vessel bound for Bristol, the master gave us so short a notice, we could not get on board; but he obliged us exceedingly, by going off with our money, and sending us to Holyhead. On the 21st August 1795, we sailed in the Bessborough, William Goddard master, and had a very pleasant passage.

In 1787 the post office inaugurated a new route to Ireland, between Milford Haven in South Wales and Waterford; five vessels of 80 tons each were employed.[130] When the Chevalier de la Tocnaye tried to sail to Dublin from Bristol in 1796 and could not, he caught the packet from Milford to Waterford and went by land thence to Dublin.[131]

Although passengers regularly travelled on merchant vessels between Dublin and Liverpool, they do not seem to have done so in large numbers until the 1770s, and Liverpool was not considered by the travelling public to be a passenger port until those years. There may have been several reasons why Liverpool did not poach the passenger trade from 'our too near neighbours of Chester' for so long.[132]

The first reason concerned the road system. As the cartographer of roads, John Ogilby, recorded in 1675,

Chester has a great intercourse with Ireland, this and Holyhead being the principal places of taking shipping for Dublin.

He also referred to the road from London to Chester as 'one of the most frequented roads in the kingdom, accordingly affording good entertainment to the traveller.'[133] Coaches were travelling in organised stages along the Chester road from the 1650s, whereas a regular coach service to Liverpool was first advertised from Manchester in 1760 and from London in 1761.[134] Road access to Liverpool came through Warrington, and the road between Prescot and Warrington

---

[130] POST 1, Treasury Book 12, p. 241.
[131] Constantia Maxwell, *The Stranger in Ireland* (1954), p. 190.
[132] The phrase was used in 1601 by Giles Brook, mayor of Liverpool; H.M.C., *Salisbury MSS* 11, p. 465.
[133] John Ogilby, *Britannia* (1675), pp. 41, 46.
[134] *Williamson's Liverpool Advertiser*, 1 Sept. 1760, 20 March 1761; A. H. Arkle, 'Early Liverpool coaching', *T.H.S.L.C.*, 73 (1921), p. 7.

was turnpiked in 1752. The preamble to the Turnpike Act stated that the road [135]

> by reason of many heavy carriages of goods and merchandises passing through the same is become ruinous and almost impassable, especially in the winter season.

Allowing for the tendency for enabling legislation to state the bleaker side of the status quo, access to Liverpool was not straightforward before about 1760 and potential travellers seem to have perceived the journey to Chester as being markedly easier. Even in 1768 Arthur Young recorded that the Warrington to Liverpool turnpike was almost as bad as the road from Wigan to Warrington which he thought 'most infamously bad' and in particular was too narrow: 'But towards Liverpool is of good breadth.'[136]

Direct access by stage coach between Chester and Liverpool also started in the 1760s, when a new machine with six able horses was advertised, on 4 June 1762, from Chester to the Woodside Ferry boathouse on three days a week; on the other three days it ran to Parkgate.[137]

We have seen that the ferries in North Wales were often dreaded by passengers, and the ferries across the Mersey could also be daunting. In the late seventeenth century Celia Fiennes found it 'hazardous':[138]

> this [the Mersey] I ferry'd over and was an hour and a halfe in the passage, its of great bredth and at low water is so deep and salt as the sea almost, tho' it does not cast so green a hue on the water as the sea, but else the waves toss and the rocks great all round it and is as dangerous as the sea.

In the early eighteenth century Daniel Defoe was more impressed by the difficulty of landing from the ferry:[139]

---

[135] F. A. Bailey, 'The minutes of the trustees of the turnpike road from Liverpool to Prescot', *T.H.S.L.C.*, 88 (1936), p. 163.
[136] Arthur Young, *A Six Months Tour through the North of England* (4 vols, 1770–1) 2nd edn, vol. 1, p. 431.
[137] A. H. Arkle, *op. cit.*, p. 10.
[138] C. Morris, ed., *The Illustrated Journeys of Celia Fiennes* (1982), p. 160.
[139] Daniel Defoe, *A Tour through the whole Island of Great Britain* (1724–6), letter 10, vol. 2, p. 664.

Here is a ferry over the Mersey, which at full sea is more than two miles over. We land on the flat shore on the other side, and are contented to ride through the water for some length, not on horseback but on the shoulders of some honest Lancashire clown, who comes knee deep to the best side, to truss you up, and then runs away with you, as nimbly as you desire to ride, unless his trot were easier; for I was shaken by him that I had the luck to be carried by, more than I cared for and much worse than a hard trotting horse would have shaken me.

Just as the Conway and Menai Straits could prove dangerous to sailing ferries, so could the Mersey. In 1750 the Rock Ferry boat sank with the loss of twelve lives, and in 1751 the Eastham and Ince boats attempted to race each other from Liverpool on a foggy morning. The Ince boat collided with a flat and six people were drowned.[140] In 1753 the Woodside ferry 'was, by the violence of the wind, overset', and eleven people drowned including a Parkgate sailor.[141] And as with the Welsh ferries, the fares were criticised:[142]

the daily impositions that are practised especially upon strangers, and which are frequently to a shameful excess . . .

The Royal Yachts, since they were usually at Parkgate, only rarely came to Liverpool. The R.Y. *Navy*, on the station from 1689 to 1693 spent a considerable time at Liverpool at first but later tended to go to Parkgate, and while there used to send overland to Liverpool for provisions.[143]

It is remarkable that the Dublin newspapers, which regularly recorded passenger arrivals from the 1730s, make very little mention indeed of Liverpool vessels before 1770. In 1742 the *Providence* of Milford brought passengers from Liverpool and a year later so did the *Vernon* of Liverpool.[144] These two examples stand out as exceptions. During 1753 *Faulkner's Dublin Journal* printed very full records of passenger traffic with Parkgate and Holyhead, without

---

[140] *Birmingham Gazette*, 12 Feb. 1750; *Chester Courant*, 1 November 1751; both quoted by A. C. Wardle, 'Some glimpses of Liverpool during the first half of the 18th century', *T.H.S.L.C.*, 97 (1946), p. 154.
[141] *Chester Courant*, 20 March 1753.
[142] W. Moss, *The Liverpool Guide* (1796), p. 7.
[143] P.R.O., ADM 51/3918.
[144] *Faulkner's Dublin Journal*, 22 June 1742, 10 Sept. 1743.

recording one single Liverpool vessel in the context of passengers.
Yet in that same year it was stated,[145]

[Liverpool] is both a convenient and very much frequented
passage to Ireland and Isle of Man, there being always vessels
going and coming from thence.

The reason for this discrepancy may be that, whereas many Liverpool ships called at Irish ports, they were frequently sailing to or
from an Atlantic crossing. *Williamson's Liverpool Advertiser* for
1756 indicates little direct trade with Ireland, but frequent calls in
Ireland by traders with America; sometimes ships advertised that
they would *not* stop in Ireland. In 1764, 63.6 per cent of all vessels
reached Liverpool via Ireland.[146] It seems that the ambitions of
Liverpool merchants lay further afield. The *Liverpool Memorandum
Book* of 1753 lists 88 ships trading with West Africa, for slaves; 108
ships trading with the West Indies and America; 20 ships in the
London cheese trade, 28 ships carrying freight to Europe, and 102
'vessels from Liverpool in the coasting and Irish trade &c. [fre-
quently take freights for different parts of Europe]'. This volume
makes no mention of passengers.[147]

It would seem, therefore, that the uncertainties of when a merchant ship might, as part of a larger journey, sail to or from Ireland,
would be less attractive to the traveller than the short-haul ships
from Parkgate or Holyhead which would sail as regularly as the
weather allowed: we have read Parkgate's boast that 'passengers will
not be detained, as at other places.'[148]

In 1758 John Wesley took ship at Liverpool:[149]

We were five in all. We had seven more cabin passengers and
many more common ones.

Two years later he again sailed from Liverpool, 'having only eight
cabin passengers, seven of whom were our own company'.[150] In that

---

[145] *Liverpool Memorandum Book*, printed for Robert Williamson (1752) in
Liverpool R.O. (920 MD 407), no page numbers.
[146] D. J. Pope, 'Shipping and trade in the port of Liverpool 1783–93', University of Liverpool Ph.D. Thesis (1970), p. 23.
[147] *Liverpool Memorandum Book* (see note 145 above).
[148] *Chester Courant*, 1 April 1777.
[149] John Wesley, *Journal*, 28 March 1758.
[150] *ibid*, 27 March 1760.

same year, 1760, the sloop *Mary Ann*, 100 tons, advertised that she had room for passengers to Dublin; she also had 'a valuable cargo'.[151]

The author of *Hibernia Curiosa*, who made detailed mention of the various means of sailing to Ireland in 1764, did not mention Liverpool at all.[152] An analysis of the passenger traffic recorded at Dublin in the following year, 1765–6, shows that nine vessels were bringing passengers to or from Parkgate, most of them regularly; three packets were sailing regularly from Holyhead; but only one arrival with passengers, of a single vessel, the *Pitt*, is recorded from Liverpool.[153] Nor was the *Pitt* a regular, for she was taking wool to Chester the same year, and was at Parkgate in later years.

In 1770 a similar situation prevailed. While eleven ships were sailing regularly (and five others less regularly) with passengers from Parkgate, and six packets were sailing from Holyhead, only two ships with passengers from Liverpool are recorded, the *Liverpool Packet* and the *John & Henry*, and each made a single visit.[154] However, at that point the tide seems to have turned, and seven ships are listed as making single visits with passengers to or from Liverpool in the first six months of 1771. In 1772 for the first time a pattern of Liverpool passenger vessels emerges, and the *Molly* (Johnson), the *Polly* (Johnson), the *Mercury* (Taylor), the *Freemason* (Shaw) and the *Hawke* (Babe) are all regularly engaged. By 1775 it is clear that the Liverpool passenger traffic was beginning to be as important as its rivals'; there were 28 recorded passenger arrivals at Dublin from Liverpool, compared with 31 from Parkgate and 50 from Holyhead. One of the Liverpool ships was the *Freemason*, Captain Eyres, with whom Wesley sailed in 1773:[155]

> We embarked again on board the Freemason, with six other cabin passengers, four gentlemen and two gentlewomen, one of whom was daily afraid of falling into labour.

Two years later he sailed with Captain Peirson on the *Hawke*, 'so fine a ship I never sailed in before'.[156]

[151] *Williamson's Liverpool Advertiser*, 4 July 1760.
[152] See the start of the next chapter.
[153] *Freeman's Dublin Journal*, 17 Aug. 1765. The survey was from Aug. 1765 to July 1766.
[154] *ibid*, 15 May, 24 July 1770.
[155] John Wesley, *Journal*, 23 March 1773.
[156] *ibid*, 30 April 1775.

This was the situation on the outbreak of the American War of Independence, which had a devastating effect on Liverpool. Earlier wars had tended to stimulate Liverpool's overseas trade, and in 1752 it had been written,[157]

> In the late war trade flourished and spread her golden wings . . . the harbour being very little known to or frequented by the enemy.

Now for the first time in eighty years there was a reason for merchants to pay more attention to the Irish Sea traffic. Parkgate had its own local worries with the loss of the *Trevor* and *Nonpareil* by shipwreck in 1775, and Holyhead temporarily lost two packets to the *Black Prince* privateer in 1780. Here is a circular from a linen merchant to allay the fears of his customers in 1779:[158]

> The Newry packet arrived safe in Liverpool the 11th inst in the morning after a pleasing passage of eighteen hours; and by a letter from the ship's broker he finds such of her linens as were for the fair were sent to Chester that night.

The new lord lieutenant of Ireland crossed the Irish Sea in 1780 in the R.Y. *Dorset*, under convoy of the *Stag* frigate.[159] Whatever was happening to the Atlantic trade, the Irish traffic kept going despite the war, and the Parkgate Customs Account shows that an average of 44 ships a year arrived there in the course of the war.[160] It seems probable that the passenger trade which had just begun to develop in the years before the war, was stimulated by the interruption to Liverpool's other trade. The Liverpool directories from 1766 make no mention of Dublin packets until 1781, when four packets are listed.[161] From 1786 the lists of packets from Liverpool are also printed in the Dublin directories. The two sets of lists do not always coincide but it is evident that four, five or six passenger packets were sailing regularly between Dublin and Liverpool from 1781 to 1800.

[157] *Liverpool Memorandum Book* (see note 145 above).
[158] W. H. Crawford, ed., *Aspects of Irish Social History, 1750–1800* (1969), p. 62.
[159] *Chester Chronicle*, 30 Dec. 1780.
[160] Parkgate Customs Account, 1776–86 (Custom House, Lower Thames Street, London).
[161] *Gore's Liverpool Directory*, 1781.

In 1796 'several packets to Dublin, for the express purpose of conveying passengers, horses, carriages and light goods' could be found by St George's Dock, at Man's Island, at 'the quay where the Dublin Packets lie, with their Packet-houses and Offices facing them; which buildings are called Nova Scotia'.[162]

The number of packets dropped off during the first decade of the nineteenth century to as low as two ships in some years, but revived in 1811; between 1812 and 1816 there were six or eight Liverpool packets, reflecting the end of Parkgate's days as a packet station.

Liverpool Passenger Packets, 1781 to 1816

| | |
|---|---|
| *Duke of Leinster* | 1781–98 |
| *Earl of Charlemont* | 1786–91 |
| *Prince of Orange* | 1781–9 |
| *Fly* | 1781–7 |
| *Hawke* | 1781–90 |
| *Hibernia* | 1787–91 |
| *St Patrick* | 1787–93 |
| *Viceroy* | 1790–8 |
| *City of Dublin* | 1792–4 |
| *Marquess of Kildare* | 1793 |
| *Clarence yacht* | 1793 |
| *Friends* | 1795 |
| *Lady Mary Fitzmaurice* | 1795–6 |
| *Mineral Spring* | 1795 |
| *Ponsonby* | 1796–1805 |
| *Thetis* | 1796–7 |
| *Beresford* | 1797–1804 |
| *Betty* | 1799 |
| *Prince* | 1799 |
| *Venus* | 1799–1800; 1807–1812 |
| *Queen* | 1800 |
| *Duchess of York* | 1801–7 |
| *Hillsborough* | 1803–4 |
| *Clement* | 1803 |
| *Lark* | 1804–6 |
| *Loughniell* | 1804–9 |
| *Earl Annesley* | 1810–16 |
| *Iberus* | 1810 |

---

[162] W. Moss, *The Liverpool Guide* (1796), pp. 6, 37.

| | |
|---|---|
| *Constitution* | 1810–12 |
| *Earl of Moira* | 1810–16 |
| *Hero* | 1810–16 |
| *Duke of Richmond* | 1810–16 |
| *Earl Wellington* | 1813–16 |
| *Alert* | 1813–16 |
| *Duke of Leinster* | 1814–16 |
| *Loftus* | 1814–16 |

This list is derived from the directories of Liverpool and Dublin (see Bibliography).

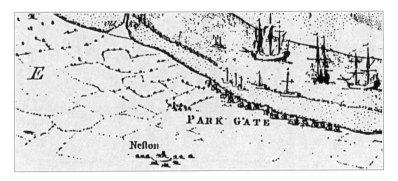

Figure 17. *Shipping at Parkgate*, from Thomas Boydell's plan of the River Dee Company's lands, 1771.

# 6 The Passengers—
## Choices and Reactions

We have seen that, of the several possible ways of reaching Dublin from the north-west of England, the usual choice was between Parkgate and Holyhead until the 1770s, when Liverpool began to strengthen its part in the passenger traffic. Before this happened, in 1764, a letter was written 'from a gentleman in Dublin to his friend at Dover in Kent, with occasional observations . . . collected in a tour through the Kingdom in the year 1764', which was published as *Hibernia Curiosa*.[1] The letter neatly sums up the possible choices of route, and because of its date, the author does not mention Liverpool at all.

> From London our first course was to West Chester, distant from Ireland about 150 miles, and from London 190. From Chester there are two passages to Dublin, either of which may be taken as shall best suit the convenience of the traveller.
>
> The one from Park-Gate, a little seaport for packets and traders, about 12 miles below Chester. The other over-land, for 80 or 90 miles, to Holy-Head, the most western point of North Wales, in the isle of Anglesey, and distant from Ireland about 23 leagues.

The author next described the passage from Bristol, which we have already quoted. He then dealt with Portpatrick:

> The shortest distance that can be made from Great-Britain to Ireland, is from Port Patrick in Galloway county, Scotland, from whence to Donaghadee in the county of Down, is about seven or eight leagues, or nearly the same distance as from Dover to Calais. But it is hardly worth while to go at least 200 miles by land extraordinary to save 40 by sea from Holyhead,

---

[1] John Bush, ed., *Hibernia Curiosa* (1764).

and therefore very few, except those whose business calls them to the North of Ireland, will go to Port Patrick for a passage.

He did not mention Whitehaven as a possible choice. Next he dealt with the question of danger, and gave the lie to those supporters of the Holyhead crossing who declared that other routes were more hazardous:

> There is, however, but little danger in crossing the Irish sea from any of these places, except at the vernal and autumnal seasons of the year, at which times, especially in the autumnal, the winds are frequently very high and tempestuous, and the channel consequently extremely rough and dangerous.

He then explained that the disadvantages of travelling by Holyhead were diminishing by reason of modern developments:[2]

> Those who shall take the Chester road, if they have much baggage to carry and are not fearful of the sea, will find the passage from Parkgate much the easiest and the most convenient, as it is very troublesome and expensive getting heavy luggage for ninety miles over the mountainous country, wide and rapid ferry ways of North Wales. However, the passage over land is, of late years, made much safer and more convenient, by the making of a turnpike road, through the country, and by the running of a coach or two from Chester to the Head, which they perform in two days very well; or otherwise you may be accommodated with horses and a guide from Chester to the Head.

In fact the author himself chose to travel from Holyhead:[3]

> After 40 hours rolling and traversing the boisterous Irish sea, for 20 leagues only, with the wind, as the sailors say, right in our teeth, there was something peculiarly pleasing on entering the beautiful bay of Dublin . . . with a fair wind, however, the passage from the Head is frequently made in 10 or 12 hours.

Despite his earlier remarks about the safety of the voyage, this traveller was apprehensive of the sea crossing, and interrogated the captain:

[2] *ibid*, pp. 2–3.
[3] *ibid*, pp. 7–9.

'But is there no insurance for a man's life for sixty miles only?'
'Oh yes, the best in the world, my noble master, a bottle of
claret, to put the want of it out of your head.'

We shall now examine the reasons why passengers chose a
particular route.

For over fifty years, from 1739 until a short time before his death in
1791, John Wesley travelled continuously, averaging four or five
thousand miles a year, spending many hours a day in usually solitary
travel, and preaching fifteen to eighteen sermons a week.[4] During
those fifty years he visited Ireland twenty-one times, and his record
of forty-two crossings of the Irish sea form a useful guide to the
choices which faced passengers.

The Dublin Methodist Society was founded in 1747 by Thomas
Williams, a lay itinerant preacher, whose letter about it to Wesley
decided him to visit Dublin that year.[5] In that same year of 1747,
Methodism was first recorded in Chester when an itinerant preacher
called John Bennett visited the city. Wesley did not himself visit
Chester until 1752.[6] From Chester, Methodism came to Neston and
Parkgate in 1756 when Edward Bennett, captain of a contract cheese
ship trading between Chester and London, discovered that his wife
and daughter Mary had developed dissenting views and he moved
house to rusticate them from the source of the contagion. In this he
was unsuccessful: the women secured a cottage in nearby Leighton
and invited Robert Roberts to preach.[7]

In 1762 a Methodist chapel was built off Parkgate Road, Neston,
which Wesley referred to as 'the small house they have just built'
and where he preached that year.[8] His interest in sailing from Parkgate rather than from Holyhead seems to have increased with the
passing of the years.

[4] Stanley Ayling, *John Wesley* (1979), p. 173.
[5] W. J. Townsend, ed., *A History of Methodism* (2 vols., 1909), 2, p. 6.
[6] F. F. Bretherton, *Early Methodism in and around Chester* (1903), pp. 26–7.
[7] John Gaulter, ed., 'Of the introduction of Methodism into the neighbourhood and city of Chester; in a memoir of Mrs Lowe of that city', *The
Methodist Magazine*, 32 (1809), p. 231.
[8] John Wesley, *Journal*, 2 April 1762.

At Holyhead, where his first crossings were made, he optimistically preached to the uncomprehending Welsh people:[9]

All the birds of the air, all the beasts of the field, understand the language of their own species. Man only is a barbarian to man, unintelligible to his own brethren!

But the local Methodist communities do not seem to have influenced his choice of port, for he preached at Parkgate only twice in eight visits after its chapel was opened; and although he was used to visiting the Chester society on his way to Parkgate, on only half the occasions that he landed in Wirral did he then go to Chester.

Because Bristol was one of his headquarters, and he often wished to visit the school he had founded at Kingswood nearby, Wesley's journeys towards Ireland often started at Bristol. But he never undertook the long sea voyage from Bristol, although he once looked for a ship there and once sailed from Fishguard.[10] On two occasions he sailed from Dublin to Bristol, and on two other occasions he sailed from Cork to Bristol or Swansea.[11] The long journey through North Wales to Holyhead was no obstacle to Wesley because, until he was about seventy years old, he preferred to travel on horseback with almost no luggage. 'I would be on horseback for life if I would be healthy,' he wrote in 1764.[12] In 1766 an admirer gave him a chaise, and from 1770 he was more likely to drive than to ride. By that date, though, the roads to Holyhead had greatly improved.

Wesley's choice of embarkation point in England usually had to do with the availability of shipping. His first four crossings to Ireland were made (because he came from Bristol) from Holyhead, and on three of these occasions he had to put up with long delays. He did not sit still, as Jonathan Swift had done when similarly delayed in 1727, but went out and preached. Because he considered that his mission was to be an itinerant preacher, he was prepared to travel by any route and preach on the way, so that after these first visits to Holyhead, he was ready to move on to another port whenever necessary. Wesley embarked eighteen times from ports in the north-west and nine of these were from Holyhead. Although only three crossings started from Parkgate, on another five occasions

---

[9] *ibid*, 6 March 1748.
[10] *ibid*, 16 March 1767; 1 Oct. 1777.
[11] *ibid*, 20 July 1749, 20 July 1750, 12 Oct. 1752, 8 Aug. 1758.
[12] Stanley Ayling, *John Wesley*, pp. 252–3.

Wesley would have sailed from there if a ship had been available. In 1778,[13]

> I had designed going from hence [Manchester] to Chester, in order to embark at Parkgate; but a letter from Mr Wagner informing me that a packet was ready to sail from Liverpool I sent my horses forward, and followed them in the morning.

On the other four occasions when he first intended to sail from Parkgate, his next choices were Whitehaven, Portpatrick and twice Holyhead.[14] In 1765 he arrived at Chester on 26 April:

> As several ships were ready to sail from Parkgate, I waited here two days. But the wind continuing foul, on Friday, 29, I crossed over to Liverpool.

He spent five days in Liverpool, preaching to full houses, before deciding that the wind was just as foul in the Mersey, and he rode to Bolton. He returned to Liverpool, but the wind remained adverse, so he went to Durham and Edinburgh, eventually reaching Ireland from Portpatrick on 1 May.[15]

As he grew older, Wesley seems to have become even less patient with delay. In April 1785 he came to Liverpool from Wigan:[16]

> Wednesday 6, I preached at Liverpool; but I found no ship there ready to sail. So, Thursday 7 (after preaching at Warrington on the way) I hastened to Chester. Neither was there any ship at Parkgate ready to sail; so, Friday 8, we took coach, and reached Holyhead between four and five in the afternoon.

Two years later, when he was eighty-four years old,[17]

> Wednesday 4, I went to Chester and preached in the evening on Heb. iii. 12. Finding there was no packet at Parkgate, I immediately took places in the mail-coach for Holyhead. The porter called us at two in the morning on Thursday, but came again in half an hour, to inform us the coach was full; so they

---

[13] John Wesley, *Journal,* 21 March 1778.
[14] *ibid,* 13 July 1752, 1 May 1765, 10 April 1785, 5 April 1787.
[15] *ibid,* 26 April to 1 May 1765.
[16] *ibid,* 6–9 April 1785.
[17] *ibid,* 4–5 April 1787.

returned my money, and at four I took a post-chaise. We overtook the coach at Conway; and crossing the ferry with the passengers, went forward without delay. So we came to Holyhead an hour before them, and went on board Le Despencer between eleven and twelve o'clock.

On his return journeys from Dublin, Wesley's landfall was dictated less by his own preference, than by the actual ship available, and here Parkgate and Holyhead share the number evenly. Seven times he landed at Holyhead; six times he landed at Parkgate, and on one further occasion he disembarked at Hoylake (not a packet station) which suggests that the ship was making for Parkgate when the wind failed.

The actual ports used by Wesley are as follows:

| Outward | | | Return | |
|---|---|---|---|---|
| Holyhead | 9 | | Holyhead | 7 |
| Parkgate | 3 | + the intention on | Parkgate | 6 |
| | | 5 further times | + Hoylake | 1 |
| Liverpool | 5 | + the intention | Liverpool | 1 |
| | | twice | | |
| Whitehaven | 1 | | Whitehaven | 1 |
| Portpatrick | 2 | | Portpatrick | 1 |
| Fishguard | 1 | | Swansea | 1 |
| | | | Bristol | 3 |

To sum up Wesley's choice of ports: he chose Holyhead and Parkgate about equally, but the weather conditions in the Dee estuary made sailing from Parkgate less reliable and he could not use it often. He used Liverpool when his approach route made it convenient to do so, and he used the more northerly ports of Whitehaven and Portpatrick only as a second or even third choice.

On both the journeys quoted in 1785 and 1787, Wesley made it clear that he did not go to Parkgate to find out whether ships were sailing from that port: he went to Chester and decided, on the basis of the weather reports from Parkgate, whether to go there or to Holyhead. This was a common practice and a feature in the popularity of Parkgate; travellers could stay in civilised inns in Chester before deciding on the short journey to Parkgate or the long journey to Anglesey. Even if the traveller did go to Parkgate he could easily return to Chester,[18]

> At 3 o'clock in the morning they went to Parkgate, the wind not being fair they returned again the next day and went there on Thursday at eleven in the morning being the 24th of September, 1736.

The same tactic was employed by the composer Handel when he travelled to Ireland in November 1741:[19]

> When Handel went through Chester, on his way to Ireland, this year, 1741, I was at the Public School in that city, and very well remember seeing him smoke a pipe, over a dish of coffee, at the 'Exchange Coffee House'; for, being extremely curious to see so extraordinary a man, I watched him narrowly as long as he remained in Chester, which, on account of the wind being unfavourable for his embarking at Parkgate, was several days.

From this account, part of which was published in the *Chester Chronicle* in 1785, there has grown the myth that Handel sailed from Parkgate on this occasion, and it has been claimed for several Parkgate houses (one of them built fifty years too late) that the great man actually stayed there.[20] But it is known from a Dublin newspaper that Handel in fact sailed from Holyhead:[21]

> and last Wednesday the celebrated Dr Handel arrived here in the packet-boat from Holyhead, a gentleman universally known by his excellent compositions in all kinds of music.

It is also known, however, that on his return journey nine months later, Handel landed at Parkgate.[22]

---

[18] G. B. Crawfurd, ed., *The Diary of George Booth of Chester*, p. 57, reprinted from *J.C.A.S.*, 28, part 1 (1928).

[19] Charles Burney, 'Commemoration of Handel', see C. Burney, *A General History of Music* (1776–89) with notes by Frank Mercer (1935), vol. 2, p. 1006.

[20] *Chester Chronicle*, 8 April 1785; for a sample myth-maker, see Hilda Gamlin, *'Twixt Mersey and Dee* (1897), p. 252; for the house, see G. W. Place, *This is Parkgate*, (1979), p. 27.

[21] *Faulkner's Dublin Journal*, 18–21 November 1741; see V. Schoelcher, *Life of Handel* (trans. J. Lowe, 1857), pp. 242–3.

[22] *Dublin News Letter*, 10–14 August 1742.

About the same time, 'two English gentlemen' found that the reports from Parkgate could not always be trusted:[23]

Just now a sailor came to inform us the wind was veering, and would certainly be fair for Dublin in four and twenty hours, so we shall leave Chester this very evening.

We are now at Parkgate . . . and have waited two days for a wind to no purpose, so that we repented leaving our old quarters at Chester.

What was worse this traveller thought that he had been deceived:

For my own part, I cursed the sailor that brought us false intelligence to Chester about the change of wind. I have learned at Parkgate, that it is a common custom of the publicans there, to send up false intelligence to Chester, that the company may come down to lie under the lash of their long bills.

### The Ports used by John Wesley to and from Ireland

|     |       | Out                                                       | Return                            |
|-----|-------|-----------------------------------------------------------|-----------------------------------|
| 1.  | 1747  | Holyhead                                                  | Holyhead                          |
| 2.  | 1748  | Holyhead                                                  | Holyhead                          |
| 3.  | 1749  | Holyhead                                                  | Bristol                           |
| 4.  | 1750  | Holyhead                                                  | Bristol                           |
| 5.  | 1752  | Whitehaven                                                | Bristol                           |
| 6.  | 1756  | Holyhead                                                  | Holyhead                          |
| 7.  | 1758  | Liverpool                                                 | Swansea ('Penklawr'— Penclawdd?)  |
| 8.  | 1760  | Liverpool                                                 | Parkgate                          |
| 9.  | 1762  | Parkgate                                                  | Parkgate                          |
| 10. | 1765  | Portpatrick (Third choice after Parkgate, Liverpool)      | Whitehaven                        |
| 11. | 1767  | Portpatrick (Third choice after Bristol, Liverpool)       | Portpatrick                       |
| 12. | 1769. | Parkgate                                                  | Holyhead                          |
| 13. | 1771  | Parkgate                                                  | Parkgate                          |
| 14. | 1773  | Liverpool                                                 | Hoylake                           |

---

[23] W. R. C[hetwood], ed., *A Tour through Ireland*, p. 32.

|  |  | Out | Return |
|---|---|---|---|
| 15. | 1775 | Liverpool | Parkgate |
| 16. | 1777 | Fishguard | Holyhead |
| 17. | 1778 | Liverpool (Second choice after Parkgate) | Liverpool |
| 18. | 1783 | Holyhead | Holyhead |
| 19. | 1785 | Holyhead (Third choice after Liverpool, Parkgate) | Holyhead |
| 20. | 1787 | Holyhead (Second choice after Parkgate) | Parkgate |
| 21. | 1789 | Holyhead | Parkgate. |

Source: John Wesley, *Journal*

If Wesley's forty-two crossings of the Irish Sea provide the most material for a study of the choices made by an individual, many other travellers recorded their decisions about which route they should take. We have already heard how Jonathan Swift was nervous about long journeys on horseback and so preferred to avoid Holyhead if possible. He seems to have embarked from 'Neston' in 1704,[24] through Parkgate to or from Dawpool in 1707 and 1709,[25] and landed at Parkgate in 1710 and 1713.[26] When he reached Chester, earlier in 1713, he learned that 'all the ships and people went off yesterday with a rare wind'. He was therefore obliged to ride to Holyhead against his will:[27]

> I would fain 'scape this Holyhead journey; but I have no prospect of ships, and it will be almost necessary I should be in Dublin before the 25th . . .

[24] P. V. and D. J. Thompson, *The Account Books of Jonathan Swift* (1984), 30 May 1704.
[25] For 1707, see *Wirral Notes & Queries*, (1893), item 28; P. V. and D. J. Thompson (see previous note), 29 June 1709.
[26] P. V. and D. J. Thompson, *Account Books*, 1 Sept. 1710, 31 Aug. 1713: J. Swift, *The Journal to Stella*, Letter 1, 2 Sept. 1710.
[27] J. Swift, *The Journal to Stella*, Letter lxv, 6 June 1713.

His unfortunate decision in 1727 to go to Holyhead has already been described:[28]

> As it happened, if I had gone strait from Chester to Parkgate, 8 miles, I should have been in Dublin on Sunday last.

The 'two English gentlemen' already referred to, travelling about 1740, found themselves windbound at Parkgate:[29]

> We have been here 13 days, and the wind is as obstinate as ever. Our baggage is stowed in a ship called the Race-Horse, but the horses have been taken out of the vessel twice. We are all out of patience.

To while away the time they went to Holywell to gaze at the 'crowds of credulous Catholics' at the shrine of St Winefride:[30]

> As we were going up the street, a man met us with this question, 'Gentlemen, do you want horses and a guide to the Head? If you should, I can furnish you as well as any man in the county.' This question put us on consultation, which was soon ended; for, with my brother's consent, we resolved to set out next morning.

They returned to Parkgate, sent their baggage, horses and servant on board th *Race-Horse* and themselves went overland with their guide to Anglesey. At Beaumaris they found the *Race-Horse* and the news that the captain had cut their horses' throats to prevent damage in a storm. They embarked in the *Race-Horse* for Dublin, only to be driven by renewed storms all the way down to Cork.

Another stormbound traveller was George Wood who, in 1748, sailed from Parkgate with Captain Berry who 'had 31 troop horses on board, besides a great quantity of merchants' goods and passengers'. The ship sailed as far as Chester bar before being driven back to Dawpool. He found a fisherman to take his party on foot, at night, across the estuary to Holywell, and so to Holyhead. There Wood was 'one of, I believe, a thousand passengers who are waiting for a fair wind to Ireland'.[31]

---

[28] Herbert Davis, ed., *Jonathan Swift, Works*, 5, (1969), p. 206.
[29] W. R. C[hetwood], *A Tour through Ireland*, p. 37.
[30] *ibid*, pp. 38–9.
[31] H.M.C., *15th Report, Appendix part 7*, (1898), p. 337.

When the actress George Anne Bellamy went with Sheridan's troop to Ireland in about 1746, she found Parkgate very crowded and decided to go to Holyhead:[32]

> Having waited several days at Parkgate, without a probability of sailing, and the place being rendered more disagreeable than it is, by the houses being crowded with passengers; Mrs Elmy prevailed upon me to endeavour to persuade my mother to go to the head. I was to urge as a reason, that our stay at Parkgate would in all probability prove much more expensive than the journey.

When she later had to return to Dublin, in 1760, it was not money but time that drove her on:

> The packet not being ready to sail from Parkgate, lest I should forfeit the penalties of my articles, by not being at Dublin in time, I set off for Holyhead.

The possibility of saving time was often a factor in the choice of route. In 1762 the Marquess of Kildare was anxious to rejoin his wife:[33]

> I propose going to the Head, except I should find a ship ready and wind fair to sail from Parkgate; which if it so happens, I may have the happiness I so much wish for, something sooner than by going through Wales.

One of the first recorded visitors who came to Parkgate, not as a passenger but for the sea-bathing, was William Sadler who came twice in the 1760s. In 1765 he wrote:[34]

> I have taken the very first opportunity of enquiring when the packet sails from Parkgate to Dublin and was informed by a person from Chester that it was very uncertain, and depended on the freight and wind; that perhaps we might stay a fortnight or three weeks and not get passage. But he likewise informed me of a much safer way, i.e. from Holyhead, where he says they sail from (Mondays, Wednesdays and Fridays) every week.

---

[32] G. A. Bellamy, *An Apology for the Life of George Anne Bellamy*, 1, p. 103; 4, p. 4 (2nd edn).
[33] B. Fitzgerald, ed., *Correspondence of Emily, Duchess of Leinster*, 1, p. 137, 20 May 1762.
[34] W. K. R. Bedford, *Three Hundred Years of a Family Living* (1889), p. 75.

It is possible to assemble a picture of the sailing conditions on the Dublin crossing, principally from Parkgate and Holyhead, from a host of accounts written by travellers. These accounts yield information on the following topics: the cost of the crossing; expenses at Parkgate; delays; the duration of the crossing; the numbers of passengers; the arrangements for cabins; and food on board.

First, therefore, the costs of the crossing.

In about 1791, James Hunter of Chester printed a map of Wirral which included sketches of five vessels of the Parkgate Packet Company, then at its zenith, together with the Royal Yacht *Dorset*. At the side of the map he indicates the fares,[35] 'From Parkgate to Dublin, £1.1, 10/6, 2/6'. These fares probably applied to the Parkgate Packet Company's ships and not necessarily to the yacht. The prices seem inexpensive compared to some earlier fares and may have been the result of competition, although it is often not clear what services are being paid for. In 1724 Daniel Duggan paid five guineas for his passage and his total travel bill was as follows:[36]

| | |
|---|---|
| Horse &c from London to Chester and Parkgate | £1. 8. 3 |
| Passage from Parkgate to Dublin | 5. 5. 0 |
| Travelling charges, London to Parkgate (158 miles) & 1/3 per day to horse charge on journey | 1. 6. 8 |

A few years later, in 1731, Mrs Delany also paid five guineas:[37]

We have secured places in the Pretty Betty. The best cabin Mrs Donellan and I have taken to ourselves, and are to pay five guineas, but I believe it will be some days before we go away.

The Royal Yacht could be much more expensive. In 1738 Lord Buttevant gave twelve guineas for the state cabin, which we have already seen described in Chapter Three, whereas his companion, George Pakenham, paid one guinea for himself and five shillings for his servant. This journey, we have seen, was interrupted at Beaumaris and had to be continued in the post office packet *Lovell* from Holyhead. The fares on this vessel were not stated, but when they reached Dublin Bay they transferred to a boat to be taken up river,

---

[35] James Hunter, *A new map of the Hundred of Wirral* (c.1791). There is a copy in the Cheshire R.O., D/3909.
[36] E. MacLysaght, ed., *Kenmare MSS*, p. 409.
[37] Lady Llanover, ed., *Autobiography . . . of Mrs Delany*, 1, p. 287, 10 Sept. 1731.

and for this,[38] 'Lord B. gave 5 guineas and I half a guinea, the passengers only 5s.' It would seem that one had to pay according to rank, as well as by quality of accommodation. The half-guinea charge from Parkgate is mentioned by several writers, but a fare which is not supported by other records is the seven shillings mentioned in a ballad, of which we shall hear more presently:[39]

> I paid the captain seven thirteens
> To carry me over to Parkgate.

An Irish shilling contained thirteen pence, to allow for the rate of exchange with England.[40] Another version of the ballad gives the fare as 'six thirteens'.[41]

On the Holyhead packets, the half-guinea fare was also commonly reported. The author of *Hibernia Curiosa* said that 'for half a guinea you are accommodated with the use of the cabbin and bed.'[42] More detail was given in 1783:[43]

> The price of a bed in one of the cabins is half a guinea, walking upon deck or in the hold, half a crown.

Sir John Carr paid one guinea in about 1805;[44] but the expenses of Sir Richard Colt Hoare in 1806 demonstrate that for many passengers, the cost of crossing the sea was not merely the price of a berth:[45]

> 23 June. Fine weather. Set sail in the evening at 8 o'clock in the Union Packet, Captain Skinner.

| | | |
|---|---:|---|
| Berths for self and son | £2. 2. 0 | |
| Berths for 2 servants | 1. 1. 0 | |
| Chaise 2.2, shipping 10/6 | 2. 12. 6 | |
| Custom house fees at Holyhead | 6. 6 | |
| Gave the steward | 17. 6 | |
| | £6. 19. 6 | |

[38] *Analecta Hibernica*, 15, pp. 116–18.
[39] Mawdsley & Son, Directory of the Hundred of Wirral (1861), p. xvii.
[40] Sir John Carr, *The Stranger in Ireland*, p. 67.
[41] Hilda Gamlin, *Memories of Birkenhead* (1892) p. 86.
[42] John Bush, ed., *Hibernia Curiosa*, p. 7.
[43] 'A short account of Holyhead to the isle of Anglesey', in *Bibliotheca Topographica Britannica*, 10 (1783), p. 12.
[44] Sir John Carr, *op. cit.*
[45] M. W. Thompson, ed., *The Journeys of Sir Richard Colt Hoare, 1793–1810*, p. 241.

Finally, Thomas Moore in 1799 found the journey from Chester to Holyhead and Dublin 'exceedingly expensive',[46]

> so I took the mail; that was three guineas and a half, which, with £1. 16s. 6d. from Holyhead, the guinea for my passage, and the other contingent expenses (in which I was obliged to conform to the other passengers) has made the whole about eight guineas. Mr M. tells me that the Parkgate way is not by the half so much.

The expenses of staying in Parkgate could be a considerable worry to some travellers. It was to William Dobbins in 1641:[47]

> Neaston; My poor wife lies here very weak, her child was born on shipboard, and she was carried ashore here, where she is very ill-accommodated. My God helps her, amongst a company of mercenary towns and extorting people as ever lived, and I dare not venture to carry her to Chester.

In 1730 Dudley Bradstreet actually ran out of money;[48]

> From Chester, I went to Parkgate, having but twenty-six shillings left, and lodged at one of the best houses in that extorting village . . . in four days my stock of money was reduced to ten shillings.

Bradstreet embarked on an elaborate confidence trick which extracted some cash and a daily dinner from the man with whom he had to share a bedroom.

When Letitia Pilkington made the crossing about 1748, she too ran out of funds:[49]

> Next day we set out for Parkgate, which was crowded with nobility and gentry, waiting for a fair wind. Here we were so long detained that my purse was quite exhausted.

Her solution was to send her son to borrow a guinea from Lady Kildare.

[46] W. S. Dowden, ed., *The Letters of Thomas Moore*, 1 (1964), p. 2.
[47] H.M.C., *MSS of the Earl of Egmont*, 1 (1905), p. 144, 8 Nov. 1641.
[48] G. S. Taylor, ed., *The Life and Uncommon Adventures of Captain Dudley Bradstreet*, p. 28.
[49] Letitia Pilkington, *Memoirs* (Dublin, 1748), 3, p. 192.

When J. P. Curran first visited England in 1773, he was greeted on the beach by a friendly innkeeper,[50]

> He pressed me to go into his house, and to 'eat of his bread' and to 'drink of his drink'. There was so much good-natured solicitude in the invitation, 'twas irresistible.

Next morning he found that his box had not, as he had arranged, been put on the coach for Chester.

> I was thinking how I should remedy this unlucky disappointment when my friendly host told me that he could furnish me with a chaise! Confusion light upon him!

Curran was so angry at this attempt to win 'a few paltry shillings' from him that he walked to Chester.

We have seen in Chapter Four that sailing delays of a month caused by the weather were not uncommon, and they could at times last twice as long. There were those passengers who concluded that the weather was, on occasion, a mere excuse when captains had other reasons for not sailing.

> The Captain talks of sailing at 12. The talk goes off; the Wind is fair, but he says it is too fierce; I believe he wants more company.
>
> [Next day.] It was fairer and milder weather than yesterday, yet the Captain never dreams of Sailing.

That was Jonathan Swift at Holyhead in 1727.[51] He further expended his spleen in this verse:[52]

> I'm fasnd both by wind and tide
> I see the ship at anchor ride
> The Captain swears the sea's too rough
> He has not passengers enough.
> And thus the Dean is forc't to stay
> Till others come to help the pay.

---

[50] W. H. Curran, *The Life of John Philpott Curran* (1819), 1, p. 33.
[51] Herbert Davies, ed., *Jonathan Swift, Works*, 5, p. 203.
[52] Harold Williams, ed., *Poems of Jonathan Swift*, 2, p. 420.

It was also at Holyhead, in 1748, that John Wesley was exasperated for the same reason,[53]

> I never knew men make such poor, lame excuses, as these Captains did for not sailing. It put me in mind of the epigram,
>
>> There are, if rightly I methink,
>> Five reasons why a man should drink:
>
> which with a little alteration, would just suit them:
>
>> There are, unless my memory fail,
>> Five causes why we should not sail:
>> The fog is thick; the wind is high;
>> It rains; or may do by-and-by;
>> Or—any other reason why.

Wesley's experience taught him to be wary of ships' captains[54]

> Hence I learned two or three rules, very needful for those who sail between England and Ireland. 1. Never pay till you set sail; 2. Go not on board till the Captain goes on board; 3. Send not your baggage on board till you go yourself.

Of course the impatient passengers, anxious to save money as well as time, may have been wrong to fret at the captains' delays. When Samuel Davies was lost with his ship the *Nonpareil* in 1775. he set sail against his better judgment:[55]

> Mrs Davies says her husband went out in very low spirits as he did not like the appearance of the weather, but the major and some other passengers pressed him to put out: which he did and was twice put back but got off a third time.

The major was Major Caulfield who, with his family and several other families, was drowned.

The length of time which sailing vessels took for the Dublin crossing varied so widely as to be largely unpredictable. We have seen that the 60-mile journey from Holyhead was not necessarily any less expensive than the 120 miles from Parkgate; nor did it necessarily take a shorter time. When Swift described his fifteen-

---

[53] John Wesley, *Journal*, 1 March 1748.
[54] *ibid*, 2 Aug. 1758.
[55] *Freeman's Dublin Journal*, 27 Oct. 1775.

hour journey to Parkgate in 1710, that was a good time for the distance and one would be lucky to better it. Lady Louise Connolly did in 1759 but was then delayed in landing,[56]

> Though we had a charming passage of 13 hours in the night air, it would not have been prudent to have landed last night.

It was certainly possible to cross to Holyhead in a shorter time, yet a shorter time was often quoted by those who, in their own case, took longer. For example, the author of *Hibernia Curiosa* took forty hours himself, and then wrote:[57]

> With a fair wind, however, the passage from the Head is frequently made in 10 or 12 hours.

Similarly, John Ferrar's journey in 1795 took twenty-one hours, but he added that 'it is frequently performed in ten hours'.[58] The poet Shelley and his first wife Harriet crossed to Holyhead in[59]

> 36 hours when we had been informed that at the most we should certainly be no more than 12 hours. There is no depending upon the word of a sailor . . .

The real difficulty in giving sailing times concerned, not merely the wind, but access to the landing points at both ends. Thus, a ship might make excellent time to the Dee estuary, but would then have to wait for the next tide to come up to Parkgate. Similarly, passengers in Dublin Bay might well take a boat up the Liffey to the quays in the city, or land at Dunlary, rather than wait for the tide to take their ship to Ringsend (a mile from the centre) or after 1796 to the Pigeon House, a dock named after John Pigeon, commander of a blockhouse there, some two miles further down river:[60]

> Thank God, we arrived safe in Dublin Bay about twelve o'clock, and by one was taken in a Dunlary hoy to Dublin Quay.

A better indication of sailing times is given by the average voyage times recorded by the Post Office packets: between Holyhead and the

---

[56] B. Fitzgerald, ed., *Correspondence of Emily, Duchess of Leinster*, 3, p. 1.
[57] John Bush, ed., *Hibernia Curiosa*, p. 9.
[58] John Ferrar, *A Tour from Dublin to London in 1795* (1796), p. 2.
[59] F. L. Jones, ed., *The Letters of Percy Byshe Shelley*, 1 (1964), pp. 283–4.
[60] Tate Wilkinson, *Memoirs of his own Times*, 1, p. 154.

Pigeon House in 1816–17 when the times were twenty-one hours out, thirteen hours back; in 1817–18, nineteen hours out and fifteen hours back.[61] Notice the effect of the prevailing west wind.

We have encountered some exceptionally long and troubled crossings, where the passengers might end up where they started, or nearer Cork than Dublin. The extreme record for an extended passage may well be the seven weeks, 15 August to 25 September, endured in 1698:[62]

> My husband and son both came safe to Chester . . . and took shipping the next day, butt were tossed up and down by stormes and tempest till the 25 September and putt in to five severall harbours; at last in an open boat without the least of shelter or subsistance, every houre expecting the fate of a mercyless sea, my great and good God of his infinite mercy landed them both safe in Dublin after haveing bin ner seven weeks cast up and down.

There is rarely any information about the numbers sailing, but the packets seem to have been very crowded indeed on some occasions. A friend of Benjamin Victor, assistant manager of the Theatre Royal, Dublin, decided to leave his ship, the *Dublin*, because it was overcrowded:[63]

> they had the happiness to quit that ship in the River Dee when under sail, finding it crowded with passengers.

Their decision was wise for them because the ship was wrecked and several actors engaged to perform at the Theatre Royal were lost, on 27 October 1758.

Wesley sailed in the *Nonpareil* with forty or fifty passengers in 1760, with sixty passengers in 1762.[64] We have heard that there were two hundred passengers on the R.Y. *Dublin* in 1738. It was estimated that nearly two hundred passengers were drowned when the *Trevor* and *Nonpareil* were wrecked in 1775; of these about thirty were aboard the *Trevor*, and it is known that the *Nonpareil*'s passengers

---

[61] 5th Report of the Select Committee on the road from London to Holyhead: Holyhead Mails & Packets (1819), appendix 4.
[62] Mary Carbery, ed., *Mrs Elizabeth Freke, her Diary, 1671 to 1714*, (Cork, 1913), p. 48.
[63] B. Victor, *The History of the Theatres of London & Dublin* (1761), p. 249.
[64] John Wesley, *Journal*, 24 Aug. 1760, 2 April 1762.

included forty-three vagrants. Occasionally some very large numbers of vagrants were put aboard Parkgate ships: in 1783 and 1784 when unusually large numbers came through Parkgate, Captain Totty carried 186 vagrants on one voyage, Captain Guile carried 211, Captain Williams carried 155.[65] The Liverpool packet *Charlemont* was carrying about 120 passengers when it sank in 1790 with over one hundred lives lost.[66] When the *King George* was wrecked in 1806, at least a hundred passengers were drowned, although some estimates put the number much higher, to 150 or even more.[67] It is quite impossible to estimate the total number of passengers a year; but the average number using the Post Office packets from Holyhead was 13,000 a year, 1816–18.[68]

The highest fares were for cabin passengers, and we can gain some insight into what the 'cabin' offered. Except perhaps for the Royal Yacht, in which Lord Buttevant engaged the state cabin for twelve guineas, a cabin passenger did not usually get a private cubicle to himself; he got a share of the single cabin or sometimes two cabins in which there were bunks. Sometimes a passenger would book the entire cabin for himself and his party, as Mrs Delany possibly did in the *Pretty Betty* [69] in 1731, though she writes of 'the best cabin', so perhaps there were two. On 19 June 1802, the log of the *Clermont* recorded that 'The cabbin taken by Mr Stewart and family', although another twenty-five names, apparently of 'cabin passengers', are listed for the same voyage.[70]

Letitia Pilkington described how she obtained a bed in a private cabin on board the R.Y. *Dublin:*[71]

and desired the steward to show me a cabin. He left me for a few minutes; and returning, told me, all the beds were engaged: but however, there was a gentleman on board, who said he would sooner sit up, than a lady be unprovided for.

[She went to bed, when] the steward once more entered the cabin, and told me, the gentleman, to whom it belonged,

[65] Cheshire R.O., QJF 211/2, 3; 212/1.
[66] *Annual Register*, 1790, p. 228.
[67] *Chester Chronicle*, 19 Sept. 1806; *Faulkner's Dublin Journal*, 23 Sept. 1806; *Lloyd's List*, 19 Sept. 1806.
[68] 5th Report, etc. (see note 61 above), appendix 8.
[69] Lady Llanover, ed., *Autobiography . . . of Mrs Delany*, 1, p. 287.
[70] B.L., Add. MSS 39770, 397–1.
[71] Letitia Pilkington, *Memoirs*, 1, pp. 299–300.

desired a moment's chat with me . . . he hoped I would not refuse him the liberty of sleeping in his own bed.

She did not mind being thus propositioned: she had dinner with the same gentleman in Parkgate where he propositioned her again.

When Tate Wilkinson crossed from Holyhead in 1757:[72]

I asked for a bed; but they were all secured, not even one for Mr Foote—as plenty of cash from the great people, had made that request impossible to be complied with. The cabin was wedged like the black-hole of Calcutta.

Wilkinson was only one of several witnesses to the overcrowding of the public cabin. When Sir John Carr crossed in the *Union* packet (which he commended) he 'quitted that consummation of human misery, a cabin after a short voyage'.[73]

The cabin could also be agreeable: on the *Prince of Wales* packet in 1791,[74]

we went down into the cabin after sunset, part of the passengers went to bed, mother and some gentlemen whom we had got acquainted with sat down to whist and others looked on . . .

A similar picture was described by J. P. Curran in 1773:[75]

When I entered, I found my fellow-passengers seated round a large table in the cabin; we were fourteen in number . . . To do them all justice, they exerted themselves zealously for the common entertainment. As for my part, I had nothing to say; nor if I had, was anyone at leisure to listen to me; so I took possession of what the captain called a bed.

We know the number of beds in the later Holyhead sailing packets. John Ferrar reported that the *Bessborough* [76]

has twenty beds in the two rooms, fitted up with mahogany, and every convenience a traveller can desire.

---

[72] Tate Wilkinson, *Memoirs of his own Times*, 1, p. 153.
[73] Sir John Carr, *The Stranger in Ireland*, p. 30.
[74] Diary of Jane Hester Reilly, 6 May 1791, in *The Nineteenth Century*, 43 (May 1898), p. 795—'A young lady's journey from Dublin to London in 1791'.
[75] W. H. Curran, *The Life of John Philpott Curran*, 1, p. 31.
[76] John Ferrar, *A Tour from Dublin to London in 1795*, p. 2.

The *Countess of Chichester* packet had, in 1819, twenty-four berths.[77]

One way of avoiding the public cabin and, in effect, having a private one, was to take one's carriage on board. Thomas De Quincey described how this was done with Lady Conybeare's coach:[78]

> The body of her travelling coach had been, as usual, unslung from the 'Carriage' (by which is technically meant the wheels and the perch) and placed upon deck. This she used as a place of retreat from the sun during the day, and as a resting-place at night.

Thomas and his companion, who were schoolboys, were shocked to see a man slip secretly into this carriage at night. Letitia Pilkington, with her son and two gentlemen, 'sat all night in Lady Kildare's coach which was lashed upon deck'.[79]

John Wesley had his coach with him in 1773 when he landed at Dublin from Liverpool,[80]

> I was a little surprised to find the Commissioners of the Customs would not permit my chaise to be landed, because, they said, the Captain of a packet boat had no right to bring over goods.

This totally unjustified attitude probably represented an attempt by the Irish Customs officers to gain some privilege for themselves, and we shall presently see a later example of the same ploy. In fact there was a well-established method of temporarily exporting such goods as carriages. When Wesley landed at Parkgate on 12 April 1787, the Customs officer recorded,[81]

> In the Prince of Wales, John Heird [the captain], Rev. John Westley, 3 horses, 1 British post-chaise, exported from this port 10 April.

[77] 5th Report etc. (see note 61 above), p. 58.
[78] Thomas De Quincey, 'Autobiography', in D. Masson, ed., *Collected Writings* (1896), p. 208.
[79] Letitia Pilkington, *Memoirs*, 3, p. 193.
[80] John Wesley, *Journal*, 30 April 1773.
[81] Parkgate Customs Account, Cheshire R.O., 942.21.NS.

Without an export certificate he would have had to pay duty on the coach when he returned to England. On his final voyage, in 1789, he stated that he shut himself into his chaise on board ship in order to read. When he landed at Parkgate, the Customs account correctly recorded that his British (that is, not Irish) post chaise had been exported from Holyhead in March last.[82]

One hazard of the passage boats was food, if the weather extended the duration of the voyage. We shall learn presently of the plight of vagrants who had inadequate food for the journey. Sir John Carr, crossing from Holyhead about 1805, imagined that he would be able to buy whatever he needed on board. But nothing was obtainable, and he was glad indeed to accept some slices of broiled mutton from Lady Tuite, his fellow passenger in the cabin.[83] Similarly, George Anne Bellamy's crossing from Holyhead in 1760 took four storm-tossed days:[84]

> As the passage is usually made in a few hours, I had not thought it necessary to lay in a sea-store.

The poet Shelley and his wife 'did not eat anything for 36 hours, all the time we were on board'.[85] By contrast, Jane Reilly had supper and breakfast in the cabin of the *Prince of Wales* Parkgate packet in 1791.[86]


It is usual for passengers to get through a port of call as quickly as possible, being only too glad to get on their way. For this reason, travellers rarely recorded very much about Parkgate as a village. An exception was George Pakenham who wrote in 1738,[87]

> Hired horses and a guide for Parkgate about 8 miles from here [Chester], this afternoon, arrived there about 6, put up at the White Swan. Sands. A neat, clean house. This is a small village close by the seaside, where the passenger ships for Dublin always lie. Subsists only by the travellers. 12 or 14 sail of good

[82] *ibid*, 14 July 1789; J. Wesley, *Journal*, 13 July 1789.
[83] Sir John Carr, *The Stranger in Ireland*, pp. 25–6.
[84] G. A. Bellamy, *An Apology for the Life*, 4, p. 7.
[85] F. L. Jones, ed., *P. B. Shelley*, 1, pp. 283–4.
[86] Diary of Jane Hester Reilly (see note 74 above), p. 796.
[87] *Analecta Hibernica*, 15 (1944), p. 115.

vessels constantly employed. Had a boiled chicken and sack whey.

Sometimes the overriding impression was of overcrowding. 'People come every day and the place is crowded,' wrote Mrs Delany in 1754.[88] Whereas Dudley Bradstreet (who was a rogue) mentioned the poorer classes of traveller,[89]

I went out among the poor half-starved wretches who were waiting for a passage.

Letitia Pilkington (who had rather soiled pretensions to gentility) recorded that Parkgate was 'crowded with nobility and gentry'. Each of them set out to prey upon the company. No wonder they did not always find the company agreeable: we have seen that Mrs Pilkington dined with a man who offered her fifty guineas for 'a night's lodging'. She refused.[90]

Travellers who were wind-bound at Parkgate were apt to get bored, but they did not have to surrender to boredom:[91]

The obstinacy of the wind made time hang heavy on our hands, therefore we resolved to take a cursory view of Liverpool.

These visitors went to see not only Liverpool but Flint and Holywell also.

Less enterprising travellers recorded their frustration:[92]

the place being rendered more disagreeable than it is, by the house being crowded with passengers.

Tate Wilkinson, engaged by the actor-manager Samuel Foote, said,[93]

We all messed together; for Foote's company, as he was well acquainted with each, was the only treat that truly dreary place Parkgate could afford.

[88] Lady Llanover, ed., *The Autobiography . . . of Mrs Delany*, 1st series, vol. 3, pp. 276–7.
[89] G. S. Taylor, ed., *The Life . . . of Dudley Bradstreet*, p. 29.
[90] L. Pilkington, *Memoirs*, 1, p. 300.
[91] W. R. C[hetwood], ed., *A Tour through Ireland*, 1, p. 32.
[92] G. A. Bellamy, *An Apology for the Life*, 1, p. 103.
[93] Tate Wilkinson, *Memoirs of his own Life*, 1, p. 151.

Thomas Moore, who hated travelling, was perhaps the least impressed visitor of all:[94]

> Dear Father, the packet will not sail today, and here I am imprisoned for one night more: the place is insipid, my companion is insipid, and all these circumstances combining with my impatience to see my beloved home, make this delay most dreadfully irksome to me.

By contrast, Mary Delany, who had several absorbing hobbies and was unlikely to become bored anywhere,[95] greatly enjoyed her visits to Parkgate. Once when she had nothing left to do, she saw a painter about to repaint an inn sign. She paid him his fee, borrowed his paints and brushes and painted the sign herself. She thought, when recollecting it later, that it was a swan, so perhaps it was the sign of the White Swan where George Pakenham stayed in 1738 and 1739.[96] She even preferred to be in Parkgate rather than Chester:[97]

> If we are delayed a day or two, which I hope we shall not, it will be pleasanter to be near the sea-side and green fields than penned up in a hot dull town.

On her final visit, in 1758, she wrote that while waiting at Parkgate, she could not think any place disagreeable with such a constant moving picture of ships, sea plants on the beach, seaweed and shells.[98]

In 1747 she left this description of the village,[99]

> Park Gate consists of about 50 or 60 houses in an irregular line by the waterside; the River Dee runs from Chester, but is not navigable farther than to this place. A few ships lie before us, and continually people passing and repassing, which is some amusement. The fields behind the houses are pleasant to walk in, but the strand before the houses rough and stony.

---

[94] W. S. Dowden, ed., *The Letters of Thomas Moore*, I, p. 13.
[95] Ruth Hayden, *Mrs Delany, her Life and her Flowers* (1980).
[96] Lady Llanover, ed., *The Autobiography . . . of Mrs Delany*, 2, p. 457.
[97] *ibid*, 2, p. 543.
[98] *ibid*, 3, p. 499.
[99] *ibid*, 2, p. 457.

# 7  The Labouring Passengers

The types of passenger we have already met—officials, the aristocracy and gentry, merchants, actors—were those most likely to leave records of their travels, but the most numerous passengers were from the lower social orders, and most of these were migrant labourers. Although there is a great deal of published information about seasonal migration in the nineteenth century,[1] the smaller but significant movements in the eighteenth century have been only spasmodically described.

Irishmen looking for work have been coming to Britain for centuries[2] and part of the Elizabethan Poor Law penalised those who brought in any 'Mannsyke, Scottish or Irish rogues'.[3] Often they came for an indefinite period, like Richard Pares who came to England 'when he was about eleven years old and has travelled up and down there ever since' until he was picked up aged fifty-four in Middlewich.[4] In 1754 a London magistrate divided Irish labourers into the worthy and the unworthy:[5]

> the Irish imported into this kingdom of the lower class are those who annually come to harvest work and when that is over return with the savings of their labour to their own country. These are useful, faithful, good servants to the farmers and as they are of great use to the kingdom, deserve protection

[1] E. J. T. Collins, 'Migrant labour in British agriculture in the 19th century', *Economic History Review*. 29 (1976); B. M. Kerr, 'Irish seasonal migration in Great Britain, 1800–38', *Irish Historical Studies*, 3 (1942); Arthur Redford, *Labour Migration in England, 1800–50* (1926); C. J. Ribton-Turner, *History of Vagrants and Vagrancy* (1887); Cormac Ó Gráda, 'Seasonal migration and post-famine adjustment in the West of Ireland', *Studia Hibernica*, 13 (1973).
[2] Dorothy George, *London Life in the 18th Century* (1925), p. 117.
[3] 39 Eliz. I c.4.
[4] Cheshire R.O., QJF 169/2/123 (1741).
[5] Saunders Welsby, *Observations on the Office of Constable . . .* (1754) quoted by Dorothy George (see note 2 above), p. 119.

and encouragement. The others are a set of fellows made desperate by their crimes . . .

Although as we shall see there were plenty of the lower orders passing through Neston for Ireland much earlier, around 1700, the large-scale annual migrations of harvesters seem to have begun in the 1720s. In 1728 a Dublin newspaper stated:[6]

> The number of Irish labourers that are to be seen in the neighbourhood of London, who are come over for harvest-work, is plain proof of the poverty of their country, and no wonder when so many of the rich inhabitants transplant themselves here for pleasure, or preferment, that the poor should follow out of necessity.

A mention by Bishop Berkeley of Irishmen going to harvest in England 'of late years' in 1735 suggests that the practice was relatively recent,[7] although in 1736 Robert Walpole wrote of the Irish 'working at hay and corn harvest, as has been usual'.[8]

There may have been obstacles which inhibited much migration earlier. In Chapter One we have discussed the official suspicion of travellers which made journeys, especially to or from a Catholic country, potentially difficult until at least the alarms of 1715 had died down. The 'Settlement Act' of 1662, revised in 1691, exempted harvest migrants from the threat of removal as 'vagabonds', but expected a certificate from the parish of origin as evidence.[9] Like the passes for overseas travel that we saw being disregarded in 1710, these certificates can rarely have been insisted upon. Yet as late as 1734 John Robinson, 'going from Whitehaven to London with intent to work at harvest', was induced to pay for a forged 'Pass by which he might travel safely'.[10] For travellers on foot, though, there were hazards even in the 1780s:[11]

> he came from Cheshire towards London with what clothes he had, except those he wore at his back, in a bundle . . . In many

---

[6] *Dublin Weekly Journal*, 8 June 1728, quoted in *Royal Society of Antiquaries of Ireland Journal* (1902), p. 187.
[7] George Berkeley, *The Querist* (1735), query 526 quoted by Cormac Ó Gráda, 'Seasonal Migration . . .', p. 49.
[8] William Coxe, *Memoirs of Sir Robert Walpole* (1798) 3, p. 348; see also William Cobbett, *The Parliamentary History*, 9, p. 1282.
[9] 1662, 14 Chas II c. 12; 1691, 3 Wm & Mary c. 11.
[10] Cheshire R.O., QJF 162/1/137.
[11] Mary Thrale, ed., *The Autobiography of Francis Place* (1972), p. 16.

places he was set upon by men, women and children, and hooted through the villages merely because he was a stranger. At one place in Cheshire . . . he was pelted with stones and called an outcomeling.

This traveller was not a harvester; but those who were, were coming through Parkgate in large numbers in the 1740s:[12]

> We are returned to Parkgate where . . . we see every day vessels coming from Dublin, with great numbers of passengers for London, of all kinds, from men of rank to the lowest station; for as our harvest in England is earlier than in Ireland, they begin about London, work their way down to the west, and get back to their own country, time enough for their business there.

The large numbers of harvesters impressed the Swedish visitor Pehr Kalm in 1748:[13]

> In the beginning of May there come from Ireland over to England a very large number of Irishmen . . . but towards Autumn . . . they return home with the money which they have been able to earn.

Greater detail of their journey was provided in the 1780s by Robert Bell:[14]

> These emigrations always took place in the beginning of autumn; at which time the roads leading to the metropolis might be seen covered with wretches, known as Spalpeens, half-naked and barefooted, with hardly the means of defraying the expenses of the journey, which their extreme frugality rendered very trifling; and sometimes without any other resource than the scanty stock of oaten bread which they carried along with them on departing from their homes.

They travelled even more frugally, according to a Chester witness forty years later:[15]

---

[12] W. R. C[hetwood], *A Tour through Ireland*, p. 34.
[13] Pehr Kalm, *Account of his Visit to England, 1748*, trans. J. Lucas (1892), 24 June, pp. 82–3.
[14] Robert Bell, *A Description . . . of the Peasantry of Ireland . . . 1780 to 1790* (1804), p. 10.
[15] *Chester Chronicle*, 6 July 1827.

An immense number of half-naked Irishmen have passed through this city towards the south, in search of honest employment . . . living chiefly on buttermilk they beg, lodging principally in stables and outhouses, and in the daytime walking without shoes and stockings.

They carried their shoes to spare them 'for certain kinds of work which could not be performed without them'.[16]

The migrants were said, at least in the 1820s, to reach Britain on three main routes: from Ulster to Scotland, from Munster to Bristol, and from Connaught (the far west) to Liverpool and, in the earlier period, to Parkgate.[17] The numbers of 'the poor half-starved wretches who were waiting for a passage' at Parkgate impressed Dudley Bradstreet in 1730.[18] Shortly after that date, the Parkgate route for harvesters was mentioned in a play called *The Brave Irishman*, written by Thomas Sheridan, father of R. B. Sheridan.[19] The first recorded performance was in 1746, but the play may have been written while the author was still a student at Trinity College, Dublin, which he left in 1739.[20]

The Irishman of the title is called Captain O'Blunder, who had travelled to London on his way to Virginia to fight the French. He was asked about his 'passage':

Devil split it for a passage. By my shoul, my own bones are shore after it. We were on the devil's own turnpike for eight-and-forty hours . . . We were brought down from Ringsend in the little young ship to Poolpheg, and then put into the great ship—the horse—ay, ay—the Race-horse they call'd it.

Poolbeg was the central part of the channel through Dublin Bay and a lighthouse stands there now. The brig *Racehorse*, Captain Davis followed by Captain Joseph Norman, was well known on this route between 1730 and 1762. O'Blunder asked the captain to stop the ship when he was seasick:

---

[16] Robert Bell (see note 14 above), p. 11.
[17] A. Redford (see note 1 above), p. 144.
[18] G. S. Taylor, ed., *The Life and Uncommon Adventures of Captain Dudley Bradstreet*, p. 29.
[19] Dr E. J. T. Collins drew my attention to this play, which is reprinted in L. Hughes and A. H. Scouten, *Ten English Farces* (1948), pp. 227–37.
[20] *ibid*, pp. 219, 222.

Oh kingrann, says I, turn her about and let us go home again: but my dear, he took no more notice of me than if I was one of the spalpeens below in the cellar going over to reap in the harvest.

He was asked how he reached London:[21]

Fait, my dear jewel, the stage-coach; I sail'd in it from Chester.

O'Blunder reports the harvesters as being in the hold, a point repeated by Robert Bell some forty years later:[22]

The holds of the packets sailing from Dublin to Parkgate and Liverpool might, at this season, be seen crowded with poor wretches, who after paying half-a-crown for their passage, had scarcely as much more to defray the expenses of their journey to the counties situated near the Metropolis.

Half-a-crown must have been the lowest rate, so the traveller in the ballad 'Billy O'Rourke' may have been more prosperous:[23]

> I paid the captain seven thirteens
> To carry me over to Parkgate:
> Before we got half over the waves
> It blew at a terrible hard rate.
>
> Says the sailor, 'To the bottom you go!'
> Says I, 'We don't care a farthing,
> For I've paid my passage to Parkgate, you know,
> And I'll hold you to your bargain!'

Here is a slightly different version:[24]

> All the men fell on bended knees
> And the ladies fell a-fainting,
> I fell on the bread and cheese,
> I always mind the main thing.
> Said the sailors all, 'To the bottom we go!'
> Says I, 'Don't care a farthing:

---

[21] *ibid*, Scene 2, p. 229.
[22] Robert Bell (see note 14 above), p. 11.
[23] Mawdsley & Son, *Directory of the Hundred of Wirral* (1861), p. xvii.
[24] This version was sung to me by Mr J. E. Allison.

> You've booked my passage to Parkgate, you know,
> And bejabers you'll stick to your bargain!'

The prospect of the long walk to London was a good reason why the harvesters sailed to Parkgate rather than to Holyhead, for they would then have been faced with an extra ninety miles through much more difficult country where they were less likely to be able to beg buttermilk. Yet they sometimes found themselves at Holyhead, in the following case because their storm-tossed ship had been obliged to seek shelter there:[25]

> The place swarms with labouring men from Ireland who are returning from harvest, and among them their wives and children, and many other poor passengers, computed at above 700 souls.

The reason why the harvesters came to England was obviously to earn money, but there was more to it. According to Castlereagh, it was the money they earned in Britain which enabled them to pay their rent in Ireland.[26] There was the attraction of the relative prosperity of England; according to Earl Temple,[27]

> The thousands of the lower Irish, who every year, in the harvest months, flock to this country, carry back with them accounts of the state of the English poor,

which was so much more favourable than their own. Arthur Young thought that they worked better in England than they did at home because they drank ale in England, not whiskey.[28]

Money earned in England meant cash in the pocket, and cash was notoriously in short supply in Ireland, mainly because exports of silver and gold from England were prohibited before 1780.[29] An attempt to circumvent this prohibition in 1751 followed an order which made Spanish pistoles, a convenient form of gold, no longer legal currency in Ireland;[30]

---

[25] H.M.C., *15th Report, Appendix, part 7*, p. 338.
[26] 11 June 1799, R. B. McDowell, *Ireland in the Age of Imperialism and Revolution 1760—1800* (1979), p. 141, quoting B.L., Add. MS 29252.
[27] William Cobbett, ed., *The Parliamentary History of England*, 34 (1819), p. 498.
[28] A. W. Hulton, ed., *Arthur Young, A Tour in Ireland*, 2 (1780), p. 44.
[29] L. M. Cullen, *Anglo–Irish Trade 1660–1800* (1968), p. 201.
[30] H.M.C., *MSS of Mrs Stopford-Sackville*, 1, 11 July 1751, p. 175.

The Government of the Bank may possibly think that we shall now attempt an extraordinary importation of English money, and may use some means to prevent it. Would it be improper to desire that some hint might be given to the Custom House officers at Parkgate that no uncommon strictness on that point was expected from them.

The annual harvest migrations, though apparently useful both to English farmers and to Irish peasants, was not universally approved. Bishop Berkeley's point, already mentioned, was to ask,[31]

whether the industry of our people employed in foreign lands, while our own are left uncultivated, be not a great loss to the country?

The authorities in Dublin were sufficiently alarmed in 1753 by the exodus of men 'to labour at the hay harvest' that they tried to prevent them from going on board ship. Their reasons were mixed: the lack of land under the plough and consequent high prices,[32]

is partly owing to the scarcity of labourers and spalpeens, who are obliged to go to England and other countries every year for employment, where they are seduced by Irish recruiting officers, who immediately send those deluded creatures to France . . .

On the English side there could be doubts about the wisdom of encouraging the migrations. After riots in Shoreditch in 1736, when the mob cried, 'Down with the Irish' and attacked a pub kept by an Irishman, Robert Walpole attributed the trouble to:[33]

greater numbers than ordinary, as is said, of Irish being here, and not only working at hay and corn harvest, as has been usual, but letting themselves out at all sorts of labour considerably cheaper than the English labourers have.

Nor were the rewards for the harvesters always what they should have been. They were often exploited by Irish gangmasters who,[34]

---

[31] George Berkeley (see note 7 above), query 528.
[32] *Faulkner's Dublin Journal*, 15 May, 23 May, 23 August 1753.
[33] See note 8 above.
[34] Robert Bell (see note 14 above), p. 12.

like West Indian negro-drivers, would call out the labourers, at break of day from the barns in which they were permitted to stretch their wearied limbs, and make then work ten times harder than their sable brethren of the torrid zone.

As a result of sleeping in damp barns,

many of them on their return were seized with agues, which continued upon them during the winter.

The journeys of these migrants between Dublin and Parkgate were subject to various hazards. Shipwreck was one of them; a large number of haymakers were saved when the *Duke of Leinster* packet boat from Liverpool was in trouble at Dublin.[35] When the Parkgate packet *King George* was wrecked in 1806 with heavy loss of life, the dead [36]

were principally labourers who had come from Ireland to assist in getting in the harvest, and were returning to their native country with the fruits of their industry.

Delays caused by bad weather could create serious distress:[37]

Not less than 140 haymakers, natives of our sister country, last week after embarking twice from Parkgate had each time the mortification of being driven back by adverse winds; the benevolent inhabitants of Neston opened a subscription for them, when the sum of £20 16s. was immediately collected by Captain Heird.

The Dublin papers also reported the 'truly deplorable situation' of these reapers.[38]

Sometimes the press gang preyed on harvesters, although they should not have been subject to the press unless they were seamen.[39] The following letter, addressed 'To King James, His Majesty in Rome', was received by the Old Pretender in 1758:[40]

[35] *Freeman's Dublin Journal*, 2–4 June 1778.
[36] *Chester Chronicle*, 19 Sept. 1806.
[37] *Chester Chronicle*, 16 Oct. 1789.
[38] *Sleater's Dublin Chronicle*, 20 Oct. 1789, quoted in *Royal Society of Antiquaries of Ireland Journal* (1897), p. 429.
[39] N. A. M. Rodger, *The Wooden World*, pp. 164–82.
[40] Royal Archives, Windsor Castle, RA SP 380/127.

Plese my king to Look upon me being Come from a man of war from Napels the Presed me in pargate when i went over to make the harvest I Come heare to you to gett Some Money to by Cloths and victuels and Cary me to Leghorn and Depend I will love you for Ever while my Name is
     Patrick Sarsfeild
   God bless King James
My grandfather fought for your father in Ireland against king William.

The writer, who was given £10, may have been the grandson of Patrick Sarsfield, earl of Lucan. In a later war, twenty-seven poor haymakers were seized by a press-gang while waiting at the Pigeon-house to take ship:[41]

> If they were able to mow hay, they could have no objection to mow the enemies of their country.

With good fortune, however, attempts to impose on the innocence of inexperienced men could be thwarted by the English law:[42]

> About 15 Irish haymakers were given whiskey by a recruiting sergeant during their passage from Ireland, and were induced to change clothes with his party of soldiers. On landing at Parkgate they found themselves in uniform, and the sergeant claimed them. But the magistrates discharged them at Chester.

Finally, while Irishmen in England seem usually to have been made welcome, at times of stress they might be regarded as a source of subversion. In 1745, just after the Battle of Prestonpans, Dudley Bradstreet was employed as a spy [43]

> to talk to my countrymen whose numbers in and about [Hackney, Highgate and Hampstead] were great, having come from Ireland to work for wages at the harvest in England.

There were particular reasons why the people of Neston and Parkgate might have felt apprehensive about so many Irish labourers passing through. About halfway along the Chester High Road, on their way to Parkgate, three harvesters in 1750 murdered their

[41] *Slater's Dublin Chronicle*, 3 Aug. 1790.
[42] *Chester Chronicle*, 6 June 1794.
[43] Dudley Bradstreet (see note 18 above, and p. 118ff).

companion 'by striking a reaping-hook into his neck and cutting him to the windpipe'. They stole his money and were found drinking in an alehouse at Shotwick. Two of the men were hanged for the murder and their bodies were gibbeted at the scene of the crime.[44] The gibbet (inaccurately marked as 'gallows') was shown on Bell's road map of 1779,[45] and the windmill built next to the gibbet in 1777[46] was at once and subsequently known as Gibbet Mill.

The effect of the murder at 'Two Mills on the Heath' was reinforced two years later, in 1752, by a violent robbery at Rake Farm, Eccleston, near Chester, by a gang of Irishmen, two of whom were hanged.[47] These dramatic crimes were kept alive in the public memory by such incidents as one in 1775 when an Irish couple exposed a new-born child in a ditch by the road to Parkgate:[48]

> They had contracted, for a small reward, to convey the child (being the offspring of an illicit amour) to the Foundling Hospital in Dublin, and that they had taken it to Parkgate for that purpose; but finding this a troublesome business, they took the resolve to desert it.

Despite these causes for alarm, the people of Parkgate seem to have regarded their Irish visitors with tolerance, even when, as in the following case, a good deal of tolerance was probably needed:[49]

> Yesterday an Irishman, who has for several years wandered about Parkgate, in a fit of insanity, laid his leg on a block and nearly chopped it off below the knee; but seeing it hang by some flesh and skin, he deliberately cut it off with a knife.

The parish register recorded his burial two days later: 'John Moors a poor man who cut off his own leg (lunacy)'.[50]

Then as later, the 'Irish joke' was a help in smoothing the relationship. In 1812 two Irishmen robbed a butcher on the Parkgate

---

[44] *Chester Courant*, 8 Sept., 25 Sept. 1750.
[45] Peter Bell, *An Actual Survey of the Great Post Road from London to Parkgate* (1779).
[46] *Chester Chronicle*, 4 April 1777.
[47] Grosvenor MSS (available through Chester City R.O.) box of papers relating to Sir Robert Grosvenor, 6th baronet. See also *Cheshire Sheaf*, Feb. 1922, pp. 2–12.
[48] *Chester Chronicle*, 2 May 1775.
[49] *Chester Chronicle*, 7 May 1784.
[50] Neston parish register, 8 May 1784.

road and made him exchange his coat for one of theirs. The butcher later discovered that his new coat had £23 in a hidden pocket, 'a sum fully compensating him for his previous terror and the loss of his coat'.[51]

A very large proportion of those who sailed from Parkgate for Dublin were vagrants who were being repatriated under the Poor Laws, and the names of over 25,000 vagrants are recorded in the meticulous accounts of the Neston House of Correction which have survived between 1750 and 1800.[52]

Here is an example of how the system worked. Hugh Ruewark was an Irishman who came to England to look for work and failed to find it. When he was arrested in January 1758 he had been begging in Middlewich, and so was declared a 'rogue and vagabond'. Under the Poor Laws, and specifically under the most recent of them, the Vagrant Act of 1744,[53] he was to be returned to his place of legal settlement, in his case his parish of origin in Kildare, not very far from Dublin. Ruewark told Thomas Swettenham, the magistrate, that,[54]

> about fifteen years ago he was hired for a twelvemonth in the parish of Kilcullen in the County of Kildare, that he served the said twelvemonth . . . Since, he hath done no act to gain him a legal settlement elsewhere, as he believes.

When the magistrate had taken this statement, he filled in the following pre-printed form:

> Whereas Hugh Ruewark and Ann his wife were apprehended in the township of Middlewich as Rogues and Vagabonds, viz. wandering and begging there, . . . it doth appear that [his] lawful settlement . . . is in the parish of Kilcullen in the County of Kildare in the Kingdom of Ireland. These are therefore to require you, the said Constable, Tythingman or other Officer of the Peace of the said township of Middlewich, to convey the said Hugh Ruewark, Ann his wife and Child named Thomas

---

[51] *Chester Chronicle*, 31 January 1812.
[52] Cheshire R.O., Quarter Sessions files (QJF 178–228).
[53] 17 Geo II c.5.
[54] Cheshire R.O., QJF 186/1/140.

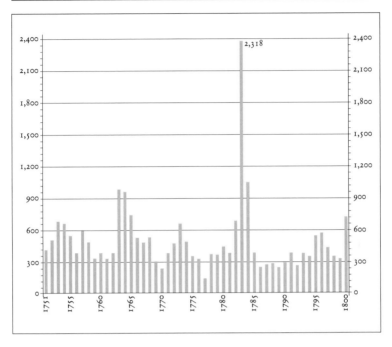

Figure 18. Graph showing the numbers of Irish vagrants repatriated
each year from the Neston House of Correction 1750–1800.

about two years old, to the township of Boughton, that being
the first place in the next precinct, through which they ought
to pass in the direct way to the said Kingdom of Ireland . . . to
be there conveyed on in like manner until they shall arrive in
Parkgate . . . to apply for a warrant to the master of any ship
or vessel bound for Ireland, that shall lie at Parkgate . . . to take
on board the said Hugh Ruewark.

It took two days to convey the Ruewark family to the gates of
Chester, and thence in the care of the constable of Boughton the
dozen miles to Neston, where they were booked in at the Old Quay
House of Correction by the master, Peter Ryder. They had to stay
in the House for four days until they were put on board a ship at
Parkgate for transmission to Dublin.

The Cheshire Quarter Sessions opened the Neston House of
Correction in 1750, half a century after it had become apparent that

considerable problems were being caused at Neston by poverty-stricken travellers. In 1698 the bench had issued this statement:[55]

> It appears unto this court that the township of Neston is very greatly overcharged and overburdened with their poor, by their being so very numerous, and also by being so charged and oppressed with passengers coming to take shipping at Neston for Ireland, and also coming back from there . . .

It was ordered that all eight townships in the parish should share the expense. The problem was not resolved, however, and in 1713 the court received a petition from the two townships in which Parkgate lay, Great Neston and Leighton, saying that they[56]

> not only provide for their own very numerous and growing poor, and pay their proportion of the yearly charge upon the whole county for relieving of vagrants constantly travelling to Ireland in great numbers, but are also under the greater burden of their passage this way and long stay here before they can get em transported . . . there being many diseased and impotent persons not capable of going to sea. Women that fall into travail and are brought to bed, helpless orphans left with us by parents which happen to die or overrun em, and others that die among us and are buried at our charge.

The petition went on to mention another problem, which would shortly be dealt with by the law; the reluctance of shipmasters to take such people:

> Besides the great difficulty and cost of prevailing with masters of ships to carry so many persons who have neither wherewithall to provide for their own sustenance or to pay for their passage . . .

An Act of the same year obliged any ship's master to take vagrants under penalty of £5.[57]

Possibly because of this pressure on Parkgate, magistrates at Nantwich and Middlewich sent their Irish vagrants on various routes, to Manchester and Liverpool as well as to Parkgate.[58] These

---

[55] *ibid*, QJF 126/2/42.
[56] *ibid*, QJF 141/1/63.
[57] 13 Anne c. 26.
[58] Cheshire R.O., QJF 168/2/66, 168/3/150, 169/2/53, 169/2/57.

directions went down badly with the Lancashire justices, who declared in 1740 that [59]

> the passing of Irish vagrants out of Cheshire to the House of Correction at Manchester, is contrary to the Act, Park Gate being the next port.

Cheshire eventually provided a solution when it was decided, in March 1750,[60]

> That it is necessary to have a House of Correction, in or near Great Neston.
>
> The magistrates have contracted for the renting or purchasing of a house called the Key House, near Great Neston. If therefore any flax dresser, manufacturer or other proper person is willing to undertake the management of the said House of Correction, in punishing offenders that shall be committed thither, and in setting them to work . . .

The principle of work was central to the idea of correction, deriving from the Act of 1575 which required that,[61]

> in every countye one or more Abyding Houses shalbe provided and called the House or Houses of Correction, for setting on worke and punishing such as shalbe taken as Rogues.

However, in this case no manufacturer was forthcoming and no work ever seems to have been provided; nor was it necessary, for the inhabitants of the House were rarely 'rogues' in need of correction, but destitute people in need of shelter, to be moved on as fast as wind and tide would permit.

The Old Key House itself stood beside Neston Key. A wooden or wood-frame building had stood on the site at the close of the sixteenth century,[62] but was replaced by a large brick building which formed a landmark on the river bank, at a time when brick was sufficiently uncommon in the area for Andrew Yarranton to describe it baldly as 'The Brick House'.[63] There is no precise record of its use

---

[59] H.M.C., *Kenyon MSS, 14th Report*, Appendix, part 4 (1894), pp. 470–1; Lancashire R.O., Kenyon MSS, no. 1207.

[60] *Chester Courant*, 13 March 1750.

[61] 18 Eliz c.3.

[62] Chester City R.O., TAO/1 (1598).

[63] A. Yarranton, *England's Improvement by Sea and Land*, map opp. p. 192.

during the seventeenth century: it may have been a store, or an inn, for in 1689 Colonel Bellingham 'lay at the Key House, at George Eaton's' after landing at Neston.[64] After the quay fell into disuse, the house was divided into three separate dwellings,[65] and in 1737 Peter Ryder, apparently the grandson of George Eaton who held the lease in 1689, was able to buy the building.[66] In 1750, therefore, Peter Ryder was the owner who leased the Old Key House to the County of Cheshire for £26 a year. Since no manufacturer offered to run it, Ryder was appointed Master of the House of Correction at an annual salary of £40.[67] A lavatory block was built, discreetly referred to in the accounts as a 'necessary house',[68] but little else was done to adapt the building.

During the fifty years from 1750, a total of 25,325 people were received at the House of Correction. Most of these were listed by name, and those that were not were described as the wives or children of named persons. The average was 506 a year, and with few exceptions the numbers varied between 300 and 600 a year. In only one year were there substantially fewer (162 in 1777), and there were two periods of remarkably high numbers: 1763 and 1764 when there were nearly a thousand a year, and 1783 and 1784 when the enormous totals of 2,318 and 1,058 vagrants passed through the House.

The reason for this huge increase in vagrant numbers in 1783 is uncertain. The weather that year was certainly unusual, starting with a wet winter and a late spring.[69] The summer of 1783 was an unpleasant one, perhaps because of earthquakes and volcanic activity in Europe. Gilbert White wrote:[70]

> This summer was an amazing and portentous one, and full of horrible phenomena: for, besides the alarming meteors and tremendous thunderstorms that afrighted and distressed the different counties of the kingdom, the peculiar haze or smoky

---

[64] 12 Nov. 1698, see *Cheshire Sheaf*, Nov. 1940, p. 53, item 7832.
[65] *Cheshire Sheaf*, 1930, pp. 61, 66 (items 6061, 6068).
[66] *ibid*, Oct. 1930, pp. 71–2 (item 6077).
[67] Cheshire R.O., QJB 3/11, July 1750; QJF 178/3, June 1750.
[68] G. W. Place, 'The repatriation of Irish vagrants from Cheshire, 1750–1815', *J.C.A.S.*, 68 (1986), p. 125.
[69] J. M. Stratton, *Agricultural Records, A.D. 220 to 1969* (1969), pp. 85–6.
[70] Gilbert White, *Natural History and Antiquities of Selborne* (1788, Penguin edn, 1941), p. 232.

fog that prevailed for many weeks . . . was quite unlike anything known within memory of man.

From 1800 to 1815 the accounts have survived in a greatly reduced form which shows the quarterly expenditure only, with no details and no nominal rolls. It is not possible to infer numbers from the expenditure, but there were peaks in 1807–8 and 1813.

By 1794, after over forty years' use by the vagrants, the condition of the building was causing concern, and the Deputy Clerk of the Peace was ordered to enquire on what terms the then owner, Joseph Lyon, would renew the lease if the county were to repair or rebuild the premises.[71] As nothing was agreed, the magistrates began looking for a new location. In 1802 it was decided to buy rather than to lease:[72]

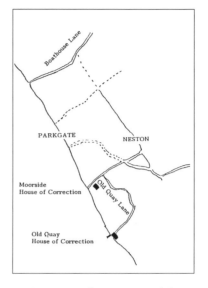

Figure 19. The positions of the Old Quay House of Correction and the Moorside House of Correction.

> to make such contract for the purchase of a house, outbuildings or other conveniences for the confinement of prisoners and vagrants to be passed to Ireland.

The house chosen was half a mile down river, at the bottom of Moorside Lane and within much easier reach of the shipping at Parkgate.

The accounts reveal many facets of the vagrants' existence while in the House of Correction: their health and mortality, their diet and their treatment. Of the three Masters, the second, William Aldcroft, was so humane and considerate that no vagrant ran away during his thirty-nine years in office.[73] But for the present we are concerned

---

[71] Cheshire R.O., QJB 3/17, Oct. 1794.
[72] *ibid*, QJB 3/18, April 1802.
[73] G. W. Place, 'The repatriation of Irish vagrants', pp. 131–7.

with those aspects which bear on the vagrants' status as passengers from Parkgate.

The vagrants were sent on board ship as soon as possible, sometimes on the day they arrived. Because their daily allowance for food is accurately recorded, the accounts tell us exactly how long the delays in sailing were. There were usually no more than about twenty in the House at any one time, so that four or five would sail on each ship. But if sailing were delayed for several weeks, the numbers would mount to the point of gross overcrowding which was transferred to the ships. The worst such occasions were in 1764, when 178 vagrants left on three ships, and in 1783, when 228 people left on two ships.[74] Because of doubts about sailing, the people often had to be taken off the ship and returned to the House; this could happen several times, the most in 1791 when some unfortunates were '5 times shipt'.[75] Delays of up to three weeks were common, the longest in 1757 when there was no sailing for sixty-five days.[76]

For over twenty years the food allowance per head was only one penny a day, which compared very unfavourably with the 6d. a day allowed by the Lancashire justices in 1740.[77] In Cheshire the allowance became 1½ d. a day in 1772, and 4½ d. a day in 1785.[78] Fortunately the Master was allowed to buy extra rations when necessary, for example in 1778, 'coarse beef at different times to make broath of, for the sick and lame people', and '4 measures of potatoes and 2 hundred herrings for the benefit of the whole'. Once the vagrants left the House, the county allowed them 'bread, boatage and passage', which originally was 2s. 1d. passage money to the captain, and 3d. bread allowance. This again compared very unfavourably with Lancashire which allowed 2s. 6d. to the captain and 1s. maintenance on board. In 1787 the Cheshire county treasurer received the following letter:[79]

> Sir, the captains of the Parkgate packets which have for upwards of twelve months past taken over the vagrants to Dublin, are (as they inform me) determined to take no more of them at 2s. 4d. a head freight, except what the law compels them to take,

---

[74] Cheshire R.O., QJF 192/2, 211/2.
[75] *ibid*, QJF 219/2.
[76] *ibid*, QJF 185/2.
[77] *ibid*, QJF 212/2.
[78] *ibid*, QJF 206/1.
[79] *ibid*, QJF 215/1.

as they too often experience that the allowance made them for sea store is often devoured before the vessel gets over the bar and by having a long passage, they must starve if the captain did not relieve them.

As a result of this petition, the maintenance allowance was doubled to 6d. and the passage money increased to 2s. 6d. The captains' letter also added, 'They are very inconvenient to people of fashion'. No doubt they were, and here the passengers on the Royal Yacht had the advantage, for the Royal Navy vessel was not subject to the law which obliged masters to take vagrants.

There is no way of telling what proportion of the vagrants were harvesters whose annual visit had ended in penury, or were long-term migrants like Hugh Ruewark. If harvesters were most likely to travel as single men, then the following figures suggest that most vagrants were not harvesters. Over the fifty years, 1750–1800, one full year has been analysed for each decade:[80]

| | | |
|---|---|---|
| Unaccompanied men | 1,029 | 44% |
| Unaccompanied women | 265 | 11% |
| Couples with children | 432 | 19% |
| Single adults with children | 592 | 25% |
| All children | 482 | 21% |

The accounts are of some value as a record of shipping. In most cases the name of the captain who was paid to take vagrants was listed, eighty-one in all; and although only eight ships are named, the ships of one third of the captains can be deduced from other evidence. In the years of very high vagrant numbers, 1783–4, the county took fright at the mounting maintenance costs and tried to have vagrants sent to Liverpool,[81]

being the nearest port for them to take shipping for the north or other parts of Ireland, being sent through the county of Chester to Parkgate, where the opportunities of getting shipping for vagrants are less frequent, and vessels very rarely sail from thence to the north of Ireland.

This claim is not supported by the evidence, despite the havoc which the War of American Independence played with shipping out of the

---

[80] G. W. Place, 'The repatriation of Irish vagrants', p. 138.
[81] *Chester Chronicle*, 9 May 1783.

Dee. During the years 1750 to 1781, the numbers sailing in each quarter with vagrants varied between 3 and 12, with an average of 6.6. The average per quarter for the year before the county's claim, 1782, was 8.5, perfectly adequate for the usual number of vagrants. It was the advent of the Parkgate Packet Company in 1785 which greatly increased the number of sailings to an average of more than twelve a quarter.

Before looking at the end of the Neston House of Correction, it is worth considering what happened to the vagrants when they reached Ireland. Here the intentions of the English law carried no weight, because there was no Poor Law in Ireland. In England the poor man

> knows that by the law the rich man is obliged to preserve him from hunger and from want. The Irish cottager, alas, has no such prospect . . . the harvesters carry back with them accounts of the state of the English poor, which only make the unfortunate Irishman look back to his own miserable hovel, to his forlorn and desperate situation, with increased feelings of anguish and misery.

So spoke Earl Temple in 1799, saying that the Irish poor would welcome the approaching union of the two kingdoms.[82] Lack of political will in the Irish parliament had prevented the strenuous efforts of people like Swift, Berkeley and many others from providing a constitutional poor law, and the Irish poor had to rely on the results of voluntary subscriptions.[83] As a result, the machinery which might conduct an Irish vagrant from London to Dublin would take him no further.

It is the record of the House of Correction which provides a useful clue to the end of the era of shipping at Parkgate. In July 1815 the *Chester Chronicle* carried this advertisement:[84]

> Irish vagrants. The magistrates of this county have given notice, by circulars, that the Dublin packets do not now sail from

---

[82] House of Commons debate, 14 Feb. 1799, in William Cobbett, *The Parliamentary History of England*, 34 (1819), p. 498.

[83] David Dickson, Trinity College Dublin, unpublished article, 'In search of the old Irish Poor Law'.

[84] *Chester Chronicle*, 28 July 1815.

Parkgate but from Liverpool. Magistrates . . . are requested to direct passes in future to Liverpool.

The final quarter of 1815 provided the last occasion that Constable Bleads of Boughton was paid for delivering vagrants 'to Great Neston'. In the accounts for the following April, he was recorded as conveying vagrants 'to Liverpool'.

The county found no further use for the Moorside House of Correction until 1822 when it was leased to a schoolmaster. The building was demolished in the early 1920s. The Old Quay House became a private residence in 1804 and remained so until the First World War, after which it became derelict and was demolished about 1941.

# 8 *Trade and the Customs*

Some Customs account books for Parkgate have survived for the years between 1776 and 1802, though they are incomplete for their last three years.[1] Unfortunately they show imports only, but they suggest that Parkgate's trade other than in passengers was very small, and that passengers became ever more important as time wore one. The Customs accounts for Chester do not survive after 1774 and therefore do not overlap with those for Parkgate. The earlier Chester accounts rarely mention Parkgate, but they indicate as we shall see that the ratio of Customs duties collected at Parkgate to those taken at Chester was very low. The fact is, however, misleading, because it overlooks Parkgate's role as a point of transfer of goods from sea-going ships to lighters, which is described in the next section.

It would perhaps be as well not to exaggerate the importance of Chester's trade at any time. In 1700 a somewhat cynical opponent of the proposed Dee navigation stated that large vessels could ascend to Chester occasionally and smaller craft at all times, and that was sufficient commerce which 'the city now hath or can ever be made capable of, by reason of the situation of it'.[2] As L. M. Cullen has pointed out, the volume of commodity traffic passing through Chester had become very small by 1700.[3] Almost a century later, in 1795, it was written that:[4]

> The maritime business of Chester is of no great extent. It chiefly consists of the coasting and Irish trade, with a small portion of trade to foreign ports.

[1] The Customs Account Book, Parkgate, 1776–1790, transcript in Cheshire R.O., 942.Z1.NES; The Comptroller's Subsidy Book, inwards, Parkgate, 1790–1802, Chester City R.O. CAP/4.
[2] 'Case of the gentlemen freeholders', B.L., 1888.C.11.1.
[3] L. M. Cullen, *Anglo-Irish Trade*, p. 43.
[4] J. Aikin, *A Description of the Country from 30 to 40 Miles round Manchester* (1795), p. 391.

A picture of Chester's trade, such as it was, in the middle of the eighteenth century is provided by a survey made in 1764 of the trade of all English ports for the five previous years.[5] The returning officer for Chester just listed commodities imported or exported by foreign or coastal trade, and did not provide the detail of his colleague at Liverpool, who broke down his list of commodities into countries of origin and destination. If we try, by reference to the Chester port books for these years,[6] to break Chester's goods down by countries, the most important of them will look like this:

| | |
|---|---|
| Foreign trade, inwards | Linen, horses, animal products such as tallow, wool, hides and skins, from Ireland. Timber, hemp and flax from the Baltic. Wine and cork from Portugal. |
| Foreign trade, outwards | By far the most important was lead, to continental countries including Mediterranean ports, and coal to Ireland. |
| Coastal trade, inwards | Goods from London, especially groceries. |
| Coastal trade, outwards | Cheese and lead, mainly to London. |

By comparing the information we have about trade at Parkgate after 1775, with examples from the Chester records shortly before that date, it is possible to give at least a flavour of Parkgate's commerce.

In sharp contrast to Liverpool, Chester had almost no American trade. In 1765, two ships came to Chester from America, while in 1771 only a single ship left Chester to cross the Atlantic.[7] During the whole of the last quarter of the eighteenth century, a single ship entered Parkgate from America, from North Carolina in 1791 with a cargo of tar and turpentine. There are scattered references to such long-distance trade in earlier years. The snow *Diligence*, which was at Parkgate in 1740 with a cargo of cheese, received an Admiralty pass in the same year to go to South Carolina.[8] In 1764 a ship which had loaded coal at Ness Colliery, near Parkgate, was bound for Philadelphia.[9] A potentially far-flung trader was the snow *Lively*, advertised while at

[5] Trade returns, B.L., Add. MS 9293, p. 109.
[6] P.R.O., E 190 1432–1436.
[7] For 1765, P.R.O., E 190 1438/1; for 1771, P.R.O., E 190 1440/10.
[8] Cheshire R.O. QDN 1/5; P.R.O., ADM 7/83 (21 Oct. 1740).
[9] University of Liverpool, Glegg Account Book, 18 Aug. 1764

Parkgate in 1786 as 'a very fit vessel for the African or West Indian trade, or any trade where despatch is required, being a remarkably fast sailer'.[10] However, as far as is known, the *Lively* was not used in the slave trade.[11]

Chester's trade with Europe was also fairly small in scale. In 1765, out of the seventy-four entries in the import accounts, six ships came from Spain or Portugal and twelve from the Baltic. In 1771, out of 129 ships leaving Chester, fourteen were bound for various European ports. During the twenty-five years from 1776, not a single ship was recorded as coming to Parkgate from Europe. Some had set out for Europe in earlier years: the sloop *Free Love* left Parkgate for Gibraltar and the Mediterranean in 1750, the brig *Princess Ann* for Cadiz in 1752, the brig *Active* for Marseilles in 1775.[12]

Glimpses of inward trade from Europe are given by the *Mary*, which reached Parkgate with a damaged cargo of flax and hemp from Riga in 1763; the *Stanislaus Angus* which unloaded timber from Danzig at 'the proper plais of discharge called the Butts' in 1765; the *Three Sisters* which brought wheat from Rotterdam in 1767.[13]

Most of Chester's foreign trade was with Dublin. D. M. Woodward has described this trade in the first half of the seventeenth century.[14] Throughout the eighteenth century, Irish trade with Britain was increasing, and Dublin was by far the busiest Irish port, taking in more than half the total Irish trade.[15] R. Craig has shown that, in 1744, over 70 per cent of ships entering or leaving Chester to or from foreign ports, were going to or from Ireland; in 1790 the proportion was nearer 90 per cent.[16] The evidence for Parkgate before 1776 is too scattered to make an estimate possible, but for the last quarter of the century, 83 per cent of ships arriving at Parkgate came from Dublin, and all but one of the rest came from other Irish ports.

The total money taken by the Customs at Parkgate, counting both imports and exports, was very small. It was only £46 in 1776, a very

---

[10] *Chester Courant*, 22 Nov. 1786.

[11] M. M. Schofield, 'The slave trade from Lancashire and Cheshire ports outside Liverpool, 1750–1790', *T.H.S.L.C.*, 126 (1977), p. 40.

[12] P.R.O., ADM 7/86 (17 Jan. 1750; 7/88 (11 Oct. 1752; 7/100 (Aug. 1775).

[13] Glegg Account Book, 2 Aug. 1763, 27 Sept. 1765, 11 May 1767.

[14] D. M. Woodward, 'The overseas trade of Chester, 1600–1650', *T.H.S.L.C.*, 122 (1971), pp. 32–8.

[15] L. M. Cullen, *Anglo-Irish Trade*, pp. 45, 15.

[16] R. Craig, 'Some aspects of the trade and shipping of the River Dee in the 18th century', *T.H.S.L.C.*, 114 (1963), pp. 90–128.

low figure probably reflecting war conditions. The nearest year before that for which we have sums of duty at both Chester and Parkgate is 1768, when £9,361 was collected at Chester and £127 at Parkgate, a mere 1.3 per cent. After 1766 the duties taken at Parkgate rarely rose above £100 until 1789 when they reached £173. From 1793 to 1797 the receipts were usually over £400, but this figure did not approach the £600 collected in 1726 (still only 6 per cent of the duties collected at Chester) which suggests that markedly more money was collected at Parkgate before the New Cut was built.[17]

The receipts in 1799 were £761, of which £500 was for exports. The increasing receipts after 1792 do not represent increased imports, nor even higher taxation, but only higher export duties. These accounts do not list the exports but do include the duties on them. The only commodity known to have been exported through Parkgate after 1792 is coal from Ness Colliery, which we shall look at in greater detail presently.

The goods listed by the Customs between 1776 and 1799 fall into six categories: vehicles, livestock, animal products, cloth, household or personal goods and the miscellaneous remainder.

The vehicles came in one at a time and can safely be assumed to have been the personal property of passengers. The number that landed can offer a rough guide to the increase in passengers. Numbers were low during the American war: 18 in 1776 but as low as 3 in 1783. The introduction of passenger vessels in 1785 (which may have allowed more space for carriages than a freight vessel could) caused a rapid increase: 22 vehicles were landed in 1786, 56 in 1789 rising to the highest number recorded, 79, in 1795.

Most of the carriages were post-chaises, followed in popularity by coaches; fourteen other varieties of carriage were landed in small numbers the most regular ones being phaetons.

The carriages were landed free of charge in most cases because they had been exported previously and were now returned, presumably with their owners. A small proportion, perhaps a quarter on average, were Irish-built and so were liable to duty.

Another but less reliable guide to the increasing number of passengers lies in the number of horses that landed. No duty was paid on horses, but the Customs staff, who had little else to do, listed them all the same. Sometimes a string of 12 or 15 horses would be

---

[17] For 1768, P.R.O., E 190 1439/8; for 1726, E 190 1406/8.

landed, indicating a commercial import, or a troop of cavalry, or a nobleman's retinue. Only once was a very large number of horses landed, in 1793 when Michael Roche imported 207 horses in eight ships within three days. Otherwise they landed singly or a few at a time. Like the carriages, the number of horses increased after the American war, and their numbers are listed at the end of this section.

Both linen and cattle are discussed separately. There were a few imports of cloth other than linen, such as fustian, woollen cloth and silk goods, but the quantities were irregular and usually quite small. Often the cloth was 'returned' as a re-import and so no duty was paid.

Animal products came in many forms up to 1790 but almost wholly ceased thereafter. The commonest were hides—cowhides, calfskins, kipskins. In some years there were goose quills, coney wool, feathers, glue, calves' valves to make rennet, and 'sheeps guts dried to make whips'. Foodstuffs were bacon, butter and beef. There were scattered imports of other animal products like wax, tallow, neats' tongues (ox tongues) and oxbones. None of these was liable to duty. The quantities of the main items are given at the end of this section.

The category of household goods contains those items which appear to be the personal belongings of passengers, many of them being re-imported and so not liable for duty. The chief items were silver and silver plate, hardware, furniture, feather beds, mattresses, pictures and musical instruments, such as single violins, guitars and harps. Some of these, like the occasional piano, may have been a commercial import or a private purchase. The names of some regular importers can be identified, like James Folliot and William Griffith, but these Chester merchants acted as shipping agents, arranging for the transport of private as well as commercial goods.

The miscellaneous category includes any other import which might have been commercial. The commonest and most regular was books, classed as bound or unbound, English ('returned' and so not liable for duty) or Irish. Books were listed by weight, and the smaller quantities were probably passengers' luggage. But some heavier boxes of books may well have been intended for the Chester book-shops. Chester had a flourishing shopping centre at this period, which included some luxury goods like books for sale.[18] Other

---

[18] S. I. Mitchell, 'Retailing in the 18th and early 19th centuries in Cheshire', *T.H.S.L.C.*, 130 (1981), pp. 37–60; pp. 55–6.

imports which may have been destined for the Chester shops were
snuff, and musical instruments. Quite a lot of French horns were
imported, with occasional buglehorns and bassoons. Broken gunbarrels were sometimes landed, probably on their way to the foun-
dry at Bersham, near Wrexham. Up till 1786 there were regular
re-imports of buckles and buttons. The only other item of any
regularity was wafers, probably for sealing documents.

How typical Parkgate's imports were of Chester's imports from
Ireland can only be estimated by looking at a sample year for which
we have the Chester port books. Here we have the difficulty that the
port books do not go into the same detail as the Parkgate accounts,
particularly as regards re-imports, which were not liable to duty. Of
the fifty-six ships arriving at Chester from Ireland in 1765, almost
all were carrying animal products or linen, with an occasional mention of books and burst gunbarrels. Only two shipments of wheat
from Dublin indicate a different pattern.

The rather slight commercial activity revealed by these Customs
accounts suggest the following conclusions. First, the number of ship
arrivals at Parkgate was not greatly affected by war conditions, but
the number of passengers greatly increased when the Parkgate Packet
Company's ships were introduced after the American war, matched
by increased but still small Customs receipts. Secondly, imports of
animal products and miscellaneous goods almost died away after
1790. Besides passengers, small numbers of cows and pigs and fluc-
tuating but small quantities of linen were the only arrivals.

But Parkgate played another role in the economy of Chester,
probably up to 1790 at least; as a point of transfer.

### Shipping, Inwards, at Parkgate

| Year | Ports of Origin | | | Customs Receipts |
|------|--------|----------------|-------|------------------|
|      | Dublin | Other Irish | Other |                  |
| 1776 | 47 | 10 |         | £ 47 |
| 1777 | 31 | 0  |         | £146 |
| 1778 | 29 | 8  | 1 (Man) | £ 65 |
| 1779 | 42 | 11 |         | £ 55 |
| 1780 | 42 | 1  |         | £ 65 |
| 1781 | 39 | 1  |         | £ 75 |
| 1782 | 37 | 0  |         | £ 96 |
| 1783 | 23 | 0  |         | £ 80 |

| Year | Ports of Origin | | | Customs Receipts |
|------|--------|----------------|-------|------------------|
| | Dublin | Other Irish | Other | |
| 1784 | 23 | 7 | | £137 |
| 1785 | 35 | 24 | 1 (Man*) | £ 99 |
| 1786 | 45 | 12 | 1 (Man) | £ 94 |
| 1787 | 40 | 19 | 3 (Man) | £ 62 |
| 1788 | 52 | 7 | | £102 |
| 1789 | 73 | 7 | | £174 |
| 1790 | 42 | 32 | | £114 |
| 1791 | 42 | 10 | 2 (Man) 1 (N.C.†) | £135 |
| 1792 | 50 | 14 | 1 (Man) | £283 |
| 1793 | 45 | 1 | 2 (Man) | £454 |
| 1794 | 31 | 2 | 3 (Man) | £379 |
| 1795 | 41 | 1 | 1 (Man) | £421 |
| 1796 | 33 | 2 | | £414 |
| 1797 | 34 | 19 | 1 (Man) | £434 |
| 1798 | 93 | 7 | | £557 |
| 1799 | 68 | 5 | 2 (Man) | £761 |

* Isle of Man.   † North Carolina

## Imports at Parkgate

| Year | Vehicles | Horses | Linen (yds) | Cows | Pigs | Mules | Sheep |
|------|----------|--------|-------------|------|------|-------|-------|
| 1776 | 18 | 104 | 3202 | 192 | — | — | — |
| 1777 | 11 | 33 | 8295 | — | — | — | — |
| 1778 | 10 | 39 | 5631 | 220 | 18 | — | — |
| 1779 | 9 | 45 | 6165 | 379 | 4 | — | — |
| 1780 | 7 | 51 | 4440 | 107 | — | — | — |
| 1781 | 13 | 16 | 6240 | — | — | — | — |
| 1782 | 8 | 11 | 1551 | — | — | — | — |
| 1783 | 3 | 26 | 3565 | 40 | — | — | — |
| 1784 | 5 | 35 | 2064 | 208 | 82 | — | — |
| 1785 | 12 | 36 | 1764 | 666 | 384 | — | — |
| 1786 | 22 | 71 | 7628 | 402 | — | — | — |
| 1787 | 29 | 143 | 2591 | 596 | 247 | — | — |
| 1788 | 29 | 125 | 961 | 170 | 39 | — | — |
| 1789 | 56 | 222 | 5613 | 384 | 75 | 5 | — |

| Year | Vehicles | Horses | Linen (yds) | Cows | Pigs | Mules | Sheep |
|---|---|---|---|---|---|---|---|
| 1790 | 43 | 253 | 3663 | 755 | 144 | 37 | — |
| 1791 | 52 | 455 | 266 | 274 | 318 | — | — |
| 1792 | 56 | 349 | 25 | 233 | 454 | 1 | — |
| 1793 | 58 | 495 | 2154 | 185 | 54 | 2 | — |
| 1794 | 67 | 339 | 600 | 60 | — | — | — |
| 1795 | 79 | 373 | 2863 | 68 | 20 | — | — |
| 1796 | 65 | 297 | 399 | 76 | 104 | — | — |
| 1797 | 53 | 158 | 700 | 528 | 479 | — | 131 |
| 1798 | 66 | 311 | 6305 | 439 | 30 | 5 | 169 |
| 1799 | 65 | 399 | 529 | 52 | 225 | 45 | — |

## Selected Imports

| Year | Cowhides | Calfskins | Bacon | Beef | Butter |
|---|---|---|---|---|---|
| 1776 | — | — | 2 cwt | — | — |
| 1777 | — | — | — | — | — |
| 1778 | — | — | 1 cwt | 1 cwt | — |
| 1779 | — | — | — | 39 tierces | — |
| 1780 | 61 | 20 doz | 8 cwt | — | 10 kegs |
| 1781 | — | 42 doz | 2½ cwt | — | 10 cwt |
| 1782 | 25 | 67 doz | 7 cwt | 3 cwt | 254 cwt |
| 1783 | 63 | 131 doz | 25 cwt | — | — |
| 1784 | 264 | 133 doz | 61 cwt 2 flitches | — | 3 cwt |
| 1785 | 240 | 77 doz | 72 cwt | 30 cwt | — |
| 1786 | 895 | 118 doz | 5 cwt | 16 tierces | 2 cwt, 1 basket |
| 1787 | 34 | 3 doz | 30 flitches | — | 20 cwt |
| 1788 | 60 | 20 doz | 35 cwt | — | 20 cwt |
| 1789 | 20 | 28 doz | 20 cwt | 4 barrels | 33 cwt |
| 1790 | — | 35 doz | 9½ cwt | — | — |
| 1791 | — | — | — | — | — |
| 1792 | — | — | 1 cwt | — | 11 firkins |
| 1793 | — | — | 1 cwt | — | — |
| 1794 | — | — | — | — | — |

No further quantities of these goods were imported up to 1800.

Selected Imports at Parkgate

| Year | Sheeps' guts | Goose quills | Glue | Calves' valves | Feathers | Snuff |
|---|---|---|---|---|---|---|
| 1776 | 71 gross | 4000 | 99 cwt | — | — | 10 lb |
| 1777 | 21 gross | — | 1 cask | — | — | — |
| 1778 | 16 gross | 56000 | 28 lb | 2 casks | — | 54 lb |
| 1779 | 16 gross | 20000 | 1 cask | — | 1 cwt | 6 lb |
| 1780 | — | — | 2 casks | 2 casks | 5 bags | — |
| 1781 | — | — | 1 h'head | — | 4 cwt | — |
| 1782 | — | — | — | — | 1 cwt | 4 lb |
| 1783 | 2 gross | — | — | — | — | — |
| 1784 | 19 gross | 2000 | 9 cwt | 2½ cwt | 1½ cwt | — |
| 1785 | — | — | — | 2½ cwt | 1¼ cwt | — |
| 1786 | — | — | 7½ cwt | 10 cwt | 6 cwt | 6 lb |
| 1787 | — | — | 8½ cwt | 14½ cwt | 4¼ cwt | — |
| 1788 | — | — | — | 1½ cwt | — | — |
| 1789 | — | — | 3 cwt | 8½ cwt | 7 cwt | — |
| 1790 | — | 78000 | — | — | 5½ cwt 6 bags | — |
| 1791 | — | — | — | ½ cwt | — | — |
| 1792 | — | — | — | 3 cwt | — | — |
| 1793 | — | — | — | — | — | — |
| 1794 | — | — | — | — | — | 16 lb |
| 1795 | — | — | — | — | — | 40 lb |
| 1796 | — | — | — | — | — | — |
| 1797 | — | — | — | — | 7 cwt | — |
| 1798 | — | — | — | — | — | — |
| 1799 | — | — | — | — | 10½ cwt | — |

'Sheeps' guts' were 'dried to make whips', and calves' valves were to make rennet.

In Chapter Two we have already seen that it was common practice to transfer goods from or to ocean-going ships to lighters for the journey through the upper part of the Dee estuary. Before the New Cut was opened in 1737, it was said that ships could reach the city on 'spring tides'.[19] It may perhaps be useful to explain that the term

[19] *Journal of the House of Commons*, 21 (24 Feb. 1733), p. 812.

'spring tide' has no connection with the season, but refers to the maximum high water that occurs on the days shortly after the new and full moon: every fortnight, in fact. In 1707 the City Council itself claimed that vessels drawing nine feet of water could reach Chester at all spring tides.[20] It is quite possible that this situation was always true during the recorded history of the Dee: when Burton in Wirral was a favoured anchorage, the hospital of St Andrew at Denhall nearby, founded in the thirteenth century, was granted the right to convey goods which were being trans-shipped through the port, in its own boat to Chester.[21] In the 1530s, just before the New Haven at Neston was started, a schedule of the rates of local Customs refers to goods 'carried by bote or lightures from the red banke, heswall, denwaull or Burton hede to this citie of Chester', with a lower rate from Shotwick.[22]

When the New Haven was built in the mid-sixteenth century, the result for the village of Neston, in effect if not in form, was to make it a town. It was therefore natural that passengers should be ferried to Neston, rather than to some uninhabited place like Hilbre. The following was written in 1620:[23]

West Chester: There is a piece of ground a mile about encompassed with water, called the Roe Dee, where barks of some 20 or 30 tons come up from Nesson, which carry passengers into and out of Ireland.

If passengers preferred to go by road to Neston, then their goods might follow by water. In 1645,[24]

I left Chester on the 16th [of April] and got as far as Neston on my way to Ireland. Our goods came down in boats . . .

We have already noted that in 1690 there were only two or three mariners in the city of Chester, but there were nineteen 'labourers in lighter boats' belonging to the city.[25]

---

[20] Chester City R.O., ML/4/601 (15 Feb. 1707); H.M.C., *Appendix to 8th Report*, 3 (1881), pp. 394–5.
[21] G. Ormerod, *History of Cheshire*, ed. T. Helsby (1882) 2, pp. 542–3.
[22] K. P. Wilson, ed., *Chester Customs Accounts 1301–1566*, p. 145. See also p. 12.
[23] Extracts from the itinerary of Henry, Earl of Huntingdon, in H.M.C. 78, *MSS of R. R. Hastings*, 4 (1947), 10–20 Aug. 1620, p. 340.
[24] H.M.C., *MSS of Earl of Egmont* (1905), p. 252 (28 April 1645), vol. 1.
[25] P.R.O., T1/11/69.

There is a clue to the transfer of cargo, before the New Cut was built, in the Exchequer port books, which mention Parkgate rarely or not at all in those years. The clue lies, to take 1723 for example,[26] in the phrase *per transary* which was often added to an entry. A *transire* was a certificate to show that no duty was payable, and was used to move goods coastwise in English waters.[27] This form was probably used to transfer goods within the estuary, since a longer journey, even to Liverpool, would probably (though not necessarily) need a cocquet, another kind of Customs certificate which required a bond to be paid, returnable when the goods were landed at another English port. Some of the coastwise port books are headed 'Chester Coketts'.[28] But if the phrase *per transary* refers to movement by lighter within the estuary, there is no indication in the port books of whether the transfer took place at Parkgate, or Dawpool (where there was a Customs officer), or anywhere else. Nor do the port books throw any revealing light on what goods, or what quantities, were transferred by lighter at Parkgate.

There is, however, considerable information in the evidence given to the Houses of Parliament in 1732, when the River Dee Bill was being considered. The cheesemongers, who claimed that they 'are concerned in at least nine-tenths of the exports from Chesters', referred to 'the usual loading places at Parkgate and Dawpool'.[29] Another petition explained why these were the usual loading places:[30]

> For some time past the navigation hath been so lost, the ships have been forced to stop at Parkgate, eight miles below Chester towards the sea, and all goods and merchandizes exported and imported from and to Chester, are sent to and from Parkgate, either by land carriage at an expence of 6s. per ton, or by small boat at an expence of 2s. per ton, to be put on board such ships . . .

This petition added that cloth usually went by land to avoid damage by water, leaving principally cheese and wine to go by river.

---

[26] P.R.O., E 190/1403/15.
[27] T. S. Willan, *English Coasting Trade 1600–1775* (1938), p. 2.
[28] For example 1749, P.R.O., E 190/1422/5.
[29] The case of the cheesemongers, B.L., 357 C.1.28.
[30] The case of the inhabitants of the County of Chester, B.L., 357 C.1.37.

Captain John Stevens gave evidence that flat-bottomed ships of 40 to 60 tons have gone up to Chester on the top of spring tides.[31]

After the New Cut was opened in April 1737, the main stream ran straight across the estuary from its new outlet on the Welsh side to its old course at Parkgate. Despite the gloomy predictions that 'in a year or two's time no ship can be brought to Parkgate',[32] Parkgate's status was actually enhanced by finding itself at the head of the old course of the river. Travelling along the New Cut was not necessarily a simple matter of sailing, but might involve being towed. The Act for erecting a lighthouse near the port of Chester, passed in 1776, made provision for the licensing of any 'tower or tracker of ships or vessels with horses'.[33] An 'old boat warn out in the towing at Parkgate' was sold by the Customs in 1759.[34]

An example of the transfer of freight just after the opening of the New Cut, is the tenor bell for Chester cathedral. This bell cracked in 1738, was sent by boat to Parkgate and thence was shipped to London to be recast. The charges for its return journey were: £4 London to Parkgate, and £1 Parkgate to Chester.[35]

From the records of the ships using the New Cut,[36] it is clear that the transfer of goods by lighter, which the River Dee Act was designed to end, was still very much in use. Although this record, the 'Register of shipping entering or leaving the port of Chester', covers twenty-nine years, the system of keeping it varied at different times. For the first five years, 1740–4, only outward shipping was recorded, and for the first four years there are frequent mentions of Parkgate. During those years, out of an annual average of ninety-two ships sailing down the Cut, an average of seventeen or nearly one-fifth called at Parkgate. Nearly all of these were cheese ships which, as we shall examine presently, had a special reason for calling at Parkgate. From 1743 onwards, the regular cheese ships were no longer shown as sailing from Chester to Parkgate, apparently because lighters were used instead to get the cheese through the Cut. During the nine years 1744–52, the phrase 'by lighter to Parkgate' or 'by sloop to Parkgate' is often used. Nearly all these were cheese

[31] *Journal of the House of Commons*, 21, p. 812.
[32] Thomas Badeslade, 'Reasons humbly offered', B.L., 190 D.15.1.
[33] 16 Geo III c.61 (1766), p. 1416.
[34] P.R.O. E 190/1433/5 (6 Feb. 1759).
[35] J. W. Clarke, 'Cheshire Bells', *L.C.A.S.*, 60 (1948), p. 96.
[36] Cheshire R.O. QDN 1/5.

shipments, an example being the *Endeavour*, which was not one of the contract cheese ships; on this occasion in 1746 she had brought hemp and flax from St Petersburg to Chester and then collected a cargo of cheese which reached Parkgate by lighter. In a few cases, other goods than cheese were brought down: in 1750 the *William & Samuel* took leather to Lisbon, and the *Seven Brothers* brought deals and iron from Gothenburg; in each case the cargo was transferred from or to lighters at Parkgate.

After 1752 the register records far fewer mentions of Parkgate, although it may be implied by the common phrase 'by sloop' usually for cheese. But a variety of small cargoes, possibly in small boats, is shown as reaching Chester from Parkgate: wine and cork, coal, linen, hides, tallow, timber, wheat, herrings, rigging.

There is also evidence of cargoes being split, presumably to lighten a ship which could sail to Chester with a twelve-foot draught. In 1754 the *John and Jane* carried balks from Riga, twenty-four tons of which came by sloop from Parkgate. The next year the *Good Intent* brought flax from Narva, one-third of it brought from Parkgate. At about the same time, 1752, a contract was made for the *Elizabeth and Rebecca* to sail from Liverpool to Rotterdam and Petersburg to load with iron and return to Chester:[37]

> in case it shall be found necessary to ease the ship, he [Joseph Deane, the master] will take one sloop load of her said cargo out at Parkgate or Dawpool.

The evidence therefore suggests that Parkgate's role as a transfer point for cargo was always important, and was strongly in evidence after the opening of the Dee Navigation as it had been before.

There remains the fact that ships which intended to sail up the Cut to Chester could rarely do so without pausing somewhere, and the natural place to pause was at Parkgate:[38]

> The Lovely Mary, Charles M'Carty master, with sundries from London arrived at Parkgate on Sunday last and as the tides are taking off, it is apprehended she cannot get up to Chester before Sunday next if wind then permits.

[37] Chester City R.O., TC/PL/1/50.
[38] *Chester Courant*, 31 March 1770.

We shall now examine more closely those aspects of trade which concerned Parkgate more particularly: linen, cheese and lead, cattle and coal.

Irish linen was exempted from British duty in 1696 and it rapidly became Ireland's most important export to Britain: 72 per cent of the value in 1738, 70.6 per cent in 1788.[39] Its use in England was 'chiefly for the wear of the common people, notably shirts'.[40] As a result, 'linen' became synonymous with clothing worn next to the skin: Admiral Smith's 'divisional system' introduced into his squadron in the Royal Navy in 1755, required the men to 'shift their linen' twice a week.[41]

Chester's share of the Irish trade was, in the eighteenth century, almost entirely in linen:[42]

They have great fairs here every year to which an abundance of merchants and tradesmen resort, but particularly from Bristol and Dublin.

Chester held three week-long fairs each year. That in February, the Horn and Hoof Fair, was for cattle and horses; the two fairs in June and September were for cloth, mainly linen.[43]

It was the Fair-time on which account the town and inns were greatly thronged. In our inn no less than 70 beds were made and mostly two in each. Great trade from Ireland hither with linen etc. for which they exchange hops chiefly.

Perhaps the culmination of this trade in Chester was the building of the Linen Hall in 1778.[44] After 1780 the trade began to be dominated by Irish wholesalers, but drapers continued to cross to the Chester fairs because they would be paid in cash or in short-dated bills.[45] The trade declined after about 1800 because the linen manufacturers

[39] L. M. Cullen, *Anglo-Irish Trade*, p. 47.
[40] *ibid*, p. 63, quoting B.L. Add. MS 21134 ff. 1, 2.
[41] N. A. M. Rodger, *The Wooden World*, p. 107, quoting B.L. Add. MS 35195 f. 9.
[42] J. Savary de Bruslow, *Universal Dictionary of Trade & Commerce* (1751), trans. Malachy Postlethwaite, 1, p. 487 (quoted by C. Armour).
[43] *Analecta Hibernica*, 15 (1944), p. 115.
[44] B. E. Harris, *Chester* (1979), p. 99.
[45] L. M. Cullen, *Anglo-Irish Trade*, p. 96.

ceased to send their cloth to Dublin but dealt between Belfast and Liverpool.

It is difficult to establish Chester's precise share in the linen trade. Duty was not payable on plain linen cloth and there was a tendency to understate the quantity imported to avoid local dues. It was said that three million yards of linen were sent to Chester a year in the 1770s, of which one-third was not endorsed on the Customs certificates. This compares with a total in 1770 of 19.6 million yards sent to Britain as a whole.[46] But the Chester port books for 1770 show only 1,181,969 yards.[47] It is therefore unsafe to compare figures for the linen trade too confidently, and one can only say that linen seems to have been considered very important at Chester. Only small quantities were actually landed at Parkgate, sometimes a few hundred yards a year, the most recorded being 8,295 in 1777.

There are many references to linen being carried to Parkgate. In 1739[48] 'Pearl Galley, Howard, to Parkgate with passengers and linen for Chester Fair'. Similarly in 1766, 'Nonpareil, Brown, passengers and linen cloth for Parkgate'.[49] In time of war this valuable trade had to be protected. In 1778 [50]

> The Active, Gwyn Brown master, and the Alexander, Hugh Williams master, arrived at Parkgate with Irish linen from Dublin for the fair, having been convoyed by the Stag sloop of war.

It was not merely the linen, but the linen merchants who formed an important part of the Parkgate scene:[51]

> 6 Oct [1775], Britannia, Brown, and Murray, Totty, with linen and linen merchants for Chester Fair.

> 8th, King George, Briscoe, with linen merchants for Parkgate.

Although linen did not pay duty, it was recorded by the Customs nevertheless, and although the Chester port books do not reveal much about Parkgate, there is mention of linen 'in the store at Parkgate' on many occasions:[52]

[46] L. M. Cullen, *Anglo-Irish Trade*, p. 60.
[47] C. Armour, p. 276.
[48] *Dublin Journal*, 29 Sept. 1739.
[49] *Freeman's Dublin Journal*, 29 Jan. 1766.
[50] *Chester Chronicle*, 17 July 1771.
[51] *Dublin Journal*, 6 Oct. 1775.
[52] P.R.O., E 190 1433/5.

8 February [1759]. In the store at Parkgate, out of the Minerva Galley, John Matthews, 127 yards rich linen.

Cheese and lead will be considered together for the good reason that the cheese ships which sailed from Chester to London often, perhaps usually, took on board a cargo of lead at Parkgate. The heavy lead served as ballast for the light cheese.

Virtually all the cheese shipped out of Chester went to London because, in 1770 [53]

> The most considerable cheesemongers in London have formed themselves into a club. They are owners of about 16 ships which are employed between London, Chester and Liverpool. They employ these ships chiefly in bringing up cheese to London. They have factors in Cheshire who buy up the cheese for them and lodge it in their warehouses in Chester.

The London cheesemongers claimed that exports of cheese, as we have seen, represented nine-tenths of Chester's trade. The stranglehold that this implied was resented and it was hoped the New Cut would loosen it:[54]

> Farmers in Cheshire are obliged to sell their cheese to the factors or brokers of the cheesemongers at their own price, upon trust, with very long credit . . . One good end to be expected from this bill, will be the destroying of that monopoly.

In 1767 the Committee of Cheesemongers named five ships as Chester ships and eleven as Liverpool ships; they agreed to limit the Chester ships to one hundred tons of cheese each, to leave room for the city's goods.[55] Over the period 1740–69, forty-two cheese ships were recorded as calling at Parkgate, although for sixteen of them, only one visit was listed.[56] The loads of cheese varied greatly, between fifteen and one hundred tons.

---

[53] James Wimpey, *Thoughts upon several interesting Subjects* (1770), pp. 39–40, quoted by G. E. Fussell, 'The London Cheesemongers of the eighteenth century', *Economic History*, I (1929), p. 395.
[54] 'The Case of the Inhabitants of Chester', B.L., 357 C.1.37.
[55] *Chester Courant*, 29 Sept. 1767.
[56] Cheshire R.O., QDN 1/5

The practice of sending lead as ballast in the cheese ships began in 1711 and became common practice thereafter.[57] Lead was first recorded being shipped from Flint in 1703 when the smelting works at Gadlys were being built by the Royal Mines Copper Company, which became the London Lead Company in 1705.[58] The company had several mines in North Wales which by 1730 were concentrated within thirty miles of the works at Gadlys, close to the small port of Bagillt.[59] Bagillt was considered a hazardous place for loading,[60] and was on the wrong side of the estuary for the main stream of the river and therefore for the larger ships. The London Lead Company described their method of shipment in 1733:[61]

> . . . do now convey their lead ore, litharge and calamine to Bagillt Mark, lying upon the said river, from whence it is carried by boats and lighters to Parkgate, at present the safest harbour for ships within the said River Dee, and where the same is put aboard the cheese ships which take it in as ballast; to be conveyed to London.

They went on to say that the boatage for the three miles from Bagillt to Parkgate was 1s. 6d. a ton. They were anxious that so heavy a commodity should not have to travel more than the shortest distance and were afraid that the River Dee Bill would cause cheese ships to deal directly with Chester, omitting Parkgate, and so increase the lead freight costs. The Bill was amended in their favour so that cheese 'brought to and put on board such ships or vessels by boats or keels' outside the Cut, paid dues at a special rate, and lead was similarly protected.[62]

The lead put on board the cheese ships at Parkgate was destined for London. Lead for other destinations might be loaded at Parkgate, Dawpool or Bagillt itself. In the years 1762–8, John Glegg's account

[57] J. N. Rhodes, 'The London Lead Company in North Wales, 1693–1792', Ph.D. thesis, Leicester University (1970), p. 316.

[58] M. Bevan-Evans, 'Gadlys and Flintshire leadmining in the 18th century', *Flintshire Historical Society Journal*, 18 (1960), p. 92.

[59] Arthur Raistrick, *Two Centuries of Industrial Welfare, the London (Quaker) Lead Company*, (1938), pp. 114–15.

[60] T. Pennant, *History of the Parishes of Whiteford and Holywell* (1796), p. 189.

[61] London Lead Company court minute book, 30 March 1737, quoted by M. Bevan-Evans, *Flintshire Historical Society Journal*, 20 (1962), p. 58.

[62] 6 Geo II c.30 (1732) clause 3.

book recorded two small vessels taking lead from Bagillt to Liverpool; two ships loading lead at Dawpool for Naples and London; one bound for Bordeaux which took on lead both at Parkgate and at Dawpool; and two ships going to Dieppe and Le Havre from Bagillt, but as these ships were recorded at Parkgate and Dawpool, perhaps only the lead came from Bagillt.[63]

During the seventeenth century, until 1664, considerable and growing numbers of Irish cattle were imported into England, and the largest numbers came into the port of Chester. In 1664, in order to protect the English fatstock market, cattle imports were prohibited between 1 August and 20 December (15 Charles II c.7). The cattle went through a variety of local ports:

> Grant to Lord Loughborough of £500 a year for 19½ years, in compensation for his surrender of the farm of duties for exporting cattle to Ireland from Chester, Neston, Liverpool and Beaumaris.

Lord Loughborough's farm was for both imports and exports.[64]

The partial ban of 1664 was replaced by a total ban in 1667, albeit by a temporary Act (19 & 20 Charles II c.12). This Act did not stop the flow of imported livestock, and enquiries into the trade in that year offer a glimpse of Parkgate's involvement. In the second quarter of 1667, three ships bearing ninety-five cattle and eighty sheep unloaded at Parkgate. In the same period, fourteen ships landed 570 cattle and 690 sheep at Flint, while smaller numbers were landed at Mostyn and Hoylake. This compares with a total of 3531 cattle and 2940 sheep landed in the Dee and Mersey during the first half of the year.[65]

A further Act to stop the loophole had to be passed in 1668 (20 Charles II c. 12). This temporary prohibition lapsed in 1679, whereupon the imports of Irish cattle and sheep resumed, with Chester more involved, at least as a landfall, than ever, accounting for many more beasts than Liverpool.[66] In 1681 a permanent ban on the import of Irish livestock was enacted (32 Charles II c.2).

---

[63] John Glegg's account book, 5 March 1764, 19 Aug. 1764, 14 March 1765, 2 Nov. 1765, 11 March, 1 Nov., 10 Dec. 1767.
[64] *Cal. S.P. Dom., 1663*, pp. 289, 303; *Cal. Treasury Books 1666–67*, p. 221.
[65] Cheshire R.O., QJF 95/2/39: D. M. Woodward, 'Anglo-Irish livestock trade of the 17th century', *Irish Historical Studies*, 18 (1973), p. 500.
[66] D. M. Woodward, 'Anglo-Irish livestock trade', pp. 502, 521.

The result of the Cattle Acts was to encourage the Irish provision trade, mainly of salt beef to France and the West Indies, while the British Navy employed its own victualling agents at Cork and Kinsale.[67] The economy of Chester must have been affected by the loss of an apparently large part of its Irish trade, but perhaps only indirectly, as the cattle trade may have been peripheral to the merchants of Chester as a whole.[68] The actual animals were landed at any convenient place in the estuary, like Parkgate. Whatever benefit this traffic gave to Parkgate was to disappear for nearly eighty years.

During the years 1745–52, there was a severe outbreak of cattle plague in England, and thirty thousand cattle are said to have died in Cheshire in 1748.[69] The details of this slaughter can be read in the claims for compensation for cows 'killed and buryed pursuant to H.M. Orders in Council'. The nearest the plague seems to have come to Neston was the two miles to Willaston, where in 1749 William Peers destroyed cattle including Come-be-times, Lovely, Crumb and Daisy.[70] The price of cattle rose sharply and Irish cattle were readmitted, the Irish Cattle Act being repealed in 1759. Although Chester's seventeenth-century cattle trade never revived, the effect on Parkgate was considerable, as ships carrying cattle and pigs then became regular visitors. These imports were encouraged by the Neston Fairs which were revived in 1776:[71]

> for all manner of cattle, as cows, horses, sheep, pigs etc., on 29 and 30 September, 2 and 3 February and 1 and 2 May, and to be continued yearly according to the old custom.

The 'old custom' had begun by charter in 1729.

The numbers of cows and pigs imported, as shown in the Parkgate Customs Account, have already been listed. In these years the numbers were not large, but they supported John Oliver, described in the Chester Directory of 1787 as 'importer of cows from Ireland to

---

[67] L. M. Cullen, *Anglo-Irish Trade*, pp. 33, 43.

[68] D. M. Woodward, 'Anglo-Irish livestock trade', pp. 505–9; D. M. Woodward, 'Overseas trade of Chester', pp. 37–8.

[69] Thomas Rigby, *The Cattle Plague in Cheshire* (1866), p. 3.

[70] Cheshire R.O., QJB/3/1749.

[71] *Chester Chronicle*, 27 Sept. 1776. 1776 was the year of the final repeal of the Cattle Acts (16 Geo III c.8), the Act of 1759 having been temporary (32 Geo II c.11). See J. O'Donovan, *The Economic History of Live Stock in Ireland*, p. 110.

Parkgate', and who is shown in the Customs accounts as an importer in 1785.

The numbers imported in the first years of the nineteenth century seem to have been considerably larger. It was recorded that in the second six months of 1810, 2,580 cows, 3,386 pigs, 1,762 sheep and 160 horses from Ireland were landed at Parkgate.[72]

Coal from the mines of Flintshire had for long been shipped to Dublin, but the rise of Whitehaven, which supplied most of the Dublin market, and the changes in the Dee navigation, both militated against the Welsh coalpits in the later part of the eighteenth century.[73]

Although there had been some very minor working for coal in Ness, at the south end of Neston parish, for many years earlier, [74] a major find of coal was made there in the late 1750s.[75] A stone quay for shipping was built at Ness Colliery in the 1760s.[76] The coal sloops sometimes took on coal only at the colliery quay, in which case they would have to come to Parkgate for Customs clearance, or obtain clearance from a Customs officer who, by special permission, would visit Ness, which was not a 'legal quay' for Customs purposes.[77] Sometimes, though, coal was only a part of the cargo. In 1764 a ship with coals from Ness called at Dawpool to collect further cargo for Philadelphia,[78] while in 1766 the *King George*, 'loaden with coles and merchant goods at Parkgate and bound for Dublin' was driven back by the wind.[79] Coal sloops sometimes carried Irish vagrants from the Neston House of Correction.[80] In 1771 some of the coal ship masters irritated the regular Parkgate trading captains by describing their ships as 'Parkgate Traders', presumably to attract cargo.[81] Coals from Ness usually

[72] *Chester Courant*, 22 Jan. 1811.
[73] T. Pennant, *History of the Parishes of Whiteford and Holywell*, p. 133; W. Cathrall, *The History of North Wales* (Manchester, 1828, 2 vols), 2, p. 214.
[74] Cheshire R.O. P.149/6/1, pew allotment, 1711, 'the Coal, Ness'.
[75] *Cheshire Sheaf*, July 1936, p. 62; W. W. Mortimer, *History of the Hundred of Wirral* (1847), p. 168; Neston parish register, 26 December 1759.
[76] Chester City R.O., AB/4/182 v.
[77] P.R.O., CUST 79/6 (28 April 1819); colliery stated not to be a legal quay, CUST 79/8 (8 Feb. 1831).
[78] John Glegg's account book, 19 August 1764.
[79] *ibid*, 18 Dec. 1766.
[80] For example, 1782, Cheshire R.O., QJF 210/1.
[81] *Chester Courant*, 12 Nov. 1771.

seem to have gone to Dublin but some also went to Chester and to Rhuddlan in North Wales.

The increase in export duties collected at Parkgate from 1792 (at £192, eight times the previous year's export duty) rising to £501 in 1799, almost certainly represents increased coal shipments from Ness Colliery. The lead exports had gone by this time. Pennant wrote that the London Lead Company 'totally withdrew at Michaelmas 1792'.[82] When Parkgate's regular shipping had ceased, the Customs staff was recommended for reduction to one man in 1820 'as the foreign trade at Parkgate is solely coals exported and cattle from Ireland'.[83]

An Act of 1662 permitted the king to appoint or delimit by commission the member ports, or places where goods might lawfully be landed, within the authority of the head ports.[84] Head ports like Chester were the seats of the principal Customs officers appointed by patent; member ports were manned by the deputies of those officers and were 'legal quays' for trade because the Customs could monitor the arrival and departure of ships; lesser creeks might be supervised by a Customs officer or by an itinerant riding officer but were not 'legal quays' and had no authority for trade.[85] After a survey of the port of Chester made in 1688 by William Carter, an order was made which mentioned Parkgate for the first time as a Customs station:[86]

> A boat to be established for the better guarding of Chester water with two boatmen at £10 per annum each, and their station to be at Parkgate and Helbre. Edward Taylor and John Bennett appointed, all as proposed by William Carter in his late survey of Chester.

Precisely what was established at Parkgate at this date, other than a boat, tends to be concealed in the records by the persistence of Neston as a direction. In the records of the Customs establishments, for example, 'Neston' remains the heading as late as 1780, after which

---

[82] T. Pennant, *History of the Parishes of Whiteford and Holywell*, p. 262.

[83] P.R.O., CUST 79/7 (8 Dec. 1820).

[84] 13 & 14 Car II c.11 (1662) para. 14.

[85] R. C. Jarvis, 'Appointment of ports', *Economic History Review*, 2nd series, 11 no. 3 (1959), p. 464.

[86] *Cal. Treasury Books 1685–89*, 8 part 4 (1923), p. 1948 (18 June 1688).

time 'Parkgate' is the heading.[87] Our first intimation of a Customs presence in Neston is 1634, when Foulke Ensdale, 'Custom man', was buried; and Clement Foster, searcher at the port is mentioned in 1640.[88]

An unusually full list of Customs officers made in 1782 indicates that warrants for two waiters and searchers for 'Neston' were authorised in 1676 and 1711. The first warrants specifying 'Parkgate' were authorised in 1724.[89] It was perhaps in that year that Parkgate, in place of Neston, acquired the status of a 'legal quay', a status which it retained until 1848.

The boat established in 1688 did not prove wholly adequate, as emerged in 1704:[90]

John Farar and Stephen Wilkinson (two of the extraordinary tidesmen, Chester port) as boatmen ibid. for the boat to be established there for boarding of ships that pass by Park Gate in the night or keep close to the Welsh side of the river which is 3 miles broad so that such ships cannot be discovered by the present boat and boatmen who are employed by the tide surveyor at Parkgate . . .

Mention of the boat at Parkgate crops up from time to time. In 1758 the Customs boat, twenty-six feet by ten feet, was for sale at Parkgate,[91] whereas in 1776 a £5 reward was offered when,[92]

the mainsail of the schooner in the service of HM Customs at Parkgate was cut away and stolen in the night between 14 and 15 August.

A 'large boat with masts, sails and tackle, in the service of the Customs' was for sale at Parkgate in 1789.[93]

Once the Customs was firmly established in Parkgate, so that ships' masters and passengers were obliged to come to the Custom House, then the village was in a position to flower, not merely as an anchorage, but as a passenger port. To be established that firmly, the

---

[87] cf. P.R.O., CUST 18/383, 400.
[88] Neston parish register (Cheshire R.O., P 149/1/1.)
[89] P.R.O., CUST 39/16.
[90] *Cal. Treasury Books 1704–5*, 19 (1938), p. 235 (17 May 1704).
[91] *Chester Courant*, 14 Feb. 1758.
[92] *Chester Chronicle*, 29 Nov. 1776.
[93] *ibid*, 28 Aug. 1789.

service needed its own building. It was the usual practice for the Custom House to be rented,[94] and a necessity at Parkgate where the entire village belonged to the Mostyn estate. The estate papers do not reveal any direct leases to H.M. Customs, and the whereabouts of the several buildings they occupied are revealed only in their dealings with Mostyn tenants. It is not known where the Custom House was that was mentioned in the first years of the eighteenth century, in a letter written by Sir Richard Middleton who died in 1716:[95]

> I cannot get Mr Vaughan's wine yet out of the Custom house if it were to save my life.

We shall see more of this remarkable letter later.

In the 1730s Joseph Howard built a house 'intended for a Custom House', a building which stood in front of all the other houses in this linear village, on the piece of land now known as the Donkey Stand, and well placed for an excellent view of the anchorage.[96] Whether it was actually used by the Customs is not known; although the evidence is uncertain it does not appear to be the building which, in 1766,[97]

> Miss Ellen Johnson has fitted up a house in a commodious manner, over the Old Custom House in Parkgate, very suitable for private lodgings.

The latter house was more probably on land nearby, to the north of Mostyn Square, leased in 1791 to George Cripps, 'on part whereof formerly stood the old Custom-House in Parkgate'.[98]

The last Custom House at Parkgate was at the southern end of the village, on the waterfront, part of the site now occupied by the Old Quay public house. We know the Crown leased this building in 1807 for two lives,[99] but this may well have been a renewal. As well as the Custom House, the Crown leased another building as a Watch

---

[94] E. E. Hoon, *The Organization of the English Customs System, 1696–1786* (1938, reprinted 1968), p. 170.

[95] Letter from Sir Henry Bunbury to Sir Steven Middleton, National Library of Wales, Plas Power c 77; for Middleton's death, *Cheshire Sheaf* new series 1, Sept. 1891, p. 141, item 237.

[96] Mostyn (Bangor) MS 5850, lease dated 1738. The house is not shown on the 1732 estate map, Mostyn (Bangor) MS 8699.

[97] *Chester Courant*, 11 March 1766.

[98] Cheshire R.O., DGA 1082, lease 108.

[99] P.R.O., CUST 79/1 (2 Oct. 1837).

House, at least from 1799 when their employee Benjamin Monk, tide surveyor, had the acumen to let to the Customs the house which he had himself leased in 1795 from Sir Roger Mostyn. It was to be seventy-five years before the Crown could rid itself of this lease, forty-six years after they had ceased to use the building.[100]

It ought to be easy to state the numbers of Customs staff at Parkgate, because the Establishment lists survive from 1688 onwards. But they do not tell the whole story, as evidenced by two lists from 1782. In one list, seven staff are shown for Parkgate: a Deputy Searcher, a waiter and searcher, a tide surveyor, two tidesmen and two boatmen.[101] A different list for the same year shows fifteen staff: all those already named, plus a Deputy Customer, a Deputy Comptroller, two weighing porters, and four more tidesmen.[102] The longer list explains the discrepancy, for the seven men on both lists were paid a salary 'per Establishment', that is, by the Crown. The other eight men derived their income 'per Incidentals'. Although they were appointed by warrant, their earnings came from the fees they collected.

Any Custom House had three senior officers, the Customer, the Controller and the Searcher, who kept separate accounts and an eye on each other. These offices were often sinecures whose holders paid deputies to do the work. Thus the Patent Customer at Chester employed a deputy at Chester and another at Parkgate, and as he paid these deputies, they might not appear on the Crown's pay lists.[103] Another possible source of confusion is that staff at Parkgate may sometimes have been on loan from Chester. For example, the establishment list for Neston in 1757 (with no mention of Parkgate at that date) shows only two men, together with a riding officer to patrol from Neston to Shotwick on the Chester establishment.[104] Yet at the same period the records of the Royal Yacht *Dorset* show that twelve Customs officers boarded the ship, four of whom are known

[100] P.R.O., CUST 79/2 (24 July 1843).
[101] P.R.O., CUST 18/400.
[102] P.R.O., CUST 39/16.
[103] See R. C. Jarvis, 'The Head Port of Chester and Liverpool, its creek and member', *T.H.S.L.C.*, 102 (1950), pp. 69–84; E. A. Carson, *The Ancient and Rightful Customs* (1972), p. 54.
[104] P.R.O., CUST 18/269.

to have been on the Chester establishment, to rummage the ship between Dawpool and Parkgate.[105]

With that proviso, that the establishment lists are probably and perhaps greatly understated, the lists for Neston up to 1780 show just two men. In 1782, as stated, the Parkgate list of Crown employees shows seven men and this number persists until 1798. In the following two years, four staff are listed, with a reduction to two in 1801.[106] Chester and Hoylake also suffered severe staff cuts in 1801. The Parkgate staff remained at two until 1812, after which it rose to four before falling to three in 1817.[107]

Not much money was collected at Parkgate. The Exchequer port books for Chester sometimes noted the amount of revenue collected at the two places, and Parkgate's share fell steadily from 6 per cent of Chester's revenue in 1726, to a mere 1.3 per cent in 1768.[108] Parkgate could not have paid the expenses of its upkeep in its later years.[109] Even Chester itself, according to the trade return of 1764, had receipts no more than 'sufficient to defray the expenses thereof', whereas Liverpool's receipts 'greatly exceeded the charges of management'. Beaumaris, which included Holyhead, had receipts 'insufficient to answer the charges of management'.[110] It is apparent that the Customs staff at Parkgate, as at Holyhead, were not there primarily to collect revenue.

The tasks of the Customs staff were: to examine cargo and thereby to discourage smuggling, an activity we shall look at more closely presently; to collect revenue and to keep accounts, which until 1787 was an extremely complicated business, apart from the fact that three sets of accounts had to be kept by the three senior officers. The surviving Parkgate Account books, showing inward traffic from Ireland and running from 1776 to 1802 have up to ten different columns for duties imposed at different times.[111] In 1787 the Consolidated Fund was formed which absorbed all these separate duties into one single heading, 'Customs'. A task which cannot be

[105] P.R.O., ADM 36/7116, March and April 1759, Sept. 1760.
[106] P.R.O., CUST (for 1785–1801) 18/417, 440, 480, 493, 510, 521.
[107] P.R.O., CUST (for 1812–17) 18/603, 605; 19/1, 15.
[108] P.R.O., E 190: for 1726, 1406/8; for 1739, 1413/5; for 1753, 1427/4; for 1759, 1433/5; for 1762, 1436/6; for 1768, 1439/8.
[109] R. C. Jarvis, in *Notes and Queries* 191 (1952), p. 40.
[110] B.L., Add. MS 9293.
[111] The duties are explained by Edward Carson in the introduction to his transcript, Cheshire R.O., 942.21.NES.

quantified and can barely be described, but which must have occupied a lot of time, was the issue and collection of *transire* certificates for goods transmitted to and from Chester by lighter. Finally, Customs officers acted as agents, usually for the central government, in a wide variety of ways.

Here are some examples of agency work, first as Receivers of Wreck in 1779,[112]

> Les Deux-Amis, French East-Indiaman, taken by the Knight privateer of Liverpool, was wrecked near Mostyn. A great part of her cargo is lodged in our Custom-house, Parkgate and Liverpool, and we are sorry to add, much damaged.

An example of a less official agency occurred in 1767 when Sir John Fielding, the Bow Street magistrate, asked the mayor of Chester, to find 'a clever custom House Officer' to help detect escaping thieves:[113]

> Yesterday Silvester Jordan and John King, two Extra-men in the port of Parkgate, received 20 guineas as a reward for apprehending the notorious Charles Pleasance.

A more humdrum duty was that advertised in 1795 and subsequent years: one might apply to William Monk, customs officer at Parkgate, for a hair-powder certificate costing one guinea; for two guineas one could obtain a certificate for any number of unmarried daughters.[114]

The names of many Customs officers at Parkgate are known, but their records rarely come to life unless there was trouble, usually in connection with smuggling. One spot of trouble which was purely personal ended before the magistrates in 1758. James Byrne and William Sanders, Customs officers, were playing cards in a Neston inn when their opponents in the game tried to leave. Byrne and Sanders urged them to stay and drink, and tried to stop them leaving with a sword and a pistol. Later the same evening, some Gayton men were returning home from Parkgate and were passing the Custom House when Byrne and Sanders attacked them: Robert Crabb declared that Byrne wrenched off his hat and wig, while Sanders pulled out a pistol and 'struck fire at him'.[115] A more honourable role was

[112] *Chester Chronicle*, 8 Jan. 1779.
[113] *Chester Courant*, 2 June 1767.
[114] *Chester Chronicle*, for example 29 May 1795.
[115] Cheshire R.O., QJF 186/1.

played in 1800 by Richard Hamond, Custom House officer (who does not appear on the establishment lists), when he sheltered Mrs Johnson, a letter carrier from Neston, when she was violently pursued by a resident who would pay only 3*d.* when 2*s.* 11*d.* postage was due, and who threatened to blow her brains out.[116]

The reason the Parkgate Account books have survived is the strange calligraphic decorations employed by Humphrey Read, the Deputy Controller who kept them. Not only were the entries elaborately decorated, but he used headings in Latin and Greek. In view of the small sums of money he collected, perhaps he had nothing better to do. He kept the accounts in his own hand from 1776 until the first quarter of 1794, with some further signs of his hand up to July. Read seems to have been only a part-time Customs officer, since he was also a surveyor who advertised that 'Noblemen's and Gentlemen's estates were carefully surveyed'.[117]

In 1779 Read sent this letter:[118]

> Dear Sir, This is to inform you that I am so imbecillited with the stone and gravel and by the weakness of my nerves together that it has rendered me incapable of performing a journey of any kind. As to the truth of the survey of the land that I made for you at the Leach near Saltney Marsh [I] am willing to testify on oath before a Justice of the Peace in this neighbourhood of the justness thereof according to the best of my ability.
>
> I am Sir with all due respects your most humble servant,
> Humphrey Read
>
> Parkgate, July 18th 1779.
>
> P.S. I have not been able to attend the Custom House these four days.

Humphrey Read was buried at Neston on 3 May 1797.[119]

The Customs service seems to have been a good employer. In 1812 John Humphreys, the waiter and searcher at Ness Colliery, died aged eighty-three:[120]

---

[116] *ibid*, QJF 228/2, 21 April 1800.
[117] *Chester Courant*, 7 Aug. 1750, quoted by *Cheshire Sheaf* (1914), p. 46.
[118] *Cheshire Sheaf* (1943), p. 39, item 8257.
[119] Neston parish register.
[120] *Chester Courant*, 11 Feb. 1812.

he had been upwards of 65 years a faithful and good officer: he never experienced an hour's illness, nor had he ever the tooth or headache, and at last dropped off 'like a pear that is mellow'.

John Edwards, tidewaiter, did not delay quite so long: when he was seventy-seven, with forty-five years' service, he applied for superannuation. His wages had averaged £54 between 1818 and 1821, and he was granted a pension of £30 a year.[121] The service was indulgent to less deserving officers; William Catterall missed eleven days' work in 1822 'when his absence was occasioned by intoxication . . . we direct you to enjoin him to sobriety and you are to keep a watchful eye on his conduct in future'. Four years later, boatman Catterall was absent from duty for fifteen days without leave and his pay was stopped for that period, but when his post at Parkgate became redundant, he was moved to another port.[122]

The Monk family seems to have done very well in the Customs service, initially at Parkgate. William Monk (1753–1831) was first recorded as a land-waiter at Parkgate in 1776 and he retired on pension in 1823 aged sixty-nine. He had married the daughter of a ship's captain and they had nine children.[123] William's brother Benjamin is known to have served as a tide surveyor at Parkgate between at least 1785 and 1804; he was Acting Controller at Chester in 1812 and died in 1832. It was Benjamin who leased the Watch House to H.M. Customs. Two of William's sons entered the service. One was Joseph, who became master of a lazarette or quarantine ship, the *Experiment*, at the quarantine station at Hoylake in 1817 and later at Bromboro Pool.[124] His elder brother Charles was acting as scribe for his father and uncle in the Controller's accounts books at an early age, for in November 1794 is the note in pencil, 'C. Monkes writing—age 13'. He was a tide surveyor at Hoylake in 1812, and probably before that, because he was living at Hoylake in 1808 when he was married in Neston church. By 1823 he was commander of the guardship *Redbreast* and superintendent of quarantine at Bromboro Pool. Charles seems to have owned considerable property: he was living in a handsome house in Neston in the 1820s, owned the even more handsome house next door in 1847, and

[121] P.R.O., CUST 79/8, 10 March 1821.
[122] P.R.O., CUST 79/9, 23 Feb. 1822; 79/13, 14 November, 2 December 1826.
[123] See the 'Monk window' at the west end of Neston parish church.
[124] P.R.O., CUST 19/15, 37, 56.

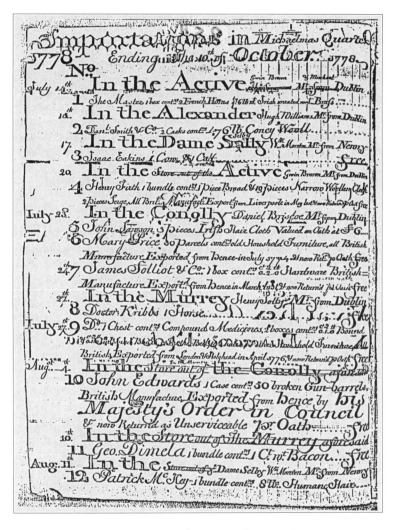

Figure 20. A page from Humphrey Read's
Parkgate account book (reduced).
Figures 20, 21 and 22 are reproduced by permission
of H.M. Commissioners of Customs and Excise.

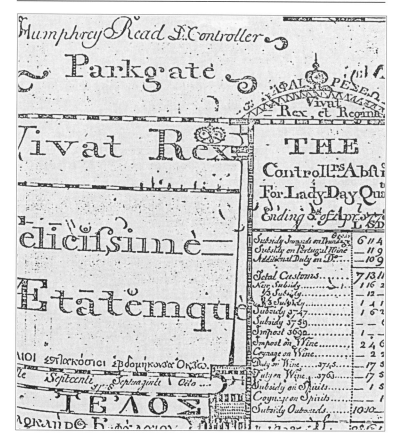

Figure 21. An example of Humphey Read's calligraphy.

Figure 22. Humphrey Read's transliteration of his name into Greek.

seems to have built a third house, definitely a gentleman's residence, in the same year.[125]


Large-scale smuggling in the North West during the eighteenth century was organised from the Isle of Man until 1765 when the island's fiscal rights were bought by the Crown,[126] and after that from the Irish village of Rush, fifteen miles from Dublin.[127] As William Gambold, captain of the Revenue cutter *Pelham*, explained in 1763, smugglers would take ship from Liverpool to the Isle of Man and there engage Irish wherries of thirty to forty tons to carry goods to the shore of North Wales, where local farmers would have carts and horses ready.[128] This kind of wholesale contraband required open sea, desolate beaches and sparsely inhabited country, and was not the sort of thing recorded in the Dee estuary, although a boat, 'soposed to have been built with intent to convey run goods from the Isle of Man' was found on the Welsh shore under Talacre in 1762.[129] The occasional Revenue cutter came to Parkgate, probably on peaceful business like the *Ross*, Captain Harman, which landed a postchaise from Dublin in 1793.[130] Captain Gambold was caught in a storm, which drowned two of his men, while trying to reach Liverpool, and found the *Pelham* cutter blown to the Old Quay near Parkgate.[131]

The sort of smuggling which troubled the Customs staff at Parkgate was very much smaller in scale, and represented opportunism by passengers or crews, usually (though not always) in an amateur way. One of the most remarkable confessions of smuggling, as well as the earliest reference to it for Parkgate, is in a letter from Sir Henry Bunbury, M.P. for Chester, to Sir Richard Middleton, M.P. for Denbigh, who died in 1716:[132]

---

[125] *Directories of Cheshire*, 1828, 1834, 1850; Tithe awards, Neston, 1847; his house The Cottage (now Beech House) bears the mark 'CM 1847'.
[126] Chester City R.O., TCP 8/72, 2 March 1752. See also, R. C. Jarvis, 'Illicit trade with the Isle of Man', *T.L.C.A.S.*, 58 (1946), p. 265.
[127] L. M. Cullen, *Anglo-Irish Trade*, p. 153.
[128] P.R.O., CUST 78/2, 14 May 1763.
[129] Clwyd R.O. (Hawarden), D/DM/734/2, 24 July 1762.
[130] Chester City R.O., CAS/17, April 1793.
[131] P.R.O., CUST 78/2, 15 Dec. 1764.
[132] National Library of Wales, Plas Power c.77.

Col. Manley says he has above two hogsheads of your wine
that I have paid for so I hope you will think of leaving orders
how it may be got by degrees when you are gone. We have had
the divil to pay here on Monday morning. They seized 26
dozen at Park Gate 5 of which are myne. Besides that the Lord
knows how many pieces of Indian silk and Indian calicoe that
the Irish ladies were running to make them fine at London this
winter so now theyl be confined to their lodgings,

    I cannot get Mr Vaughans wine yet out of the Custom house
if it were to save my life.

If this was the attitude of such pillars of the established order, it is
no surprise that smuggling, or at least the intention to smuggle, was
more or less endemic. One way in which we hear that smuggling has
been attempted is the sale of seized contraband. In 1767, thirty-four
gallons of brandy and five gallons of rum were for sale at Parkgate,
while in 1774 Irish muslins and poplins, rum, brandy, geneva, raw-
coffee and tea were sold.[133] In 1778 an even longer list was offered:
Irish printed muslins, cotton and linen, printed linen handkerchiefs,
Irish poplin, brandy, rum, geneva, rectified spirits of wine and Bohea
tea, which goods had been seized and condemned.[134] In 1789 an
auction in the Long Room, Parkgate (all Custom Houses had a Long
Room, whatever its shape, after the one in London) offered, as well
as the fabrics and alcohol already mentioned, Irish whiskey; whereas
in 1800 some more mundane goods were for sale: starch, hair pow-
der, vinegar, whisky and wine.[135]

    Because of the great difficulty in proving an offence of smuggling,
those involved in a dispute with Customs officers were more likely
to be charged with assault. Thus in 1757 Henry Davis of Neston,
Customs officer, met William Hughes on the seashore. What had
happened previously we are not told, but Hughes

put his hands into his [Davis'] pocketts and search'd em and
made an offer to strick him but did not.

Next day Hughes went to Davis' house and assaulted him, then 'got
the pocker and swore he would break it about his jaws'.[136] Hughes

[133] *Chester Courant*, 3 March 1767, 21 June 1774.
[134] *Chester Chronicle*, 7 Aug. 1778.
[135] *ibid*, 13 March 1789, 3 Jan. 1800.
[136] Cheshire R.O., QJF 185/4, 3 Nov. 1757.

was indicted for assault but he sailed as a mariner on board a ship bound for Barbados; the ship was captured by a French privateer and Hughes was taken to St Sebastian, whence (the Quarter Sessions was told) he was about to return.[137] Similarly in 1725 Edward Onslow, tide surveyor at Parkgate, was hit in the face with a large key and threatened with pistols after a dispute concerning the seizure of 'fifty pounds worth of silks'.[138]

A case of smuggling where the contraband disappeared and the offender were charged with assault occurred in 1733. Peter Paynter, Customs officer at Parkgate,[139]

> saw Timothy Deally mariner going thro Neston on horseback (about ten o'clock) with a large sack this informant took to be tea and coffee. He demanded of him to see what he had in the said sack or bag. Deally answered he should not and struck this informant with a stick . . .

After further struggles involving a pistol, help arrived, and Paynter obtained the bag, locking it in a room in a nearby house,

> but some women got in and threw the bag out of the window, by which means it was conveyed away . . .

Deally was described as 'a Yacht man'. If crew members of the Royal Yacht were caught smuggling, they were liable to be dismissed the service: for example, in March 1739 John Oglethorpe, James Rishton and John Higgins, all able seamen, were all dismissed for smuggling, the last-named specifically for bringing counterfeit money from Dublin.[140] This was the R.Y. *Dublin*. But the same vessel seven years later was described in these terms:[141]

> I am glad that the stuff for cousin Price was sent by one of the crew of the yacht, for I think there is not the least danger but she will get it safe, for these fellows have an excellent hand conveying a bundle ashore without the knowledge of the officers, who, unless properly fee'd, would convert it to their own use.

---

[137] *ibid.*, QJF 186/3/89.
[138] *ibid*, QJF 153/2/80.
[139] *ibid*, QJF 161/2/71.
[140] P.R.O., ADM 36/898, March 1739.
[141] H.M.C., *15th Report, Appendix VII* (1898), p. 334.

Sometimes goods were not even safe in the Custom House. Mary Fletcher of Parkgate was charged with stealing a box of gold and silver ingots from the Custom House in 1763.[142]

A more determined and less amateur degree of smuggling may be detected in a story of smuggled soap. It should first be explained that ships from Ireland had customarily used soap waste as ballast, and in 1729, finding that duty had been imposed on it, some merchants and shipmasters of Liverpool had petitioned the House of Commons (in vain) to be allowed to continue, free of duty.[143] At Parkgate in 1757, the Customs officers discovered forty-six dozen parcels of soap concealed in the ballast of a ship called the *Chester Packet*. The soap was loaded on to a cart and taken to the Custom House, but while it was being unloaded, six or seven men (only one of whom was identified: John Lucas, mariner of Parkgate who belonged to the ship) seized the cart and drove it away with one of the officers still in it. The cart was recaptured after about fifty yards.[144] The master of the *Chester Packet* was John McCullough who built the brig *Kildare*, 'well-known in the Dublin and Chester trade',[145] and sailed her from 1759 until his death; he lived in Parkgate and died there in August 1768.[146] Although this man has been mistakenly identified with another John McCullough who, in the 1780s, was involved with the Brittany contraband entrepot of Roscoff,[147] there is no evidence that Captain McCullough of the *Kildare* was more than a trader who, in the matter of soap, chanced his arm with the law.

Of course one hears only of those smuggling ventures which fail. In 1728 Thomas Brown, tidesman, laid aside two printed linen gowns which he had found in the ship *Recovery* at Parkgate. A local man called to a sailor on the ship, falsely using Brown's name (so the sailor maintained) to throw the dresses down to him.[148]

At Holyhead the Customs officers were similarly kept busy with attempts to circumvent the revenue, and in 1764 it was again soap:[149]

[142] *Chester Courant*, 5 April 1763.
[143] A. C. Wardle, 'Some glimpses of Liverpool during the first half of the 18th century', *T.H.S.L.C.*, 97 (1946), p. 147.
[144] Cheshire R.O., QJF 185/2/211.
[145] *Williamson's Liverpool Advertiser*, 30 Sept. 1774.
[146] Neston parish register, burial 8 Aug. 1768.
[147] G. I. Hawkes, 'Illicit trading in Wales in the 18th century', *Maritime Wales*, 10 (1986), p. 103. The references in this article should be treated with caution.
[148] Cheshire R.O., QJF 156/3/51.
[149] P.R.O., CUST 78/2, 31 May 1764.

The Justices never would give any penalty on the masters of the packets unless proof could be made of their being privy to the importation of the sope from Ireland, which the officers could not possibly prove.

In 1808 the Post Office authorities learned of

a disgraceful practice which is stated to have obtained on board the Packets from Holyhead to Dublin of smuggling articles of Dry Goods in bags attached to the mails.

The mate of the packet *Uxbridge* was charged after ten pieces of cambric and muslin were found in his Dublin bedroom.[150]

Jane Hester Reilly's account of her arrival at Parkgate in 1791 underlines the point that, for the law-abiding traveller, the Customs are always a part of the routine:[151]

we arrived about ten o'clock at Parkgate, but the tide not being quite in we could not get close to the shore, but went some part of the way in a small boat and were carried by the men the rest of the way. We found chaises on the beach to take us to the inn where we dressed as soon as we could get the luggage from the Custom House.

Miss Reilly sailed on the *Prince of Wales* packet, but passengers on the Royal Yacht were sometimes able to avoid a visit to the Custom House if the officers came to them. On several occasions the officers stayed on the ship for two or three days,[152] and this is known also to have happened at Holyhead.[153]

Some passengers resented the customs. When J. P. Curran reached Parkgate in 1773 he endured 'the usual pillage at the custom-house'.[154] After the Act of Union in 1800, Sir John Carr could see no reason for it:[155]

---

[150] POST 41/1, p. 244 (31 Oct. 1808).
[151] Jane Hester Reilly, 'A young lady's journey from Dublin to London in 1791', *The Nineteenth Century*, 43 (May 1898), pp. 796–7.
[152] P.R.O., ADM 36/7116, 2–5 March, 13–14 March, 15–17 April 1759.
[153] P.R.O., ADM 36/898, 13 Oct. 1737.
[154] W. H. Curran, *The Life of John Philpott Curran* (1819), I, p. 32.
[155] Sir John Carr, *The Stranger in Ireland*, p. 23.

> Here [Holyhead] the traveller is assailed by these detestable, corrupt harpies, called custom-house officers, merely because the sea divides one part of the united kingdom from another.

This harsh view may have been justified at Holyhead, where a parliamentary committee described the Customs arrangements for examining baggage as 'very vexatious' in 1819.[156] Sometimes, though, the officers were provoked, as at Holyhead in 1738:[157]

> Lord B[uttevant] quarrelled with the collector about searching the baggage, which had hindered us from going away the next day, if I had not gone and made it up. Lord B. in the wrong for the officer came in a civil manner to do his duty, but I was not then by. He would have stopped it from going on board and I had much ado to satisfy him, because he had been called a rascal, but at last he gave me a permit without any examination.

It will be remembered that John Wesley was refused permission to land his chaise at Dublin in 1773, 'because, they said, the Captain of a packet-boat had no right to bring over goods'. As Wesley added, 'Poor pretence!'.[158] The Irish Customs sometimes tried to separate passengers from freight, presumably for their own convenience, and seem to have invented their own rules to that end. The Select Committee of 1819 reported that the Irish Customs were then forbidding the packets to carry stage-coach parcels, thus handing the monopoly of such goods to the *Henrietta*, a trading vessel sailing once a fortnight. It had been earlier recommended, in 1815, that the packets should be allowed to carry parcels, but without lasting effect.[159] Similarly, the Irish Customs tried, from at least 1802 to 1816, to use their own mail boats in competition with the English ones organised from Holyhead, despite having accepted £9,000 a year not to do so, even to the extent, in 1813, of refusing to hand the mail at Dublin to the regular packet captain.[160]

[156] 5th Report from the Select Committee on the Road from London to Holyhead etc.: Holyhead Mails and Packets (1819).
[157] *Analecta Hibernica,*. 15, (1944), p. 118.
[158] John Wesley, *Journal*, 29 or 30 April 1773.
[159] 5th Report (see note 156) above.
[160] POST, 12/10.

Although regular traders and packets ceased to sail between Parkgate and Dublin in 1815, there must have been enough occasional traffic to justify, after the visit of a committee in 1819, a staff of one tide surveyor and two boatmen, obtainable by shedding four other staff by natural wastage. By 1821 the Custom House was no longer in use and permission was gained from London to let it, so business must have been transacted at the Watch House, a very simple building of two small rooms connected by an outside stair. The Crown hoped to rid itself of the lease of the Custom House but their landlady, Mary Corkran, declined to receive it:[161]

> I am getting very far advanced in years and would much rather receive the rent which is mainly the chief of my support.

So the Crown had to pay £25 a year until she died in 1831.[162] It was decided in 1826 that the Parkgate boat, initiated in 1688, was to be discontinued; the boat and its men were sent to Liverpool, and the rummaging and supervision of ships going to Chester was to be organised at Hoylake.[163] That left one man, William Harrop, probably doing nothing for eighteen months before he was sent away to 'Blythnook', and in August 1828 the Customs presence at Parkgate, which had lent so much to the village's status for 140 years, was at an end.[164] Ness Colliery was supervised from Chester. However, Harrop did not actually leave for nearly a year, and the Crown was still stuck with the Watch House, a decrepit building, difficult to lease and often needing repair. Benjamin Monk, who died in 1832, had leased the Watch House to the Crown in 1799 for three lives. The third life, his nephew Charles, clung to the lease until he died aged ninety-three in 1874.[165]

In 1848 the 'legal quay' within the port of Chester was redefined as 880 yards of the Chester waterfront, and this was the formal end of Parkgate's right to trade.[166]

A curious legacy of Parkgate's Customs officers was inherited when the Royal Navy took over responsibility for the Coastguard service (founded in 1822) from the Customs in 1856. Some bureaucrat seems

---

[161] P.R.O., CUST 79/17, 22 Oct. 1830.
[162] P.R.O., CUST 79/2, 3 Aug. 1843.
[163] P.R.O., CUST 79/15, 10 Aug. 1828.
[164] P.R.O., CUST 79/18, 8 Feb. 1831.
[165] P.R.O., CUST 79/4, 18 April 1874.
[166] *Chester Chronicle*, 7 Jan. 1848.

to have decided that Parkgate was a port, without knowing that he was well over thirty years out of date. So, Parkgate was made a detachment of the Hoylake coastguard station, a row of coastguard cottages was built with a boathouse, and four men were installed in 1858.[167] Eventually the Admiralty realised that the station had nothing whatever to do, and it was closed about 1875.[168]

Finally, the days of the Customs and the concomitant smugglers are still perversely remembered in tales of 'smugglers' tunnels'. There are no tunnels, but a common feature of local houses built in the eighteenth or early nineteenth centuries is a cellar with a vaulted brick ceiling. The vaulting was designed to create a cool temperature and at least two of these 'cellars' are above ground. If the far end of the cellar is obscured by goods, it looks like a tunnel. There is an inextinguishable rumour that a tunnel ran from a house near the church to the Old Quay, a distance of over one thousand yards, downhill, starting in solid rock and ending in swampy ground. This advertisement of 1770 indicates the probable origin of the story:[169]

To be let, a dwelling house opposite the church in Great Neston, walled garden, cellared and vaulted under.

[167] P.R.O., ADM 175/9.
[168] Reminiscences of A. G. Grenfell in *The Griffin* (Sept. 1899), pp. 199–200; typewritten notes by A. G. Grenfell in the possession of A. D. J. Grenfell; *Directory of Cheshire* (1874).
[169] *Chester Courant*, 16 July 1770.

Figure 23. The former Customs House at Parkgate, in use at least from 1807 until 1821, is the house on the right. It was demolished in 1963.

Figure 24. The Watch House, Parkgate, as it was in 1979.

# 9 *The Village of Parkgate*

The road from London to Chester was well established as a route for passengers by the mid-seventeenth century, and well before Parkgate was itself established as a point of embarkation. There was a regular coach service from London in the 1650s. When John Cresset complained that the roads were being spoiled, and robbers encouraged, by such vehicles, he said that stage coaches had been set up from London to Norwich 'thirty years ago' (before 1672), to Exeter twenty to thirty years before, to Chester twenty years before (i.e. about 1652) and to York eighteen years before. Cresset's proposed remedy was to suppress 'all hackney stage coaches and caravans'.[1] An advertisement in the *Mercurius Politicus* of 1657 stated that a stage-coach service left London for Chester on three days a week, a four-day journey for 35s. In 1659 the journey took five days.[2] The route to Chester was, therefore, one of the earliest long-distance routes to be well organised in post stages, and we have already noted that John Ogilby called it, in 1675, 'one of the most frequented roads in the kingdom'.[3]

At no time did a stage-coach run directly between London and Parkgate, although coaching advertisements might sometimes make it appear so. The fares for journeys setting out from the *Golden Lion* inn, Charing Cross, London, in carriages 'well guarded and lighted' in 1786 were stated to be,[4]

> To Holyhead, £3 7s. 6d.; Liverpool, £1 16s.; Parkgate, £1 16s.; Chester £1 16s.; every even at 6 o'clock except Saturday. Outside ½ price.

However, these are fares and not through coaches. Whereas in 1791 the Royal Mail was running from Chester to London every evening in twenty-six hours, and the Royal Chester was running on the same

---

[1] *Cal. S.P. Dom., 1672–73* (1901), pp. 64, 346–8 (19 Oct. 1672).
[2] J. Parkes, *Travel in England in the 17th century* (1925), pp. 83–4.
[3] John Ogilby, *Britannia* (1675), p. 41.
[4] *The Times*, 12 Dec. 1786 (then *The Daily Universal Register*).

route three days a week,[5] the coach leaving Chester for Parkgate in that same year was the Mercury, six days a week in summer, three in winter.[6] So the traveller would have to change coaches in Chester.

The first regular coach service to Parkgate of which any record has been found was in 1761, when,[7]

> We hear from Parkgate that the Chester or new Flying Machine, and their own numerous post-chaises, have set that place all on wheels.

The Flying Machine mentioned was 'a new machine, on steel springs', from the *Golden Talbot* in Chester at 8 a.m. on Tuesday, Thursday, Saturday, returning 5 p.m. from the *George & Three Pigeons* in Parkgate, 2s. 6d. inside, 1s. 3d. outside.[8] A year later 'a new machine with six able horses' was travelling to Parkgate every Monday, Thursday and Friday.[9]

In 1789 John Paul, formerly of the *Pied Bull* in Chester, took over the *White Lion* and revitalised the coach services, so that the editor of the *Chronicle* could say,[10]

> The rapid advancement, made within the last few years, in stage-coach travelling, both in point of pleasure and expedition, is really astonishing.

Stage-coach travelling was more often described as dangerous; in 1805 two Parkgate postilions, John Parry and Robert Morris, were convicted for dangerously driving a coach and four at a gallop through Northgate Street in Chester.[11]

Because coaches to Parkgate were advertised 'to meet the Packets', in times of adverse weather the coaches could not be relied upon to run, so that in 1795, it was stated that 'The Parkgate Coach goes at uncertain times'.[12] As the packet service declined, especially after 1801, the coach service to Parkgate was often included in the service

[5] *Directory of Chester* (1791).
[6] *ibid*; see also advertisements in the *Chester Chronicle*, 1792–4.
[7] *Chester Courant*, 30 June 1761.
[8] *ibid*, 23 June 1761.
[9] *ibid*, 4 June 1762.
[10] *Chester Chronicle*, 17 April 1789.
[11] *ibid*, 1 March 1805.
[12] *Chester Guide* (1795).

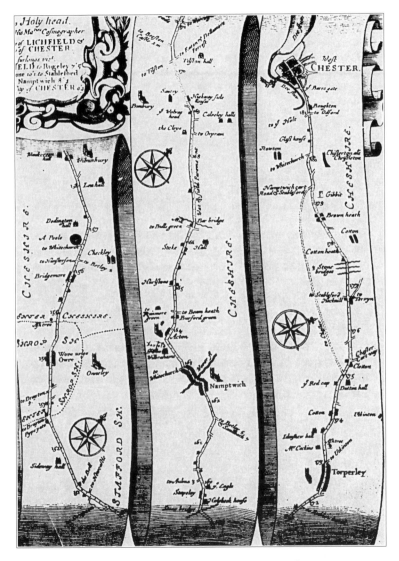

Figure 25. From Ogilby's *Britannia* (1675), plate 23.

to the Mersey ferries. In 1811 the Prince of Wales post coach ran from the *White Lion* in Chester to Neston, Parkgate, Tranmere Ferry, 'to Mr Ball's, Nova Scotia'.[13] During the bathing season, however, coaches were organised direct to Parkgate. In 1816,[14]

> New Coach from Chester to Parkgate, great convenience for Sea Bathing! The Princess Charlotte, White Lion to the George Inn.

Between 1820 and 1828 the Royal George coach was running regularly to Parkgate. After that date, coach services to Chester no longer appear in the newspapers although there were connections to the Mersey ferries.

Before the establishment of regular coaches, as well as afterwards, travellers used to hire horses or post-chaises. One local horse-hirer was John Jones who advertised in 1750 that he had [15]

> hired a black mare to Thomas Holland, wearing a brown sailor's jacket, a striped waistcoat, a worsted cap; he said he was going to Chester, but 'tis suspected he is gone the Bristol road.

John Jones was later described as a 'post chaise man'.[16] Many chaise-hirers are recorded in the parish registers, and one hears of chaises in advertisements for articles lost:[17]

> Dropt or taken from behind a post-chaise about ½ mile this side Neston a brown portmanteau trunk containing shoes etc. 5 guineas reward and no questions asked to Captain Seton at Parkgate.

John Seton was master of the *Royal Charlotte*.

Some travellers who could not afford either post-chaise or stage-coach, arrived by waggon, as Letitia Pilkington and her son did in about 1748; 'A most tiresome way of travelling!'.[18] The hazard of armed robbery on the highway was occasionally reported on the approaches to Parkgate. A post boy was robbed of the mail by two footpads a mile from Neston in 1794, and Andrew Ram was robbed

---

[13] *Chester Chronicle*, 27 July 1811.
[14] *ibid*, 1816.
[15] *Chester Courant*, 6 Feb. 1750.
[16] Neston Parish register, 14 March 1764.
[17] *Chester Courant*, 5 June 1770.
[18] Letitia Pilkington, *Memoirs*, 3, p. 185.

at pistol point while journeying from Parkgate to Chester in 1760. The footpad, James Armstrong, was sentenced to death for this latter robbery.[19]

We have noted in Chapter Five that the roads through North Wales were very poor, and the road approaches to Liverpool were not much better, until at least the late eighteenth century. Arthur Young travelled through the northern counties between June and December 1768.[20] He catalogued 122 roads during this journey with comments on each one: some were very good, but he found his journey through Lancashire and Cheshire a great trial. Although Young did not venture into Wirral, he described the Liverpool to Altrincham turnpike as [21]

> If possible this execrable road is worse than that from Preston. It is a heavy sand, which cuts into such prodigious ruts, that a carriage moves with great danger.

He went on to advise travellers to avoid any journey north of Newcastle under Lyme:[22]

> Until better management is produced, I would advise all travellers to consider this country as sea, and as soon thinking of driving into the ocean as venture into such detestable roads.

With travellers' tales like these, it is no wonder that passengers from the south of England should steer clear of Liverpool and keep to the established route to Chester. One advantage of Parkgate, therefore, was that it lay a short journey by road from Chester. Only one traveller is known to have mentioned the state of the road to Parkgate: in 1791 Jane Hester Reilly said that [23]

> The road is narrow and bad; towards Chester it grew broader but was very bad still.

A detailed road map of the route from London to Parkgate was surveyed by Peter Bell in 1779. It describes nineteen stages, the last

---

[19] *Cheshire Sheaf*, June 1915, p. 34; *Chester Courant*, 10 June, 9 Sept. 1760.
[20] Arthur Young, *A Six Months Tour through the North of England* (1770–1), 2nd edn, 4, pp. 423–5 (Letter XLI).
[21] *ibid*, p. 432.
[22] *ibid*, p. 435.
[23] Jane Reilly, 'A young lady's journey from Dublin to London in 1791', *The Nineteenth Century*, 43 (May 1898), p. 797.

of which was from Chester to Parkgate.[24] The traveller took the Chester High Road (as opposed to the Low Road which ran from Neston to Burton and Shotwick) and which can be shown to have been an ancient highway.[25] At 'Enderton' (Hinderton) he turned to pass through Neston, but the Parkgate road ran no further than the boundary of the old Neston Park; the route followed Moorside Lane down to the shore. The final half-mile followed the shore to Parkgate, where there was no roadway and no sea wall, as may be seen from the Mostyn estate map of 1732.[26] This unsatisfactory final stage was corrected by the Wirral Turnpike Act of 1787,[27] which governed the route from Chester to Parkgate, of which the only new part was the short stretch, following a footpath, across the fields from Neston to Parkgate.

The first map to show Parkgate was, as we saw in Chapter One, Greenvile Collins' chart published in 1693. The makers of land maps were rather slower to show the blossoming settlement, the first map of Cheshire to show Parkgate was that by Thomas Badeslade in 1741.[28] The earlier cartographers of Cheshire, including Badeslade, showed no roads in Wirral at all: the first to do so was Kitching in 1764. But his roads were not surveyed and are mere indications of routes with no pretence of accuracy. For that we have to await Burdett's survey of 1777.[29] Before Bell's specialised road map of 1779, Daniel Paterson published the first edition of *Paterson's Roads*, in 1771.[30] This work which went through fifteen editions up to 1811, described the routes to Parkgate, adding, 'the Traveller who takes shipping at Parkgate saves the land travelling through Wales'.[31] The work was given a new lease of life in 1822 when Edward Mogg

[24] Peter Bell, *The Actual Survey of the Great Post Road from London to Parkgate* (1779), p. 19.

[25] Geoffrey Place, 'The Chester High Road (A540)', *Bulletin of the Burton & District Local History Society* (1977), 1, pp. 11–18.

[26] Mostyn MSS (Bangor) 8699.

[27] 27 Geo III c. 93. See also Geoff Dodd, 'The turnpikes of Wirral', *Journal of the North Western Society of Industrial & Archaeological History*, 2 (1977), pp. 21–27.

[28] Harold Whitaker, *A Descriptive List of the Printed Maps of Cheshire 1577–1900* (Chetham Society, 1942), pp. 58–9.

[29] P. P. Burdett, *A Survey of the County Palatine of Chester* (1777).

[30] Daniel Paterson, *A new and accurate description of all the direct and principal cross roads in Great Britain* (1771); H. G. Fordham, *Paterson's roads: Daniel Paterson, his maps and itineraries 1738–1825* (1925).

[31] *Paterson's Roads*, 13th edn (1803).

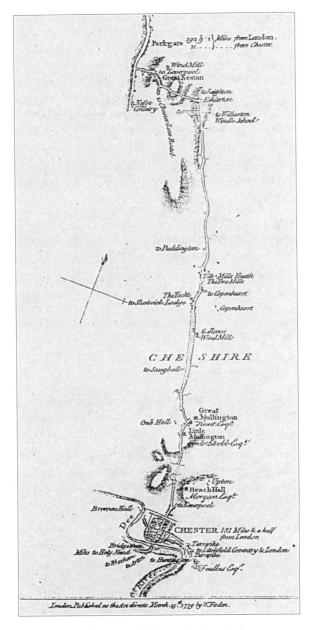

Figure 26. Chester to Parkgate: the last nineteen stages,
drawn by Peter Bell, 1779.

reissued it, the last edition being published in 1832. Unfortunately Mogg did not revise the descriptions, and Parkgate was given the details appropriate to 1803.

Some travellers between Parkgate and Chester chose to avoid the High Road, perhaps when its condition was poor in bad weather, by riding on the sands of the estuary. Using the sand roads could be dangerous: in 1687 Robert Selby was drowned when trying to get to Neston along the shore,[32] and in the same year the bishop of Chester, Thomas Cartwright, sent his coach[33]

> after dinner to Nesson, to fetch Sir Charles Porter and his lady to Chester, which found his children set in a stage coach, broke in the quicksands, three miles from Chester.

Porter was lord chancellor of Ireland and had landed on the R.Y. *Portsmouth.* For Henry Prescott, the deputy registrar of the diocese, the sand route was agreeable after a 'plentifull dinner'.[34]

> Wee sitt past 4, mount, call at Park Yate, where after 2 bottles good claret, remount, ride by the seaside to Burton, return in a cool sweet evening.

A less fortunate traveller was Arthur Carr who[35]

> mistakenly forded the Dee near Shotwick while riding to Park-gate to embark for Ireland and was drowned trying to return.

The sand roads ran across the estuary as well as along its shore. One reason was the lack of adequate roads along the Flintshire shore. Turnpike Acts were obtained for that area in 1768 and 1770,[36]

> before which our roads were scarcely passable. If either Sir Roger Mostyn's family or our own wanted to get to Chester, we were to reach the sea-side; then to Flint as we could, and from thence at low water cross the ford of the Dee, a way not always unattended by danger.

[32] Chester City R.O., c/1/13, 13 Sept. 1687.
[33] Joseph Hunter, ed., *Diary of Thomas Cartwright* (Camden Society 22, 1843), p. 37.
[34] John Addy, ed., *The Diary of Henry Prescott* (Record Society of Lancashire and Cheshire, 1987), p. 180 (17 July 1708).
[35] Chester City R.O., c/1/13 (23 April 1698).
[36] Thomas Pennant, *History of the Parishes of Whiteford and Holywell* (1796), p. 53.

Celia Fiennes crossed from Flint to Burton in 1698 and well described the source of the danger:[37]

> the sands here are so loose that the tyde does move them from one place to another at every flood, that the same place one used to foard a month or two before is not to be pass'd now for as it brings the sands in heaps to one place so it leaves others in deep holes, which are cover'd with water, and loose sand that would swallow up a horse or carriage, so I had two guides to conduct me over.

After 1728, when Neston market was established, people often crossed the estuary on foot to Parkgate. In 1791 a farmer called Williams was drowned crossing the sands to Neston market,[38] while in 1819 a vegetable seller returning to Flint from Parkgate mistook the signal lights and was rescued just as the tide was about to overwhelm him and his horse.[39] A fictional account of a man crossing from Parkgate described [40]

> the cheerful chatter, laughter and fragments of Welsh airs sung in chorus by a hearty crowd of cockle and mussel gatherers, fishermen, and farmers' wives on their way to market on the Cheshire side—men, women (they were in the majority) and children on foot, on ponies and donkeys, and in little carts.

These travellers could have sailed across the estuary on the ferry which plied between Flint, Bagillt and Parkgate from at least the 1780s until 1860. In 1786 a correspondent, noting the proposal for a Wirral turnpike, recommended that there should be a good horse-ferry between Parkgate and Flint, because at that time travellers had to leave their horses behind.[41] Three years later, a pair of innkeepers in Flint and Bagillt advertised,[42]

> they have fitted up a large commodious two mast and row boat for the conveyance of passengers, horses and cattle etc., well manned with sober and experienced boatmen.

---

[37] C. Morris, ed., *The Journeys of Celia Fiennes* (1949), pp. 182–3.
[38] *Chester Chronicle*, 5 Aug. 1791.
[39] *ibid*, 17 Sept. 1819.
[40] Samuel Sidney, *Gallops and Gossips in the Bush of Australia* (1854), p. 182.
[41] *Chester Chronicle*, 14 April 1786.
[42] *Gore's Liverpool General Advertizer*, 5 Nov. 1789.

The supply of sober boatmen may not have been maintained, for in 1799,[43]

> The Friends passage boat was, in consequence of carrying too much sail in a gale of wind, overset on her passage from Flint to Parkgate. Two women were drowned. Another passage boat was sailing in company with the Friends. The Flint and Parkgate boats have been used to carry too much sail in trying to outsail each other, to the great danger and terror of the passengers.

Nevertheless the ferry continued to sail once a day, every day, as a surviving scrap of timetable from 1847, illustrated on page 253 (figure 28), makes clear. When Richard Ayton made the crossing in 1814,[44]

> we took our passage, together with a crowd of other passengers, being packed and crammed into our places with as little regard for our ease in such a state of stowage as though we had been dead cargo.

Yet he preferred the ferry to trying to ford on foot, because

> it is only the hardy and heroic few, who can walk in mid-day without breeches, that would attempt such an expedition.


The Mostyns of North Wales have proved to be a remarkably tenacious landowning family. By acquisitive dynastic marriages and a policy of attending to their own affairs, they became masters of large estates in North Wales without suffering the fate of overweening ambition. When Thomas ap Richard ap Hywel, who died in 1558, adopted the surname Mostyn from his largest estate, centred on the Flintshire village of Mostyn, he was drawing together strands of family connection and land acquisition dating back to 1200.[45] Lord Mostyn still lives in Mostyn Hall today.

The civil war between king and parliament found Colonel Sir Roger Mostyn on the royalist side as governor of Flint Castle until

---

[43] *Chester Chronicle*, 27 Dec. 1799.
[44] Richard Ayton, *A Voyage round Great Britain*, 1 (1814), p. 76.
[45] A. D. Carr, 'The making of the Mostyns, the genesis of a landed family', *Transactions of the Honourable Society of Cymmrodorion* (1979), pp. 137–57.

he had to surrender it in 1643. Although he was made a baronet in 1660, he reckoned he had spent a fortune, allegedly £60,000, in the king's service.[46] The family fortunes were, therefore, in serious need of repair. This was done by careful exploitation of mineral resources, mainly coal and lead—'Mr Roger Mostyn' wrote a paper for the Royal Society of London describing an explosion caused by fire damp at the Mostyn mine in 1675.[47] The traditional family method of astute marriages also continued.

The first Thomas Mostyn (ap Richard ap Hywel) had a brother Piers who founded a family at Talacre, near Mostyn, and this branch now represents the direct male line of the Mostyns. In 1655 Anne Mostyn of Talacre married d'Arcy Savage of Leighton (Wirral), and their daughter, Bridget, became heiress of estates in Cheshire: Leighton, Neston, Thornton Hough, Beeston and Peckforton. The Mostyns of Mostyn gained these estates when Thomas, who became the second baronet, married Bridget Savage in 1672.[48] The Mostyns remained landlords of these estates, which included the whole village of Parkgate, for 177 years, until they were sold in 1849.

The Mostyns, being a Welsh family based on their Welsh lands, never lived in Cheshire; but they seem to have taken a personal interest in the development of Parkgate, which undoubtedly benefited from an active management policy. The sixth baronet, at least, was known as a considerate landlord: in 1821 Sir Thomas reduced the rents of his tenants by 25 per cent, instructing his agent [49]

> to remember his poor tennants—he considered himself and them all of one family, and if they suffered, he suffered also.

The probable reason for the rebate of rents was the very severe winter the year before, 1819–20, followed by a wet, cold spring and summer in 1821.[50] There were two particular ways in which Parkgate benefited from having a strong landlord who could stand up to the

---

[46] Lord Mostyn and T. A. Glenn, *History of the Family of Mostyn of Mostyn* (1925), p. 145.

[47] *The Philosophical Transactions and Collections* [of the Royal Society of London], 2 (abridged by) John Lowther (first pub. 1705, 4th edn 1731), Chapter 3 (Mineralogy), para. 7, no. 4, pp. 378–81.

[48] Mostyn and Glen (see note 46 above), p. 156.

[49] *Chester Chronicle*, 18 May 1821.

[50] J. M. Stratton, *Agricultural Records*, pp. 99–100.

city of Chester. The first centred on anchorage dues and the second concerned the right to a market.

Chester claimed certain rights over the Dee estuary, notably dues for anchorage, so that when one of its own aldermen petitioned to use some of the city's stones from the Old (Neston) Quay to develop the nearby colliery, permission was granted 'without prejudice to the Corporation's right to the ancient Port Dues or Anchorage'.[51] A manorial lord might claim rights on his own shores, as Richard Savage did at Neston in 1661. He deputed John Bridges of Great Neston to collect anchorage dues from vessels at all roads and havens within the lordship of Neston.[52] Similarly in 1711 John Matthews of Parkgate leased from Sir Roger Mostyn the duties and fees for anchorage within the manors of Great Neston and Leighton.[53] At these times the amount of business at Parkgate was probably not large enough to disturb Chester's sensibilities; but when Sir Roger Mostyn applied to the Crown for a charter to provide Neston with a market and fairs (of which more later) Chester responded with an Assembly Order:[54]

> The water bailys of this city do immediately demand anchorage, due to this city, at Parkgate, and insist upon the same as this city's right.

The city's right, if any, was obscure, and it is noteworthy that the River Dee Act of 1732, in many details careful to protect established interests, made no mention of such rights.[55] But opinion in Chester was sensitive at the time the Bill was being discussed. One citizen wrote,[56]

> Parkgate has already encroached too much on this antient City; Trade and Manufactures are set up there to your Prejudice, and more intended . . .

---

[51] Chester City R.O., AB/4/209, 17 Jan. 1763.
[52] Mostyn (Bangor) MS 5346. (D'Arcy Savage was Lord of the Manor of Neston.)
[53] Mostyn (Hawarden) MS 2935.
[54] Chester City R.O., AB/4/31, 14 Oct. 1730.
[55] 6 Geo II c.30.
[56] Printed letter, *Some few observations on a late libel, entitled a reply to the Cheesemongers* (July 1732) in the Grosvenor Papers: Richard Grosvenor, 4th baronet (miscellaneous papers: trade).

Or, as another writer put it, 'When Chester is runing to Parkgate, it's time to look about you'.[57] In Sir Roger Mostyn, who opposed the Bill as M.P. for Flint, Parkgate had a landlord who was well able to stand up to this sort of pressure.

In the matter of a market, Sir Roger Mostyn succeeded in 1728 when two previous landlords had failed. The first was the earl of Derby who, probably just before he sold the manor of Neston in 1599, laid plans not merely for a market and fairs, but for 'libertie for the lading or landing of all kinds of merchandise' (that is, for a 'legal quay'), and for the farm of the Customs.[58] Nothing came of this plan, but in 1677 Sir Thomas Mostyn, the 2nd baronet, seems to have petitioned for a market, if one may judge from Chester's alarmed response:[59]

> Great endeavours have beene and are used for the procureing a patent from his Majesty for the setting upp a market and Faires att Nesson neare unto this Citty, which if once effected would tende to the subversion of the trade of this Citty and consequently to the great impoverishment thereof.

Chester sent its own petition to the king with successful results:[60]

> No grant pass of any fair or market at Neston is to be made without notice [to the city of Chester].

There was no further move for fifty years, when in 1728 Sir Roger Mostyn petitioned:[61]

> That Great Neston is not only the largest and best town in this Hundred, but very much the most conveniently situated for a market being placed very near the middle of the Hundred, and in the midway between Chester and Hoylake, and is itself the port for all or most of the ships of any bulk that have any trade with the City or County of Chester.

---

[57] Another printed letter, *To the citizens of Chester* (Feb. 1732), in Grosvenor Papers, Sir Robert Grosvenor, 6th baronet.
[58] Mostyn (Bangor) MS 5203.
[59] Chester City R.O., AB/2/186 (7 Sept. 1677).
[60] *Cal. S.P. Dom., 1677–78* (1911), p. 368 (21 Sept. 1677).
[61] P.R.O., SP 36/151 f.25.

If Chester opposed this petition at the enquiry following a writ of
*ad quod damnum*, its opposition is not recorded in the city's records.
The enquiry decided that,[62]

> it would not be to the damage or prejudice of ourselves or of
> others nor would be harmful to neighbouring markets . . .

In this way did Neston gain the right to a weekly market on Fridays,
and a fair three times a year, in February, after Whitsun and in
September, emphasising its importance and increasing its value to the
Mostyns, who owned all Parkgate and the greater part of Neston.

The Sir Roger who was granted the market charter was the third
baronet, and died in 1734. His grandson, Sir Roger the fifth baronet,
showed an interest in the shipping activities at Parkgate and owned
shares in the *Princess Royal* packet.[63] In 1779 he was party to a
proposal to apply to parliament for an Act for making a dock at
Parkgate. This plan was an echo of a provision in the River Dee Act
of 1732, whereby the undertakers would have to build a wet dock
capable of holding twenty ships, if it did not prove possible for
cheese ships drawing fourteen feet of water to pass down the river
from Chester.[64] Although this clause was not activated, the cheese
ships tended to call at Parkgate anyway, as we have seen. The 1779
plan may have been intended to encourage the cheese ships to
continue calling at Parkgate, or to encourage the ship-repairing
business which had long been a speciality of the port. The plan
provided for a wet dock measuring sixty by eighty yards, next to a
dry dock of sixty yards square.[65] The cost was estimated at £6,000,
of which Sir Roger put up £1,000. But the fourteen other promoters
put up only £1,200 between them and nothing further was heard of
Parkgate dock.[66]

The fourth baronet, Sir Thomas, was landlord when Neston common was enclosed. Sir Thomas' principal interests were hunting and
racing, yet the following letter of 1747 from his Neston agent

[62] Mostyn (Bangor) MS 5205, translated by P. H. W. Booth in *Cheshire
History*, 5 (Spring 1980), pp. 18–21.
[63] R. Craig, 'Shipping and shipbuilding in the Port of Chester', *T.H.S.L.C.*,
116 (1964), p. 54.
[64] 6 Geo II c.30, para. VI.
[65] Mostyn (Bangor) MSS 7172, 7264.
[66] *Chester Chronicle*, 13 Nov. 1778, 8 Jan. 1779.

suggests that he took a personal interest in his estates, without seeking to override local opinion:[67]

> I spoke to some of the heads of the town a bout the Common and they all a gree to go about to Messaure it and to gett Commisingers for a Lotting it out so they desire you would Rite to Mr Glegg about it.

John Glegg of Gayton was the neighbouring landowner. Neston common was surveyed for enclosure in 1751, there being 118 landholders who would get shares, and the enclosure map is dated 1765.[68]

While considering the positive lead in development at Parkgate provided by the landowners, it is worth remembering the point made in Chapter Two, that certain other possible sites for a Dee anchorage did not develop. Dawpool, several miles further from Chester, lay at the end of a long, straggly lane; the anchorage was backed by high cliffs of clay, so that access from the land was far from easy. Moorside, at the end of the lane from Neston and half a mile from Parkgate, might have been suitable had not the ground by the river been very wet, as evidenced by the field names, Moor on one side and Marsh Field on the other.[69] The prime candidate, if any site was to develop before Parkgate was firmly established, must have been Neston Quay, where only one house was ever built. Leaving aside questions of navigation, which have already been considered, there seems also to have been a different attitude on the part of the landowners. The site at Neston Quay was split, with Chester owning the quay and the Cottingham family owning the land on which the house stood. Development was actually prevented by Charles Cottingham's lease to Peter Ryder in 1700; it contained a covenant not to erect any building within a hundred yards.[70] Compare this with several leases of about the same date at Parkgate, where the consideration for each lease specified the building of a house instead of an entry fine.[71]

The business acumen shown by the Mostyns in encouraging Parkgate to develop in the eighteenth century, followed by some personal

---

[67] Mostyn (Bangor) MS 7320.
[68] Cheshire R.O., DHL 31/1, 2.
[69] Tithe map for Great Neston, 1847.
[70] Cheshire R.O., DHL 3/9, 11.
[71] Mostyn (Bangor) MSS 4387, 4389, 4398.

involvement in its welfare as a bathing resort in the nineteenth century, was to be matched by their readiness to move their investment elsewhere, as we shall see in the next chapter.

In the summer of 1753 a new and celebrated book was on sale in Chester, for 2s. 6d. if bound in calf or '2/– sewn'.[72] It was Dr Russell's book *On the Use of Sea-Water*,[73] and it was to stimulate the 'rush into the sea',[74] which transformed the fortunes of many seaside places all round the coasts of Britain. Parkgate, with its existing clientele of passengers waiting to take ship for Ireland, was only too glad to provide a new interest for its restless visitors, and to attract a new clientele of those eventually to be called 'holidaymakers'. From the 1760s onwards, the status of Parkgate as a port was complemented by its role as a resort.

People had of course bathed in the locality before, but not in large numbers. When a sailor, Griffith Thomas, was in 1705,[75]

> happening to bathe himself naked near Parkgate upon a shelving bank of sand and not knowing how to swim, he fell out of his depth and called for help, but drowned.

In 1757 the curate of the nearby village of Burton, the Revd Robert Washington, was drowned whilst bathing in salt water.[76] What Russell's book did was to make popular the idea that sea water was a health giving mineral water in the same sense as the mineral springs which had made the fortunes of the spa towns; and only one spa, Scarborough, was by the sea.[77] As a later analyst put it, 'Sea water is in fact a mineral water to all intents and purposes.'[78]

The first known visitor to Parkgate for the sea bathing, William Sadler in 1763, was disappointed:[79]

---

[72] *Chester Courant*, 28 Aug. 1753.
[73] Richard Russell, *A Dissertation on the Use of Sea-Water in the Diseases of the Glands* (first English edn, 1752).
[74] From William Cowper's poem 'Retirement' (1782), line 524; see H. S. Milford, ed., *Cowper's Poetical Works* (1967), pp. 109–20.
[75] Chester City R.O., c/1/25, 25 May 1705.
[76] *Chester Courant*, 1 Aug. 1757; see also P. H. W. Booth, ed., *Burton in Wirral: a history* (1984), p. 114.
[77] J. A. R. Pimlott, *The Englishman's Holiday* (1947), p. 51.
[78] A. B. Granville, *Spas of England* (1841), 2, p. 6.
[79] W. K. R. Bedford, *Three Hundred Years of a Family Living*, (1889), p. 73.

The accommodation here is tolerable, but the place is very disagreeable. Here is no coffee-house, no newspaper, and almost no company. We are several leagues from the ocean, and consequently sea water is not to be had here in perfection. There is no bathing but in the spring tides, which continue but seven days in a fortnight . . .

Nor did Sadler find the natives at all agreeable:

The inhabitants of this place are an amphibious mongrel breed of an animal, half-English and half-Irish, and as unconversible as their brother monsters of the deep.

At least the accommodation was tolerable. As well as its inns which put up the passengers, Parkgate's householders began, in the 1760s, to advertise rooms or whole houses to let.[80]

The house where the late Captain Brown lived in at Parkgate is completely fitted up, and a new bath made in the same, where ladies and gentlemen may be accommodated with genteel board and lodging during the bathing season.

By 1775, when the *Chester Chronicle* was first published,[81] Parkgate's status as a resort was clearly established:[82]

The great resort of people of rank, at this season of the year, for the purpose of bathing in the sea, has made this place vie with Brighthelmstone, Southampton etc., and it is imagined it will still improve, as its situation, as well for prospect and serenity of air, as its convenience for bathing, is much more eligible than any other place of resort for that purpose.

Parkgate's most celebrated sea-bathing visitor was Emma Lyon, the future Lady Hamilton, who stayed at Parkgate for several weeks in 1784 with her small daughter and her mother.[83]
She came from London to Cheshire because her daughter had been left with Emma's grandmother in Hawarden, and she found it necessary to explain to her protector, Charles Greville, that she was

[80] *Chester Courant*, 26 May 1767.
[81] Herbert Hughes, *Chronicle of Chester* (1975), p. 3.
[82] *Chester Chronicle*, 3 July 1775.
[83] Walter Sichell, *Emma, Lady Hamilton* (1907), pp. 71–2.

not being extravagant in choosing Parkgate. Abergele was too expensive because,[84]

> It is grown such a fashionable place. And High Lake as 3 houses in it and not one of them as is fit for a Christian. Has to where I am, I find it very comfortable, considering from you. I am in the house of a laidy, whoes husband is at sea.

The interest in Emma's letters (she was calling herself Mrs Hart at the time, perhaps because the presence of a daughter required the appearance of a married name) for the student of Parkgate lies in their portrayal of the sea-bathing cure. She was suffering from some kind of skin complaint:[85]

> I must not forgett to tell you my knees is well, as I may say. There is hardly a mark, and my elbows is much better . . . You can't think how soult the water is. And there is many a laidys bathing here. But Greville, I am obledged to give a shilling a day for the bathing horse and whoman, and twopence a day for the dress. It is a great expense, and it fretts me wen I think of it.

If Emma's London doctor (referred to as Mr W.) was following the prescriptions of Dr Russell, then the nearest description of an ailment that seems to fit Emma's case is called, 'Of various Foulnesses of the Skin'. For this Russell prescribed,[86]

> every morning anti-scorbutic medicines and the sea-water, and deterge the skin with Quercus Maritimus taken from the shore.

By *quercus maritimus* he meant a seaweed of the *fucus* species: bladder-wrack or tang. Russell was in favour of drinking sea water, but his disciple Dr J. Speed laid more emphasis on bathing in later editions of Russell's book.[87] Emma therefore did all these things:[88]

> I have not took but 2 of those things from Mr W. as the sea-water has done me so much good. I have drunk a tumbler

---

[84] Alfred Morrison, *The Hamilton and Nelson Papers* (1893) 1, p. 85, letter 125 (15 June 1784).

[85] *ibid*, p. 87, letter 126 (22 June 1784).

[86] R. Russell (see note 73 above), p. 80.

[87] J. Speed, *Dr Speed's Commentary on Sea Water*, added to later editions (e.g. the third, 1755) of Russell's *Use of Sea Water*.

[88] A. Morrison, *Hamilton and Nelson Papers*, 1, p. 89, letter 128 (3 July 1784).

glas every morning fasting, walked half-a-hour, and then bathed and breakfasted. I have the tang appleyd to me kne and elbows every night going to bed, and every day washed them twice a-day in the sea-water, and the are just well. Therefore as long as I stay, I had better go on in my old whay, for I can take Mr W.'s prescription at home, but not sea-water, tang &c

At a time when women frequently bathed naked,[89] and as they were doing at Parkgate, in 1813,[90] it is notable that Emma paid for the horse that pulled a bathing van into and out of the water, for a 'whoman' who was the 'dipper', ensuring that the customer got wet but did not drown, and for a bathing dress. Just before Emma's visit, in 1782, a local innkeeper advertised that he had the very latest bathing machine, incorporating a 'modesty hood' or awning that screened the bather from vulgar eyes.[91]

> Joseph Manlove of the George Inn, Parkgate, informs the Ladies, Gentlemen and others that, for their better accommodation during the bathing season, he has purchased an additional bathing machine on entire modern construction, in which Ladies may bathe with the utmost ease and secrecy. Price for a single bathing, 8d., and every lady will (if desired) be attended by a female servant . . .

It was customary, as in Emma's case, for bathers to take the sea-water cure under medical prescription. Doctors were naturally anxious to safeguard their mystique:[92]

> The general and indiscriminate use of bathing is allowed on all hands frequently to lay the foundations of a train of maladies, and instead of being a harmless or salutary amusement, is often destructive to health and enjoyment ... the advice of a physician should always be taken.

The same author explained that the 'tonic effect' of cold water required a bathe in the early morning, and 'the first plunge is the only one that can be attended with any utility'. Because bathing was

---

[89]  For example, see cartoons of 1803 and 1820 in *History Today*, 33 (July 1983) on cover and p. 21.
[90]  Richard Ayton, *A Voyage round Great Britain*, 1 (1814), p. 76.
[91]  *Chester Chronicle*, 10 May 1782.
[92]  John Feltham, *A Guide to all the Watering and Sea Bathing Places* (1803), p. 433.

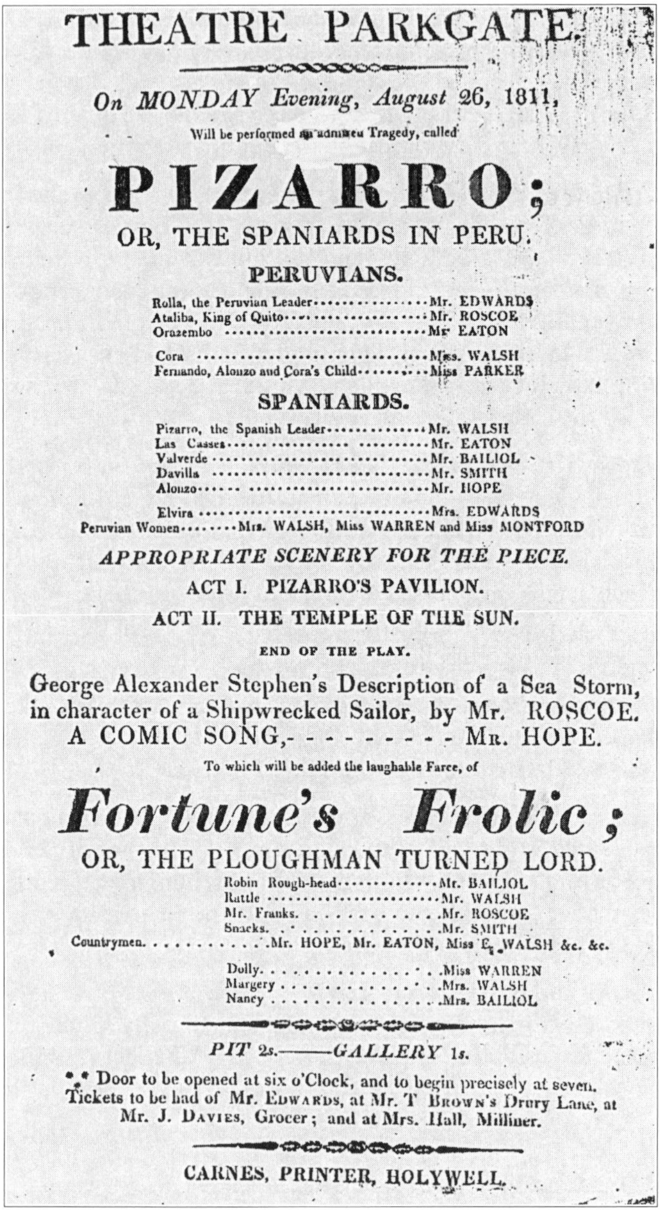

# THEATRE PARKGATE

On *MONDAY Evening, August* 26, 1811,

Will be performed an admired Tragedy, called

# PIZARRO;

## OR, THE SPANIARDS IN PERU.

### PERUVIANS.

Rolla, the Peruvian Leader················Mr. EDWARDS
Ataliba, King of Quito···················Mr. ROSCOE
Orazembo ·································Mr EATON

Cora ····································Mrs. WALSH
Fernando, Alonzo and Cora's Child········Miss PARKER

### SPANIARDS.

Pizarro, the Spanish Leader··············Mr. WALSH
Las Casses·····························Mr. EATON
Valverde ······························Mr. BAILIOL
Davilla ·······························Mr. SMITH
Alonzo·······························Mr. HOPE

Elvira ································Mrs. EDWARDS
Peruvian Women········Mrs. WALSH, Miss WARREN and Miss MONTFORD

*APPROPRIATE SCENERY FOR THE PIECE.*

ACT I. PIZARRO'S PAVILION.

ACT II. THE TEMPLE OF THE SUN.

END OF THE PLAY.

George Alexander Stephen's Description of a Sea Storm, in character of a Shipwrecked Sailor, by Mr. ROSCOE. A COMIC SONG,--------- Mr. HOPE.

To which will be added the laughable Farce, of

# *Fortune's Frolic;*

## OR, THE PLOUGHMAN TURNED LORD.

Robin Rough-head··············Mr. BAILIOL
Rattle ·····················Mr. WALSH
Mr. Franks. ············Mr. ROSCOE
Snacks. ·············Mr. SMITH
Countrymen. ··········Mr. HOPE, Mr. EATON, Miss E. WALSH &c. &c.

Dolly. ···············Miss WARREN
Margery ··············Mrs. WALSH
Nancy ················Mrs. BAILIOL

*PIT* 2s.——*GALLERY* 1s.

•.• Door to be opened at six o'Clock, and to begin precisely at seven. Tickets to be had of Mr. EDWARDS, at Mr. T BROWN's Drury Lane, at Mr. J. DAVIES, Grocer; and at Mrs. Hall, Milliner.

CARNES, PRINTER, HOLYWELL.

Figure 27. Theatre programme at Parkgate, 1811.

largely done before breakfast, a lot of time had to be filled by visitors. William Sadler had complained in 1763 that 'here is no coffee-house', and this need was filled by 1776 when an Assembly Room had been established. Two young men who visited Parkgate in that year recorded their expenses for an assembly, for billiards and at playing cards, as well as for bathing.[93] The Billiard House or Assembly House was built behind the building now known as Balcony House (though its balcony was not built until 1868)[94] and it must have been very prosperous, for its annual rent was raised from eight guineas in 1784–9, in stages to £25 in 1804.[95] No doubt the personality of its manager was important; George Harrison, master of the billiard room, was 'a most lively and eccentric character', who had married Widow Grimes, 'head bathing woman to the ladies who frequent the place', in 1801.[96]

There was another house in use as an Assembly Room in Parkgate from at least 1787, the house already mentioned as situated on the Donkey Stand.[97] In 1811 this house was converted into a bath house:[98]

> warm and cold, for the convenience of invalids, with an outlet for the accommodation of those who prefer the open sea.

Parkgate's praises as a resort were regularly sung in a way that suggests that they were promising rather than established. In 1788[99]

> Parkgate bids fair to become, in a short time, the only fashionable Summer retreat in this part of the kingdom; a revival which will not be so much wondered at, when the convenience for sea-bathing, with the elegance and cheapness of the accommodation, are considered.

The problem of how to occupy visitors in a small village was ever present, and from time to time the dances and card games provided at the Assembly Room would be augmented by a company of actors. A playbill from one such visit is here reproduced.[100] The most

---

[93] Cheshire R.O., DBC/ACC 1063.
[94] Cheshire R.O., LU Ne 2004/1, 2.
[95] Cheshire R.O., DHL 52/6.
[96] *Chester Chronicle*, 7 Oct. 1814; Hilda Gamlin, *'Twixt Mersey and Dee* (1897), p. 260.
[97] Mostyn (Bangor) MSS 5039, 5041; *Chester Courant*, 16 June 1812.
[98] *Chester Courant*, 26 March 1811; *Chester Chronicle*, 8 April 1882.
[99] *Chester Chronicle*, 23 May 1788.
[100] Playbills in a private collection. See also *Notes & Queries*, 10th series III (1905), pp. 289, 355, 397, 457.

striking improvement for the benefit of visitors for the sea-bathing was the Parade, the name now given to the road which runs along the front of the houses and is bounded by the sea wall. We have seen that there was no roadway in front of the houses in 1732, merely a beach.[101] The concave face of the wall and absence of mooring posts or rings suggests that it was not intended that ships should moor beside it. Sir Thomas Mostyn bought the stones of the Old Quay from the City of Chester in 1799,[102] and tradition has it that he used them for the sea-wall at Parkgate. The first mention of a 'quay wall' so far discovered is in 1800,[103] and the first stretch to be built was the central part from the Middle Slip (by the Watch House) to the house just mentioned, used as an assembly room and later as a bath house: by going round this house, the sea wall enclosed the bastion known as the Donkey Stand.[104] Because a part of the routine at the inland spas was the daily promenade of visitors, so did the bathing resorts also provide a promenade. In 1811,[105]

A grand, brilliant and splendid display of fireworks will be exhibited on the shore beneath the Terrace at Parkgate on Saturday August 10th by Signor Saxoni.

Parkgate then, as now, was well situated for visits to the cities of Chester and Liverpool. A landlady offering 'genteel board and lodging' in 1767 added,[106]

There is a good post-chaise and horses, when any of the company please to take an airing.

One place of interest for the tourist from Parkgate was St Winefride's Well at Holywell, remarkable as a place of Catholic pilgrimage throughout the years of religious intolerance.[107] Not only was it [108]

---

[101] Mostyn (Bangor) MS 8699.
[102] R. H. Morris, *Chester in the Plantagenet and Stuart Reigns* (1894), p. 459, n. 2.
[103] Cheshire R.O., QJF 228/2 (21 April 1800).
[104] Estate map surveyed in 1811, Mostyn (Bangor) MS 8702.
[105] *Chester Chronicle*, 9 Aug. 1811.
[106] *Chester Courant*, 26 May 1767.
[107] Christopher David, *St Winefride's Well, a history and guide* (1971), unpaginated.
[108] *Analecta Hibernica*, 15 (1944), p. 118.

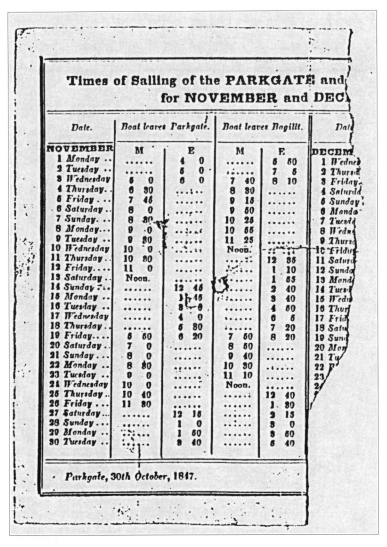

| Times of Sailing of the PARKGATE and for NOVEMBER and DEC⟩ | | | | | |
| --- | --- | --- | --- | --- | --- |
| Date. | Boat leaves Parkgate. | | Boat leaves Bagillt. | | Dat⟩ |
| | M | E | M | E | DECEM⟩ |
| **NOVEMBER** | | | | | |
| 1 Monday .. | ...... | 4 0 | ...... | 5 50 | 1 Wednes |
| 2 Tuesday .. | ...... | 5 0 | ...... | 7 5 | 2 Thursd |
| 3 Wednesday | 5 0 | 6 0 | 7 40 | 8 10 | 3 Friday |
| 4 Thursday.. | 6 30 | ...... | 8 30 | ...... | 4 Saturd |
| 5 Friday ... | 7 45 | ...... | 9 15 | ...... | 5 Sunday |
| 6 Saturday.. | 8 0 | ...... | 9 50 | ...... | 6 Monda |
| 7 Sunday. .. | 8 30 | ...... | 10 25 | ...... | 7 Tuesd |
| 8 Monday... | 9 0 | ...... | 10 55 | ...... | 8 Wedn |
| 9 Tuesday .. | 9 30 | ...... | 11 25 | ...... | 9 Thurs |
| 10 Wednesday | 10 0 | ...... | Noon. | ...... | 10 Friday |
| 11 Thursday.. | 10 30 | ...... | | 12 35 | 11 Saturd |
| 12 Friday.... | 11 0 | ...... | | 1 10 | 12 Sund |
| 13 Saturday .. | Noon. | ...... | | 1 55 | 13 Mond |
| 14 Sunday .. | ...... | 12 45 | | 2 40 | 14 Tues |
| 15 Monday .. | ...... | 1 45 | | 3 40 | 15 Wedn |
| 16 Tuesday .. | ...... | 3 0 | | 4 50 | 16 Thur |
| 17 Wednesday | ...... | 4 0 | | 6 5 | 17 Frid |
| 18 Thursday .. | ...... | 5 30 | | 7 20 | 18 Satu |
| 19 Friday.... | 5 50 | 6 20 | 7 50 | 8 20 | 19 Sun |
| 20 Saturday .. | 7 0 | ...... | 8 50 | ...... | 20 Mon |
| 21 Sunday ... | 8 0 | ...... | 9 40 | ...... | 21 Tu |
| 22 Monday .. | 8 30 | ...... | 10 30 | ...... | 22 F |
| 23 Tuesday .. | 9 0 | ...... | 11 10 | ...... | 23 |
| 24 Wednesday.. | 10 0 | ...... | Noon. | ...... | 24 |
| 25 Thursday .. | 10 40 | ...... | ...... | 12 40 | |
| 26 Friday ... | 11 30 | ...... | ...... | 1 30 | |
| 27 Saturday... | ...... | 12 15 | ...... | 2 15 | |
| 28 Sunday ... | ...... | 1 0 | ...... | 3 0 | |
| 29 Monday .. | ...... | 1 50 | ...... | 3 50 | |
| 30 Tuesday .. | ...... | 3 40 | ...... | 5 40 | |

Parkgate, 30th October, 1847.

Figure 28. Timetable of the Parkgate to Bagillt ferry, November 1847.

much frequented by the Papists, who come over every year
from Ireland in great numbers to perform their devotions,
there being many virtues attributed to the water

but it also attracted many less reverent visitors who came to view,
or to scoff at, 'great crowds of credulous Catholicks'.[109]

Despite the encomiums of the *Chester Chronicle*, Parkgate was by
no means the only place for sea-bathing in the locality. Pre-eminent
was Liverpool, where a spring of chalybeate water, 'extremely bene-
ficial, perfectly innocent and adapted even to weak stomachs' had
been exploited in 1773.[110] The North Pleasure and Salt Water Baths,
'at the end of the New Quay, near the Ladies Walk at Liverpool',
opened in 1765, and large numbers of the labouring classes used to
visit Liverpool to bathe, usually naked, on half a mile of beach, land
later occupied by Prince's Dock.[111] In 1794 'a set of elegant and
commodious sea-baths' was built there.[112] The opening of the New
Hotel, Hoylake, in 1793 provided further rivalry.[113]

Nevertheless, Parkgate earned a second reputation as a place for a
salubrious holiday. One visitor, John Riland, published a poem
extolling Parkgate's air compared with the 'taint contaminate of
poison'd atmosphere' in Birmingham in 1791. It includes the lines,[114]

> Haply escaped from thence, 'tis mine, PARKGATE to visit,
> This air salubrious, free from noxious taints,
> Which much pollute that which I've left behind,
> And make unhealthy living in the town.

At much the same time, in 1790, Reginald Heber (the hymn-writer
and future bishop of Calcutta) arrived at Parkgate:[115]

> We had a fine day and the children bore the journey without
> being coach-sick. The lodging-houses are small but we occupy
> the whole of this except for three apartments. If the weather

---

[109] W. R. C[hetwood], *A Tour through Ireland*, p. 37.
[110] Thomas Houlston, *Essay on the Liverpool Spa Water* (1773); *Williamson's Liverpool Advertiser*, 28 Aug. 1773.
[111] *Williamson's Liverpool Advertiser*, 31 May 1765.
[112] J. Aikin, *A Description of the Country from 30 to 40 miles round Manchester* (1795), p. 357; *Chester Chronicle*, 2 Sept. 1791, 6 June 1794.
[113] *Chester Chronicle*, 19 July 1793.
[114] W. K. R. Bedford, *Three Hundred Years of a Family Living*, pp. 127–8.
[115] R. H. Cholmondeley, *The Heber Letters 1733–1832* (1950), p. 59.

holds fair I think the sea air and bathing will be of service in strengthening both Mama and her babes.

The fashionable concentration on health as a reason for the visit meant that a number of visitors to Parkgate were recorded for unhappy reasons:[116]

> Mr Jobbern of Wolverhampton, attorney at law, on his return from Parkgate, where he had been for the benefit of sea-bathing, was suddenly arrested by the cold hand of Death in a chaise at Whitchurch.

One aspect of this concern for health was the establishment of a charitable fund:

> The benevolent inhabitants of Parkgate and Neston are establishing a fund to enable those whose poverty precludes them from the salutary benefits of sea bathing [to enjoy it].

Each visitor was to be invited to subscribe one shilling.[117] This fund continued to provide for invalid visitors until 1881, when its capital was used to establish a convalescent home at Parkgate, run by the Chester Royal Infirmary.[118] The house was sold in 1925 and the proceeds, still called the Parkgate Convalescent Fund, are now used to pay for the convalescent treatment at home of patients of the Infirmary.[119]

The service which supported both the travellers and visitors was the inn. Amongst the many inns mentioned during the eighteenth century, the *George Inn* became pre-eminent. It was apparently formerly called the *Three Pigeons*, renowned in Dublin under that name,[120] and later as the *George and Three Pigeons*, from which a coach used to leave for Chester in 1761.[121] It was the innkeeper of the *George*, Joseph Manlove, who advertised the new bathing machine with modesty hood in 1782. Manlove's son-in-law and successor, Thomas Spencer, ran the *George Inn* for twenty years until he decided in 1808 that Parkgate's days as a passenger station were

---

[116] *Chester Chronicle*, 21 Sept. 1792.
[117] *ibid*, 20 Aug. 1790.
[118] *ibid*, 1 July, 7 Oct. 1882.
[119] Enid Mumford, *Chester Royal Infirmary 1756–1956* (1956); Chester City R.O., HI/122–124.
[120] *Faulkner's Dublin Journal*, 12 June 1753.
[121] *Chester Courant*, 23 June 1761.

numbered. He moved to Holyhead where he took the *Eagle and Child* inn,[122] which he ran as a successful inn for the packet passengers for at least the next twenty years.[123] The *George* in Parkgate was rebuilt in 1819 and reopened as the *Mostyn Arms Hotel*.[124]

[122] *Chester Chronicle*, 15 April 1808.
[123] James Sparrow, *Biography of J. M. Skinner* (1866), drawing at end of book.
[124] *Chester Chronicle*, 9 July 1819.

# 10  *The Aftermath*

We have seen that the last regular shipping to visit Parkgate sailed in 1815. In that year, at the end of July, the Cheshire magistrates advised that 'the Dublin packets do not now sail from Parkgate but from Liverpool', although vagrants were still being brought to the Neston House of Correction at Moorside until at least that time. The last of the Parkgate packet ships, the *Loftus* and the *Bessborough*, were finally listed in the *Directory of Dublin* for 1814 and 1815 respectively. The closure of Parkgate's shipping could have been foretold for at least eight years. The Parkgate Packet Company seems to have been run down between 1807 and 1809, following the loss of the *King George* in 1806. The records of the Dee pilots show that, between 1803 and 1823, there was a complete shift from men living at Parkgate to those from Wales. Finally, we have seen that Thomas Spencer the innkeeper correctly read the writing on the wall when he moved from Parkgate to Holyhead in 1808.

The reasons for the decline of the Parkgate anchorage were various, but there were two principal causes. The first was the gradual alteration of the main channel of the River Dee from the English to the Welsh shore, deliberately induced by the engineers of the River Dee Company; and the second was the steady improvement of the roads to Holyhead, resulting in an increase in the packet services there and better harbour facilities. As a background to these factors, there was a continual growth in the Irish passenger traffic at Liverpool, where reliably deep water became more important with the increase in the size of ships.

How much the Parkgate anchorage was used after 1808 is uncertain. The two packet ships still sailing, together with the R.Y. *Dorset*, were sufficient in 1810 to justify the reference, 'Parkgate, from whence the packets sail to ireland'.[1] However, the references to Parkgate in gazetteers can be misleading: we have seen that *Paterson's Roads*, which stated accurately in 1808 that at Parkgate 'passengers

---

[1] D. and S. Lysons, *Magna Britannia*, 2 (1810), p. 715.

frequently take shipping to Dublin to save the land travelling through Wales', continued to state that 'this place is also noted as a station whence packets sail for Ireland, which they generally do four times a week', as late as 1829.[2] Similarly, George Ormerod, who collected the information for his *History of Cheshire* in 1813, wrote it up by 1819, causing his 1882 editor to state that the packet service 'continued some years after 1816'.[3]

In 1811,[4]

> the carriage, horses and suite of Dr Cleaver, Archbishop of Dublin, were safely landed [at Parkgate] on 10th April from on board the Beresford, his lordship's strength now permitting exercise in the open air.

The *Beresford* was a Liverpool vessel which has not otherwise been recorded at Parkgate, and it may be that most merchant vessels calling there were, by this time, casual visitors. In the final six months of 1810, large numbers of livestock were landed at Parkgate, as we have already noted, and we have seen that livestock carriers were usually occasional visitors to the Dee.[5] The final visit of the R.Y. *Dorset* to Parkgate in October 1812 recorded the names of the last passengers known to have landed there.

By June 1814 it seems to have been assumed that there was no longer a reliable passenger service from Parkgate, if one may judge from the editorial comment on a new coach service between Chester and Holyhead:[6]

> It will be particularly convenient to the gentlemen of Liverpool, as in the event of accident in the sailing of packets from that port, they will be always sure of conveyance by this coach.

Even then, the decay of Parkgate was not regarded as inevitable. In December 1815 there seem to have been plans to revive the Parkgate Packet Company:[7]

---

[2] *Paterson's Roads*, (14th edn 1808, 15th edn 1811, 16th edn 1822, 17th edn 1824, 18th edn 1826–32).
[3] George Ormerod, *History of Cheshire* (2nd edn 1882) ed. T. Helsby, 2, p. 534.
[4] *Chester Courant*, 23 April 1811.
[5] *ibid*, 22 Jan. 1811.
[6] *Chester Chronicle*, 3 June 1814.
[7] *ibid*, 1 Dec. 1815.

A general meeting of the Parkgate New Packet Proprietors will be held in Chester. It was resolved that subscriptions should be paid up 50% and should close on 1st February.

Unfortunately nothing further was reported of this venture.

What happened next was the advent of steam power, which was accepted so quickly over the next few years that no revival of Parkgate could be considered except in the context of steam. The first steam boat to be seen on the Mersey, the *Elizabeth*, was recorded there on 5 July 1815.[8] The ship had been built in 1812 at Port Glasgow, but at once steam vessels began to be made locally and started operating in 1816 on the Mersey ferry routes: to Runcorn, to Eastham and to Ellesmere Port.[9] The sudden improvement in the conditions for crossing the Mersey made the use of Liverpool all the more attractive to travellers. In April 1817,[10]

the elegant new steam packet, the Princess Royal, has commenced going from the Parade Slip, Liverpool, twice a day to Eastham, where she meets coaches to Chester, Shrewsbury, Holyhead &c.

These coaches included the Hibernia Hero Light Post Coach to Chester via Neston. A month later another steam ferry began running between Liverpool and Tranmere, and for a short period a steam boat called the *Ancient Briton* was running between Parkgate and Bagillt on the Welsh shore.[11] The *Ancient Briton* was working on the Mersey in 1819 and Parkgate's ferry reverted to sail. By 1818 there was a steam packet running from Chester to Flint and Bagillt every day.[12] As we have seen, steam ships took over the Irish Sea crossing from Holyhead, and from Liverpool, in 1822.

Those Chester interests who hoped that the new technology might yet turn the fortunes of the Dee, began by supposing that Parkgate might still be used. In 1821,[13]

---

[8] A. C. Wardle, 'Early steamships on the Mersey 1815–20', *T.H.S.L.C.*, 92 (1941), pp. 85–100.
[9] C. L. D. Duckworth and G. E. Langmuir, *West Coast Steamers* (1953), p. 24.
[10] *Liverpool Mercury*, 18 April 1817.
[11] *ibid*, 6 June 1817.
[12] *Pigot's Commercial Directory* (Manchester 1818), p. 107.
[13] *Chester Chronicle*, 29 June 1821.

> We congratulate the public on the probability of the establishment of a steam packet, to ply between Parkgate and Dublin: we have learned that subscription is on the tapis for the purpose.

Within two months, though, the plan was being related, not to Parkgate, but to Dawpool:[14]

> one of the largest class of steam vessels would always have sufficient depth of water to come into and sail out of Dawpool.

A public meeting discussed the idea at Chester Town Hall and Thomas Telford was appointed engineer.[15] However, when the plan was presented by Telford in March 1822, it was for an artificial harbour nearly a mile from Dawpool lane. A semi-circular harbour was to be joined to the shore by a floating roadway 800 feet long, and linked to Heswall by a new road.[16] The cost was said to be £30,000 and the proposal was dropped.[17]

One final attempt to provide a steamer service to Dublin was tried in 1823, when a Liverpool steam ship, the *Mountaineer*, was engaged to sail from Gayton Lane End, one mile down river from Parkgate, although the advertisements referred to Dawpool. Because the backers hoped to prove that a journey from the Dee would save two hours compared with the time for crossing from Liverpool, a certificate from the Chester post office, confirming the time of arrival at Chester of the coach from London, was taken on board the *Mountaineer*. In the event, the *Mountaineer* was able to deliver the London newspapers four hours earlier at Dublin than those sent through Holyhead. The ship returned from Dublin in 13½ hours.[18] However, nothing more was heard of this plan either.

We have seen that, when the Parkgate Customs staff was reduced to one man in 1820, 'the foreign trade at Parkgate is solely coals exported and cattle from Ireland'.[19] Although cattle as such were not liable for duty, it was undoubtedly thought necessary to keep an eye on the cattle ships for contraband, and one may presume that the end

---

[14] *ibid*, 24 Aug. 1821.
[15] *ibid*, 7 Sept., 14 Nov. 1821.
[16] Cheshire R.O., D. 3940.
[17] *Chester Chronicle*, 29 March 1822.
[18] *ibid*, 25 July, 1 Aug., 8 Aug. 1823.
[19] P.R.O., CUST 79/7, 8 Dec. 1820.

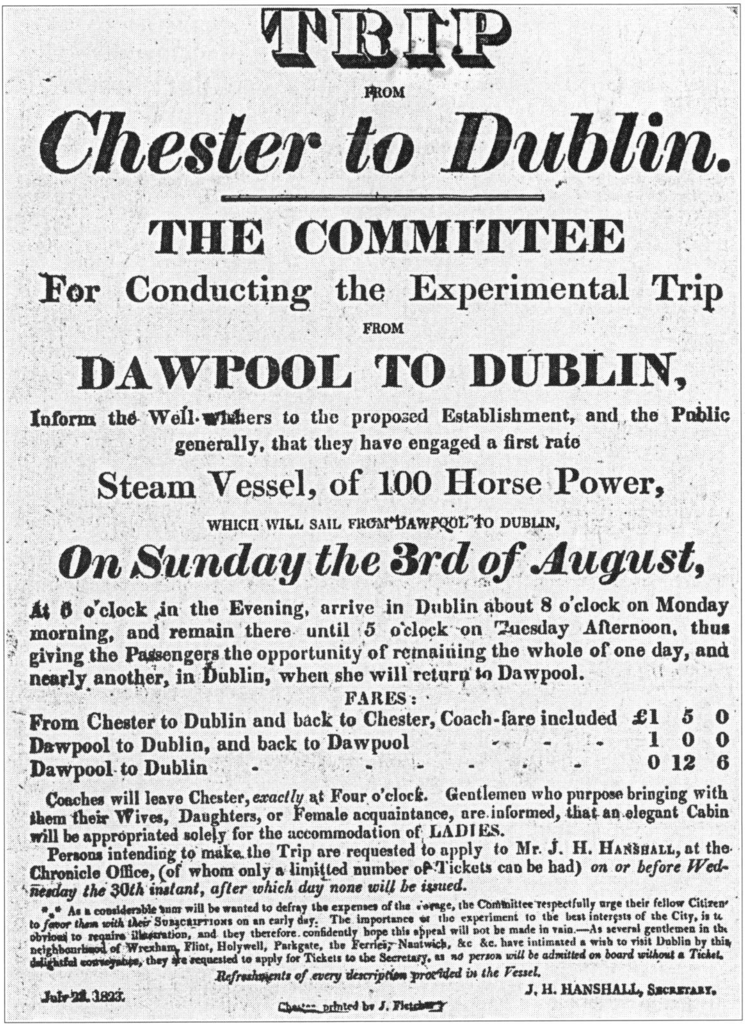
# TRIP

FROM

# *Chester to Dublin.*

## THE COMMITTEE

For Conducting the Experimental Trip

FROM

## DAWPOOL TO DUBLIN,

Inform the Well-wishers to the proposed Establishment, and the Public generally, that they have engaged a first rate

### Steam Vessel, of 100 Horse Power,

WHICH WILL SAIL FROM DAWPOOL TO DUBLIN,

### *On Sunday the 3rd of August,*

At 6 o'clock in the Evening, arrive in Dublin about 8 o'clock on Monday morning, and remain there until 5 o'clock on Tuesday Afternoon, thus giving the Passengers the opportunity of remaining the whole of one day, and nearly another, in Dublin, when she will return to Dawpool.

FARES:

| | | | |
|---|---|---|---|
| From Chester to Dublin and back to Chester, Coach-fare included | £1 | 5 | 0 |
| Dawpool to Dublin, and back to Dawpool - - - | 1 | 0 | 0 |
| Dawpool to Dublin - - - - - - - - | 0 | 12 | 6 |

Coaches will leave Chester, *exactly* at Four o'clock. Gentlemen who purpose bringing with them their Wives, Daughters, or Female acquaintance, are informed, that an elegant Cabin will be appropriated solely for the accommodation of LADIES.

Persons intending to make the Trip are requested to apply to Mr. J. H. HANSHALL, at the Chronicle Office, (of whom only a limitted number of Tickets can be had) *on or before Wednesday the 30th instant, after which day none will be issued.*

*** As a considerable sum will be wanted to defray the expenses of the voyage, the Committee respectfully urge their fellow Citizens to *favor them with their* SUBSCRIPTIONS on an early day. The importance of the experiment to the best interests of the City, is too obvious to require illustration, and they therefore confidently hope this appeal will not be made in vain.—As several gentlemen in the neighbourhood of Wrexham, Flint, Holywell, Parkgate, the Ferries, Nantwich, &c &c. have intimated a wish to visit Dublin by this delightful conveyance, they are requested to apply for Tickets to the Secretary, as *no person will be admitted on board without a Ticket.*

*Refreshments of every description provided in the Vessel.*

July 22, 1823. J. H. HANSHALL, SECRETARY.

Chester, printed by J. Fletcher

Figure 29. Advertisement for the voyage of the *Mountaineer*, 1823.
(original in private hands)

of the Customs presence in 1828 followed the end of cattle imports at Parkgate. The coal exports, however, were to continue until the middle of the century, and Ness Colliery formed an important part of the economy of Neston. An arm of the river, the Colliery Gutter, curled round to the stone quay built there in the 1760s and allowed coal sloops to load there independently of the conditions at Parkgate. In 1851 the colliery was employing 120 men, and the census recorded that the sloop *Mary* was lying off Ness Colliery at the time.[20] The colliery closed in 1855, to be reopened with new shafts (but with no further use of its quay) twenty years later.[21]

An occupation which former mariners may have followed was fishing. During the years before 1815, the occupation of fisherman was recorded only rarely in the Neston parish registers,[22] possibly because men may have fished while temporarily home from the sea. Thomas Price, who was drowned when his fishing boat overturned near the Point of Air in 1765, was said to have kept a public house at Parkgate.[23] In 1809 Richard Jones and his young son William from Parkgate were drowned while fishing near Beaumaris.[24] From the 1760s Parkgate had a herring curing house, established by William Williamson 'for drying, salting or curing herrings'.[25] These processes produced 'red' herrings which were smoked, or 'white' herrings which were salted, encouraged by bounties for herring fisheries and for salting fish, while salt tax was not collected if it was used for curing.[26] Cured herrings from Parkgate were being sold in Liverpool in 1766, in Chester in 1778.[27] Fresh herrings from Parkgate were advertised for sale in Chester in 1783 and 1809, though not necessarily caught by Parkgate fishermen.[28] The curing house must have stopped production by 1804, as the Parkgate Packet Company was then renting its premises.[29] In 1829, when storms caused a great deal of damage to fishing boats, a correspondent requesting charity stated,[30]

[20] Census, 1851, Parish of Neston (Ness).

[21] *Chester Chronicle*, 23 June 1855.

[22] For example, James Roberts 1787, Charles Edwards 1799, Peter Evans 1807.

[23] Clwyd R.O., Hawarden, Wreck book, D.DM.734/2, 13 Nov. 1765.

[24] *ibid*, 6 Dec. 1809.

[25] Mostyn (Bangor) MS 5017.

[26] W. C. Smith, *A Short History of the Irish Sea Herring Fisheries* (1923), pp. 23–4.

[27] *Williamson's Liverpool Advertiser*, 19 Nov. 1766; *Chester Chronicle*, 18 Feb. 1778.

[28] *Chester Chronicle*, 18 Feb. 1778, 21 Oct. 1809.

[29] Cheshire R.O., DHL 52/5, p. 18.

[30] *Chester Chronicle*, 10 July 1829.

All the seafaring men belonging to Parkgate have been at one time or another in the service of the navy, and fought and bled in defending the liberties of their country.

By 1822, Parkgate was existing chiefly on its reputation as a resort:[31]

The inhabitants of this place derive their principal support from the expenditure of the visitors who reside here in the bathing season.

After the Napoleonic wars, some efforts were made to improve the resort. When the steamship *Ancient Briton* was put on the ferry route across to Flint, a new pier was built, probably beside the *Boat House* inn. This pier had to be repaired in 1821 after storm damage.[32] The *George Inn*, inherited from her husband in 1814 by Esther Briscoe, was reopened as the *Mostyn Arms Hotel* in 1819:[33]

the above INN is re-opened and fitted up in the first style of elegance. The house has been considerably enlarged. Several parlours, sitting rooms, bedrooms (supplied with excellent bedding) have been added to it. From these extensive alterations, she will be enabled to accommodate whole private families, with complete suites of apartments, finished in a very superior manner.

Occasionally one gets a glimpse of the numbers of visitors involved. On two occasions in the summer of 1829, the *Chester Chronicle* reported that arrivals were divided between the hotel and lodgings as follows: at the end of July, eleven at the hotel and thirty-four in lodgings; two weeks later, nineteen at the hotel and forty-two in lodgings.[34] In July 1824, thirty-eight gentlefolk were named as visitors to Parkgate, including the landowner, Sir Thomas Mostyn, his brother-in-law Sir Edward Lloyd, and his neighbour Sir Watkin Williams-Wynn. In one year, there was a grimmer reason for Parkgate's popularity. Asiatic cholera reached Britain for the first time in

---

[31] Edward Mogg, ed., *Paterson's Roads* (1822), p. 217.
[32] *Chester Chronicle*, 6 April, 13 July 1821.
[33] *ibid*, 9 July 1819.
[34] *ibid*, 24 July, 11 Sept. 1829.

1832 and was greatly feared, but Parkgate was free of it. The place was [35]

> thronged with company who have flocked in from all quarters to this always salubrious and now highly favoured spot.

In 1831 Sir Thomas Mostyn, sixth and last baronet, died, and his estate passed to the husband of his eldest surviving sister, Sir Thomas Champneys. In the same year the husband of another sister, Sir Edward Lloyd, was created 1st Baron Mostyn, and their son, Edward Mostyn Lloyd (who was heir both to the barony and the Mostyn estates) adopted the surname Mostyn by royal licence.[36] When Edward Mostyn succeeded to the estates in 1840, he set several improvements in hand. A number of dilapidated buildings were knocked down, the ferry pier was again repaired, and the approach road at the north end of the village was paved with stone. These moves were popular:[37]

> The inhabitants are highly pleased with the prompt manner in which Mr Mostyn has conceded to their wishes and suggestions.

It would seem that the whole of the promenade was completed or repaved during the 1840s.[38] Most important of all, Edward Mostyn or his family came to stay at Parkgate in the summer of several years.[39] In smaller ways too the landowner showed his support: he installed a new billiard table in the old Assembly Room, and gave a haunch of venison for the dinner after one of the annual regattas.[40]

All this investment may, however, have come too late. In 1830 a Liverpool merchant, James Atherton, realised that the Mersey was no longer the barrier it had been before the coming of steam ferries, and bought 170 acres of sandhills near Liscard, on the Wirral shore opposite Liverpool.[41] The resort he built there was described in 1841:[42]

[35] *ibid*, 6 July 1832.
[36] *ibid*, 22 April 1831.
[37] *ibid*, 14 May 1841.
[38] *ibid*, 15 June 1849.
[39] *ibid*, 14 May 1841, 6 June 1845.
[40] *ibid*, 30 Sept. 1842, 3 July 1841.
[41] W. W. Mortimer, *The History of the Hundred of Wirral* (1847), p. 300.
[42] A. B. Granville, *Spas of England* (1841), 2, p. 4.

of late years a new sea-bathing place has been created exclus-
ively for the accommodation of the wealthier classes in and
about Liverpool who, having now nearly deserted the once
fashionable Parkgate, on the Cheshire coast, gladly availed
themselves of the new establishment to which the emphatic
title of New Brighton has been given.

Because Parkgate once more seemed to be on the way down, and for
other reasons to be examined presently, Edward Mostyn sold all his
Cheshire estates; and Parkgate, every yard of which had belonged to
the family throughout its recorded history as a settlement, went
under the auctioneer's hammer in 1849. Mrs Briscoe raised a mort-
gage to buy her hotel and then died; the hotel closed and the building
became a school in 1855.[43] The resort had a struggle to survive. In
August 1854,[44]

There does not seem to be many people here at present, and
Grandmama thinks Parkgate much duller than it used to be.

Its fortunes were revived, in a small way, by the coming of the
railway in 1866, combined with the introduction of Bank Holidays
in 1871.

For 177 years, from 1672 to 1849, the whole of Parkgate and the
greater part of Neston, forming an estate of about 1,500 acres,
belonged to the Mostyn family. Some of the functions of local
government were performed by the manor courts of Great Neston
and of Leighton and Thornton, some of whose records between 1828
and 1847 survive.[45] The steward of the manor appointed a bailiff, and
the jurors appointed constables, burleymen (who dealt with straying
livestock and broken fences) and leavelookers (who looked after
trading and the market). When the steward's authority ceased in
1849, such duties were accepted, rather unwillingly, by the parish
vestry, which appointed a standing committee for general (civil)
purposes in 1855.[46]

[43] G. W. Place, 'John Brindley (1811–1873) Cheshire schoolmaster, the opponent of atheism', *T.H.S.L.C.*, 133 (1984), p. 124.
[44] Letter from Kitty James to her father, 4 Aug. 1854 (privately owned).
[45] Mostyn (Bangor) MS 6250.
[46] Neston churchwardens' accounts, 23 Nov. 1855 (Cheshire R.O.,
P.149/9/2).

As well as his official responsibilities as landowner, we have seen that Edward Lloyd Mostyn was prepared to involve himself personally in the fortunes of Parkgate. However, his great inheritance brought with it great financial problems. His grandfather, Sir Roger Mostyn the 5th baronet, left a son and six daughters when he died in 1796, and his will allowed his daughters an annuity until marriage and £10,000 when they married.[47] The estate, which was entailed, was left to trustees, and if his son, who became Sir Thomas the 6th baronet, died without male heirs, the trustees were to sell the estate and pay any remaining daughters £10,000 each.[48] In addition, the estates had been subject to continual mortgages since at least 1699.[49] When Sir Thomas died unmarried in 1831, the surviving five daughters went to the High Court of Chancery to establish that they were entitled to £10,000 each and that the trustees had power to obtain these sums.[50] The eldest surviving daughter was Charlotte, wife of Sir Thomas Champneys, but they had no children. The heir presumptive was therefore the eldest son of the next sister, Elizabeth, whose husband Sir Edward Lloyd had been created Lord Mostyn in William IV's coronation honours; this son, Edward, added Mostyn to his surname to conform to his grandfather's will. When Sir Thomas Champneys died in 1839, Edward Lloyd Mostyn assumed control of the estate.[51] The financial encumbrance of the estate was growing rapidly: in 1840, over £60,000 was owing on the mortgages, in 1843 this sum was raised to £100,000, and the decision to sell at least part of the estate was taken.[52] The estate had been formally disentailed in 1840, and Edward Mostyn's aunt Charlotte died in 1845, his mother having died three years earlier.[53] It is possible, therefore, that much of Edward Lloyd Mostyn's concern for the welfare of Parkgate may have been intended, in the long run, to fatten it for sale.

There was another reason for selling the Neston estate, besides the negative need to pay off debts of £100,000. It had always been the way of the Mostyns to plan and develop for the future, and future

---

[47] Abstract of Title no. 1 (1849 sale of Neston estate), p. 1.
[48] *ibid*, p. 3.
[49] Supplemental Abstract of title of the Mostyn estates in Cheshire, 1699–1793.
[50] Abstract of Title no. 1, p. 18. (Some of the Neston sale papers are in the Cheshire R.O., DHL 29.)
[51] Abstract of title no. 1, p. 29.
[52] Abstract of Title no. 1, p. 41; no. 3, p. 80.
[53] 1850 Sale Papers; Abstract of further disentailing assurances.

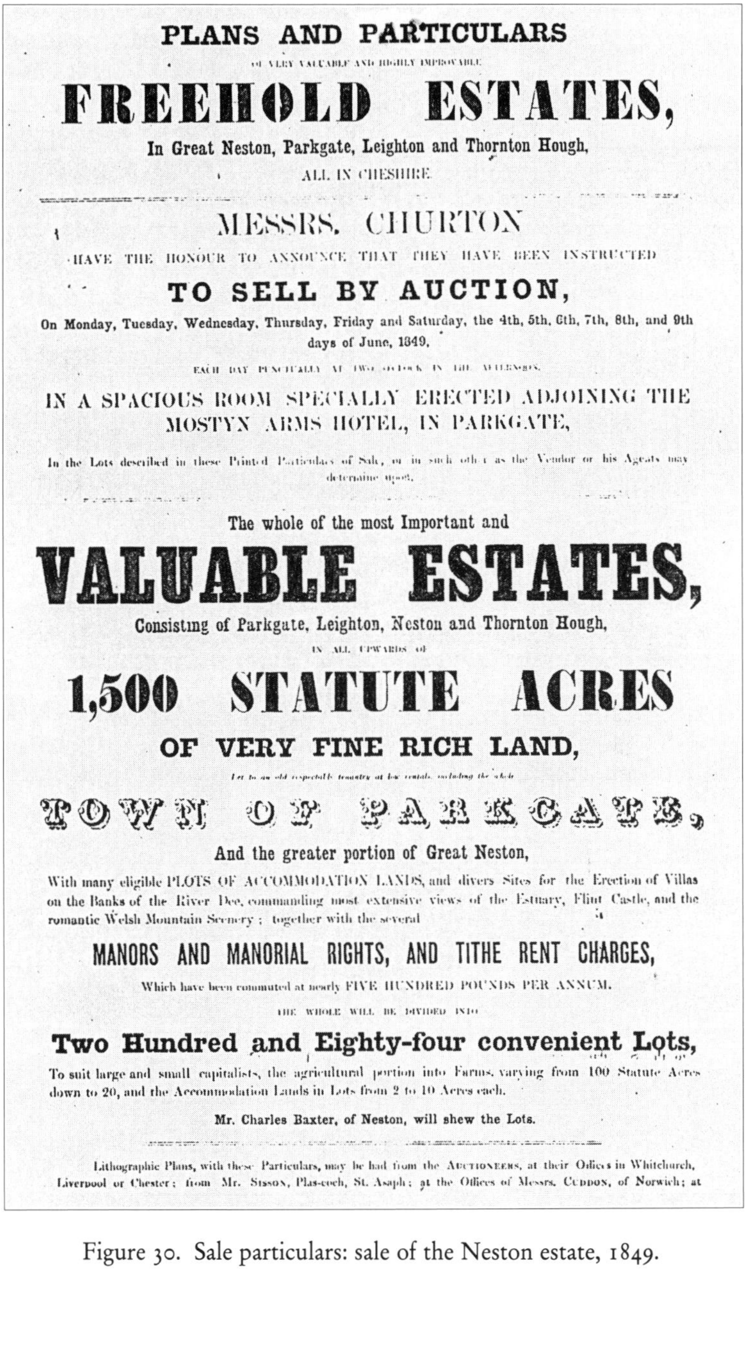

PLANS AND PARTICULARS

OF VERY VALUABLE AND HIGHLY IMPROVABLE

FREEHOLD ESTATES,

In Great Neston, Parkgate, Leighton and Thornton Hough,

ALL IN CHESHIRE.

MESSRS. CHURTON

HAVE THE HONOUR TO ANNOUNCE THAT THEY HAVE BEEN INSTRUCTED

TO SELL BY AUCTION,

On Monday, Tuesday, Wednesday, Thursday, Friday and Saturday, the 4th, 5th, 6th, 7th, 8th, and 9th days of June, 1849,

EACH DAY PUNCTUALLY AT TWO O'CLOCK IN THE AFTERNOON,

IN A SPACIOUS ROOM SPECIALLY ERECTED ADJOINING THE MOSTYN ARMS HOTEL, IN PARKGATE,

In the Lots described in these Printed Particulars of Sale, or in such other as the Vendor or his Agents may determine upon.

The whole of the most Important and

VALUABLE ESTATES,

Consisting of Parkgate, Leighton, Neston and Thornton Hough,

IN ALL UPWARDS OF

1,500 STATUTE ACRES

OF VERY FINE RICH LAND,

*Let to an old respectable tenantry at low rentals, including the whole*

TOWN OF PARKGATE,

And the greater portion of Great Neston,

With many eligible PLOTS OF ACCOMMODATION LANDS, and divers Sites for the Erection of Villas on the Banks of the River Dee, commanding most extensive views of the Estuary, Flint Castle, and the romantic Welsh Mountain Scenery; together with the several

MANORS AND MANORIAL RIGHTS, AND TITHE RENT CHARGES,

Which have been commuted at nearly FIVE HUNDRED POUNDS PER ANNUM.

THE WHOLE WILL BE DIVIDED INTO

Two Hundred and Eighty-four convenient Lots,

To suit large and small capitalists, the agricultural portion into Farms, varying from 100 Statute Acres down to 20, and the Accommodation Lands in Lots from 2 to 10 Acres each.

Mr. Charles Baxter, of Neston, will shew the Lots.

Lithographic Plans, with these Particulars, may be had from the AUCTIONEERS, at their Offices in Whitchurch, Liverpool or Chester; from Mr. SISSON, Plas-coch, St. Asaph; at the Offices of Messrs. CUDDON, of Norwich; at

Figure 30. Sale particulars: sale of the Neston estate, 1849.

prosperity did not appear to lie in Parkgate. One day in 1844 a Liverpool surveyor, Owen Williams, landed on the beach of Llandudno Bay with a friend who had come for a meeting of the mining company which was extracting copper from the Great Orme. He remarked that the bay would make a fine watering-place, and his suggestion was reported to Edward Lloyd Mostyn who commissioned Williams to plan a new resort.[54] An Enclosure Act for the area had been obtained in 1843, at which time Lady Champneys possessed the Gloddaeth estate which lies inland of the bay. After her death in 1845 her nephew Edward controlled the estate, and the Enclosure Award of 1848 gave him 832 acres out of 955.[55] The leaseholds of building sites were auctioned in Conway in August 1849, under strict development regulations. The Llandudno Improvement Act which appointed Town Commissioners was piloted through Parliament in 1854 by Edward Lloyd Mostyn as M.P. for Flintshire, just before he succeeded as the second Baron Mostyn. He was himself the first chairman of the Board of Commissioners.[56]

But Parkgate had gone:[57]

> Who'll buy a town? – a pretty town indeed – the town of Parkgate, which above all other towns has the singular privilege of being sold by auction. Many a town has been battered to pieces, but Parkgate has only to be brought to the hammer.

And so, over six days in June 1849, the village of Parkgate was sold in ninety-six lots.[58] The various tides that had brought it prosperity had finally all receded.

[54] Owen Williams, letter to the *Llandudno News Sheet*, 9 Aug. 1882 (Aberconwy Area Library, Llandudno, D 7801/A 176387).
[55] Alan Stuart, 'The growth and morphology of coastal towns in North Wales' (MA thesis, 1959, U.C.W. Aberystwyth), pp. 224–34.
[56] Harold Carter, *The Towns of Wales* (1965), p. 302.
[57] *Liverpool Albion*, quoted by *Chester Chronicle*, 1 June 1849.
[58] 1849 Sale Particulars, Mostyn (Bangor) MS 5366.

# *Bibliography*

## UNPUBLISHED SOURCES

*Aberconwy Area Library, Llandudno*
Letter by Owen Williams

*Bodleian Library, Oxford*
Gough maps

*British Library*
Harleian MS 2004 f. 137; Add. MS 39,769

*Cheshire Record Office, Duke Street, Chester*

| | |
|---|---|
| DBC | Birch, Cullimore & Co. |
| DCC | Cowper papers |
| DGA | Gamon & Co. papers |
| DHL | Hayes, Lyon papers |
| DPB | Potts & Ball papers |
| EDT | Tithe Awards |
| LU NE | Local undertakings, Neston |
| P | Ecclesiastical parish records |
| QDN | Dee navigation |
| QJB | Quarter Sessions books |
| QJF | Quarter Sessions files |
| D | Deposited plans |

*Chester City Record Office, Town Hall, Chester*

| | |
|---|---|
| AB | Assembly minute books |
| CAP | Assessments |
| GB | Guild Books |
| HI | Chester Royal Infirmary |
| ML | Mayors' letter books |
| QAP | Point of Ayr lighthouse trust |
| QCR | Crownmote records |
| QSE | Quarter Sessions: examinations |

TAO     Treasurer's draft accounts
TC      Town Clerk
Grosvenor MSS, Eaton Hall (obtainable through Chester City R.O.) Papers
of the 4th and 6th baronets

*Clwyd Record Office, Hawarden*
Wreck book (D.DM.734.2)

*HM Customs & Excise, Museums & Records Unit, Room M10E,
Custom House, Lower Thames Street, London EC38 6EE.*
Parkgate Customs account

*House of Lords Record Office*
1733 petitions

*John Rylands University Library of Manchester*
Mainwaring MSS

*Lancashire Record Office, Preston*
Kenyon MSS

*Liverpool City Record Office, Central Libraries, William Brown
Street*
Diary of Sir Willoughby Aston

*Liverpool Museum, William Brown Street*
Ship bowls

*Maritime Records Centre, Albert Dock, Liverpool*
Liverpool shipping registers

*Mostyn MSS*
a)      Archives of U.C.N.W. Bangor, cited as 'Mostyn (Bangor)'
b)      Clwyd Record Office, Hawarden, cited as 'Mostyn (Hawarden)'

*National Library of Wales, Aberystwyth*
Plas Power documents

*National Maritime Museum, Greenwich*
Yacht models and paintings

*Neston*
Neston parish register (microfilm in Neston Public Library)

*Post Office Archives, Freeling House, 23 Glasshill Street, London SE1 0BQ.*
POST 1, 12, 29, 41, 42, 58, 59, 94

*Public Record Office, Chancery Lane, London*
CHES 2   (Palatinate of Chester)
E 190    (Exchequer)
SP 36    (State Papers)
TI 11    (Treasury)

*Public Record Office, Kew, Richmond*
ADM 7, 8, 36, 51, 175        (Admiralty)
CUST 18, 19, 39, 78, 79      (Customs)
CO 5, 33                     (Colonial)
WO 5                         (War Office)

*Royal Archives, Windsor Castle*
Stuart papers

*University College of North Wales, Bangor (see Mostyn)*

*University of Liverpool: Sidney Jones Library, special collections*
John Glegg, account book

## BOOKS, ARTICLES AND THESES

Aiken, J., *A Description of the country from 30 to 40 miles round Manchester* (1795).

*Analecta Hibernica* no. 15 (Dublin, 1944): Journal of G. E. Pakenham, pp. 114–25.

*Annual Register*, 1790, 1806.

*The Antiquarian Repository*, ed. F. Grose (4 vols, 1809).

Arkle, A. H., 'Early Liverpool coaching', *T.H.S.L.C.* 73 (1921), pp. 1–32.

Armour, C., 'The trade of Chester and the state of the Dee navigation, 1600–1800', Ph.D. thesis, London University (1956).

Ayling, Stanley, *John Wesley* (1979).

Ayton, Richard, *A Voyage round Great Britain* (8 vols, 1814–25).

Bailey, F. A., 'The minutes of the trustees of the turnpike road from Liverpool to Prescott', *T.H.S.L.C.* 88 (1936), pp. 159–200.

Barber, E., 'Parkgate, an old Cheshire port', *J.C.A.S.* n.s. 8 (1911), pp. 5–25.

Baskerville, S. W., 'The establishment of the Grosvenor interest in Chester 1710–48', *J.C.A.S.* 63 (1980), pp. 59–84.

Becket, J. V., *Coal and Tobacco: the Lowthers and the Economic Development of West Cumberland, 1660–1760* (Cambridge, 1981).

Bedford, W. K. R., *Three Hundred Years of a Family Living* (Birmingham, 1889).

Bell, Peter, *An Actual Survey of the great Post Road from London to Parkgate* (1779).

Bell, Robert, *A Description of the Condition and Manners, as well as of the moral and political character, education &c., of the peasantry of Ireland, such as they were between 1780 and 1790* (1804).

Bellamy, George Anne, *An Apology for the Life of George Anne Bellamy* (2nd edn, 1785, 6 vols).

Berkeley, George, *The Querist* (Dublin, 1735).

Bethell, J. P., 'The Dee estuary: an historical geography of its use as a port', M.Sc. thesis, U.C.W., Aberystwyth (1953).

Bevan-Evans, M., 'Gadlys and Flintshire leadmining in the 18th century', *Flintshire Historical Society Journal*, 18 (1960), pp. 75–130; 20 (1962), pp. 32–60.

*Bibliotheca Topographica Britannia*, ed. J. Nicholls (10 vols, 1780–1800).

Bingley, William, *North Wales* (1804).

Blome, Richard, *Britannia* (1673).

Booth, P. H. W., ed., *Burton in Wirral, a History* (Burton, 1984).

Boydell, Thomas, *Plan of the lands and premises of the River Dee Company* (1771).

Bradstreet, Dudley, *The Life and Uncommon Adventures of Captain Dudley Bradstreet*, ed. G. S. Taylor (1929).

Bretherton, F. F., *Early Methodism in and around Chester, 1749–1812* (Chester, 1903).

British Library: pamphlets about the Dee navigation:
The Case of the Cheesemongers (BL 357 C.1.28)
The Case of the Citizens of Chester (BL 816 M.8.38).
The Case of the Gentlemen, Freeholders and other the inhabitants of the County of Flint (BL 1888 C.11.1.3).
The Case of the Inhabitants of the County and City of Chester (BL 357 C.1.37)
Thomas Badeslade: Reasons humbly offered to the consideration of the public (BL 190 D.15.1.5)

Brooke, Richard, *Liverpool as it was during the last quarter of the 18th century* (Liverpool, 1853).

Burdett, P. P., *A Survey of the County Palatine of Chester* (1777, reprinted 1974 by the Historic Society of Lancashire and Cheshire).

Burney, Charles, *A General History of Music* (1788–9) with notes by Frank Mercer (2 vols, 1935).

Bush, John, ed., *Hibernia Curiosa* (1769).

Callender, Professor, 'The Lord Lieutenant of Ireland and his yacht', *The Mariner's Mirror*, 14 (1928), pp. 58–61.

Cannell, H., *see* D. Eagle.

Carr, A. D., 'The making of the Mostyns: the genesis of a landed family', *Transactions of the Honourable Society of Cymmrodorion* (1979), pp. 137–57.

Carr, Sir John, *The Stranger in Ireland* (1806).

Carson, E. A., *The Ancient and Rightful Customs* (1972).

Carte Générale des Costes d'Irlande et des Costes Occidentales d'Angleterre, levées et gravées par ordre exprez du Roy (1693).

Carter, Harold, *The Towns of Wales* (Cardiff, 1965).

Cartwright, T., *The Diary of Thomas Cartwright*, ed. Joseph Hunter (Camden Society, 22, 1843).

Cathrall, W., *The History of North Wales* (Manchester, 1828).

Charnock, John, *Biographia Navalis* (6 vols, 1794–8).

*Chartulary of Chester Abbey*, ed. J. Tait (Chetham Society, Manchester, N.S. 82, 1923).

*Cheshire Sheaf*: O.S. 1878–86; N.S. 1891; 3rd series 1896–1965.

Chetwood, W. R., *A Tour through Ireland in several entertaining Letters*, ed. W. R. C. (1748).

Cholmondeley, R. H., *The Heber Letters, 1783–1832* (1950).

*Clarendon: The Correspondence of Henry Hyde, earl of Clarendon, and of his brother Lawrence Hyde, earl of Rochester*, ed. S. W. Singer (2 vols, 1828).

Clarke, J. W., 'Cheshire bells', *L.C.A.S.* 60 (1948), pp. 86–116.

Clemens, P. G. E., 'The rise of Liverpool, 1665–1750', *Economic History Review*, 2nd series 29 (1976), pp. 211–25.

Cobbett, William, *Cobbet's Parliamentary History of England* (36 vols, 1800–1820), 34 (1819).

Colledge, J. J., *Ships of the Royal Navy, an Historical Index* (2 vols, Newton Abbott, 1969): Vol. 1, Major Ships.

Collins, E. J. T., 'Migrant labour in British agriculture in the 19th century', *Economic History Review*, 29 (1976), pp. 38–59.

Collins, Greenvile, *Great Britain's Coasting Pilot* (1693).

Connell, K. H., *The Population of Ireland, 1750–1845* (1950).

Cowper, William, *Poetical Works*, ed. H. S. Milford (Oxford, 4th edn, 1967).

Coxe, William, *Memoirs of the Life and Administration of Sir Robert Walpole, Earl of Orford* (3 vols, 1798).

Craig, Robert, 'Some aspects of the trade and shipping of the River Dee in the 18th century', *T.H.S.L.C.* 114 (1962), pp. 99–128.

——, 'Shipping and shipbuilding in the port of Chester', *T.H.S.L.C.* 116 (1964), pp. 39–63.

Crawford, W. H., *Aspects of Irish Social History, 1750–1800* (1969).

Crawfurd, G. B., ed., *The Diary of George Booth of Chester*, reprinted from *J.C.A.S.* 28 part 1 (1928), pp. 5–96.

Cullen, L. M., *Anglo-Irish Trade, 1660–1800* (Manchester, 1968).

Curran, W. H., *The Life of the Rt Hon John Philpott Curran* (2 vols, 1819).

*Cymru A'r Môr, see Maritime Wales.*

David, Christopher, *St Winefride's Well, a History and Guide* (Nass, 1971).

Davies, H. R., *A Review of the records of the Conway and Menai Ferries* (Cardiff, 1942).

Davies, P. N., McBride, P. W. J., Priestman, K., 'The Mary, Charles II's yacht', *International Journal of Nautical Archaeology and Underwater Exploration* (1973), 2:1, pp. 59–73.

*Davies, R.: Journal of the Rev. Rowland Davies*, ed. R. Caulfield (Camden Society, 1857).

Davis, Ralph, *The Rise of the English Shipping Industry in the 17th and 18th Centuries* (1962).

*Dee, River: The Dee Regulation Scheme*, Welsh Water authority, Dee & Clwyd division (undated pamphlet, *c.*1986).

Dee navigation pamphlets: *see* British Library.

Defoe, Daniel, *A Tour through the whole Island of Great Britain* (1724–6; reprinted 1927, 2 vols).

Delany, Mary, *The Autobiography and Correspondence of Mary Granville, Mrs Delany*, ed. Lady Llanover (6 vols, 1862–3).

*De Quincey, Thomas, Collected Works*, ed. David Masson (14 vols, Edinburgh 1889–90).

*De Quincey Memorials*, ed. A. H. Japp (1891).

Dickson, David, 'In search of the old Irish Poor Law', unpublished article (undated, *c.*1980), Trinity College, Dublin.

Directories—

    *Commercial Directory, James Piggot* (Manchester, 1818).

    *Directories of Cheshire* (1828, 1834, 1850, 1874).

    *Directories of Chester* (1787, 1791).

    *Directory of the Hundred of Wirral*, Mawdsley & Son (Birkenhead, 1861).

    *Gore's Directory of Liverpool* (1769, 1772, 1774).

    *Wilson's Directory of Dublin* (1782–1816).

*Mortimer & Harwood's Directory of Birkenhead* (1843).

Dodd, A. H., 'The roads of North Wales, 1750–1850', *Archaeologica Cambrensis* (vol. 80, 1925), pp. 121–48.

Dodd, Geoff, 'The turnpikes of Wirral', *Journal of the North-West Society of Industrial & Archaeological History*, 2 (1972) pp. 21–7.

Dore, R. N., 'The sea approaches: the importance of the Dee and the Mersey estuaries in the Civil War in the North-West', *T.H.S.L.C.* 136 (1986), pp. 1–25.

Duckworth, C. L. D., and Langmuir, G. E., *West Coast Steamers* (Prescott, 1953).

Dunlop, Robert, *Ireland under the Commonwealth* (2 vols, Manchester, 1913).

Dyer, F. E., 'The journal of Grenvill Collins', *The Mariner's Mirror* 14 (1928), pp. 197–219.

Eagle, D. and Cannell, H., *Oxford Literary Guide to the British Isles* (Oxford, 1st edn 1977; 2nd edn 1981).

Elis-Williams, M., *Packet to Ireland: Porthdinllaen's challenge to Holyhead* (Gwynedd archive services, Caernarfon, 1984).

Enfield, William, *An Essay towards the History of Liverpool* (Liverpool, 1773).

*Evelyn, Sir John: Diary* ed. E. S. de Beer (6 vols, Oxford, 1955).

Eyes, John, *A Survey of the River Dee* (1740). *See also* Fearon.

Falconer, William, *An Universal Dictionary of the Marine* (1776 edn).

Fearon, S. and Eyes, J., *A Description of the Sea Coast of England & Wales* (1738).

Feltham, John, *A Guide to all the Watering and Sea-Bathing Places* (1803).

Fenwick, G. L., *A History of the ancient City of Chester* (Chester, 1896).

Ferrar, John, *A Tour from Dublin to London in 1795* (Dublin, 1796).

Fiennes, Celia, *The Illustrated Journeys of Celia Fiennes, 1685–c.1712*, ed. C. Morris (1982).

Fordham, H. G., *Paterson's Roads: Daniel Paterson, his Maps and Itineraries, 1738–1825* (1925).

Fransson, J. Karl, 'The fatal voyage of Edward King, Milton's Lycidas', *Milton Studies* 25 (Pittsburgh, 1990), pp. 43–67.

Gamlin, Hilda, *Memories of Birkenhead* (Liverpool, 1892).

———, *'Twixt Mersey and Dee* (Liverpool, 1897).

Gastrell, Francis: *Notitia Cestriensis*, ed. F. Raines (Chetham Society, Manchester, 1845, vol. 8).

Gaulter, John, ed., 'Of the introduction of Methodism into the neighbourhood and city of Chester; in a memoir of Mrs Lowe of that city', *The Methodist Magazine* 32 (1809), pp. 187–231.

Gavin, C. M., *Royal Yachts* (1932).

George, M. Dorothy, *London Life in the 18th Century* (1925).

Glasgow, T., 'The Elizabethan navy in Ireland, 1583–1603', *The Irish Sword* 8 (Dublin, 1965–6), pp. 291–307.

Glenn, T. A., *see* Mostyn.

Greenwood, C., *Map of Cheshire* (1819).

Grenville, A. B., *Spas of England* (2 vols, 1841).

Granville, Mary, *see* Delany.

Gresswell, R. Kay, 'The origin of the Dee and Mersey estuaries', *Geological Journal* 4, part 1 (Liverpool, 1964), pp. 77–86.

*The Griffin: Magazine of Mostyn House School, Parkgate* (1892–1901).

*Hamilton, Emma, Lady: The Hamilton and Nelson Papers of Alfred Morrison*, ed. A. W. Thibeaudeau (2 vols, 1893).

Hanshall, J. H., *History of the County Palatine of Cheshire* (Chester, 1823).

Hardwick, M., *Literary Atlas and Gazetteer of the British Isles* (Newton Abbott, 1973).

Harris, B. E., *Chester* (Edinburgh, 1979).

Hawkes, G. I., 'The Point of Ayr lighthouse', *Maritime Wales* 9 (1985), pp. 42–3.

———, 'Illicit trading in Wales in the 18th century', *Maritime Wales* 10 (1986), pp. 89–107.

Hayden, Ruth, *Mrs Delany, her Life and her Flowers* (1980).

Helsby, T., ed., *see* G. Ormerod.

Historical Manuscripts Commission—

> *Chester Corporation, 8th Report App. 1* (1881).
>
> *8th Report, App. 3* (1881).
>
> *Fortescue MSS, 1* (1892); *4* (1905).
>
> *Townshend, 11th Report App. 4* (1887).
>
> *Kenyon MSS, 14th Report app. 4* (1894).
>
> *Earl of Dartmouth, 3, 15th Report, App. 1* (1896).
>
> *Sir R. Puleston, 15th Report App. 7* (1898).
>
> *Mrs Stopford-Sackville, 1* (1904).
>
> *Earl of Egmont, 1* (1905).
>
> *Salisbury, 11* (1906).
>
> *Marquis of Ormonde, n.s. 6* (1912); *n.s. 8* (1920).
>
> *R. R. Hastings, 4* (1947).

*History Today* 33 (July 1983).

Her Majesty's Stationery Office: British National Archives—

> *Calendar of Charter Rolls*

*Calendar of Inquisitions Post-mortem*

*Calendar of State Papers, Domestic*

*Calendar of State Papers, Ireland*

*Calendar of Treasury Books*

*Calendar of Treasury Papers*

Hoare, Sir Richard Colt: *Journeys 1793–1810*, ed. M. W. Thompson (Gloucester, 1983).

Hogg, T. J., *Life of Percy Bysshe Shelley* (1858), ed. E. Dowden (1906).

Holdsworth, William, *History of English Law* (16 vols: vol. 6, 1920; vol. 10, 1938).

't Hooft, C. G., 'The first English yachts, 1660', *The Mariner's Mirror* 5 (1919), pp. 108–23.

Hoon, E. E., *The Organization of the English Customs System 1696–1786* (1938, reprinted Newton Abbott, 1968).

Houlston, Thomas, *Essay on the Liverpool Spa Water* (Liverpool, 1773).

*House of Commons Journal*, vols 21, 22 (1732, 1733).

*House of Lords Journal*, 24 (1733).

Hughes, Herbert, *Chronicle of Chester* (1975).

Hughes, L. and Scouten, A. H., *Ten English Farces* (Austin, Texas, 1948).

Hughes, Mervyn, 'Telford, Parnell and the Great Irish Road', *Journal of Transport History* 4 (1963–4), pp. 199–209.

Hughes, Thomas, *The Stranger's Handbook to Chester* (Chester and London, 1856).

Hunter, James (publisher), *A new map of the Hundred of Wirral* (c. 1791).

Jackson, T. V., 'The Irish Post Office, 1638–1700', *Bulletin of the Postal History Society* 100 (March–April 1959), pp. 1–4.

Jarvis, R. C., 'Illicit trade with the Isle of Man', *T.H.S.L.C.* 58 (1946), pp. 245–67.

———, 'The head port of Chester and Liverpool, its creek and member', *T.H.S.L.C.* 102 (1950), pp. 69–84.

———, 'Appointment of ports', *Economic History Review*, 2nd series 11, 3 (1959), pp. 455–66.

Kalm, Pehr, *Account of his Visit to England, 1748*, translated by J. Lucas (1892).

*Kenmare: The Kenmare MSS*, ed. E. MacLysaght (Dublin, 1942), Irish MSS Commission.

Kerr, Barbara, 'Irish seasonal migration in Great Britain, 1800–1838', *Irish Historical Studies* 3 (1942), pp. 365–80.

King, Edward, *Obsequies to the Memory of Mr Edward King* A.D. *1638* (1694 edn).

Langmuir, G. E., *see* Duckworth.

*Leinster, Correspondence of Emily, Duchess of Leinster*, ed. B. Fitzgerald (2 vols, Dublin, 1949), Irish MSS Commission.

Leland, John, *The Itinerary in Wales of John Leland, c.1536–39*, ed. L. Toulmin-Smith, vol. 3 of 5 (1907–10).

*Liverpool: Municipal Archives and Records, 1700–1835*, ed. Sir James Picton (1836, reprinted Liverpool, 1886).

*Lloyd's: Lloyd's Lists*.

*Lloyd's Register of Shipping*.

Lloyd, G., 'The canalization of the River Dee in 1737', *Flintshire Historical Society Transactions* 23 (1967–8), pp. 35–41.

Lloyd-Jones, D., and Williams, D. M., *Holyhead, the Story of a Port* (1967).

*Lucian: Liber Luciani de Laude Cestrie*, ed. M. V. Taylor (Record Soc. L. & C., 1912).

Lysons, D. and S., *Magna Britannia* (6 vols, 1806–22), vol. 2, part 2 (1810).

McBride, P. W. J., *see* P. N. Davies.

McDowell, R. B., *Ireland in the Age of Imperialism and Revolution, 1760–1801* (Oxford, 1979).

McGowan, A. P., *The Royal Yachts* (3rd edn, 1977).

McGurk, J. J. N., 'The recruitment and transportation of Elizabethan troops and their service in Ireland, 1594–1603', Ph.D. thesis, University of Liverpool, 1982.

Mackay, John, *An abridged plan of the River Dee and Hyle Lake* (1732).

Macready, W. C., *Macready's Reminiscences and Selections from his Diary and Letters*, ed. Sir F. Pollock, 2 vols (1875).

*Maritime Wales (Cymru A'r Môr)* 9 (1985); 10 (1986).

Markland, J. H., 'Some remarks on the early use of carriages in England', *Archaeologia* 20 (1824), pp. 443–77.

*Moore, Thomas: The Memoirs, Journal and Correspondence*, ed. Lord John Russell (8 vols, 1853).

*Moore, Thomas: The Letters*, ed. W. S. Dowden (1964).

*Morris, Lewis, Richard, William and John, Letters*, ed. J. H. Davies (2 vols, Aberystwyth, 1907).

Morris, R. H., *Chester during the Plantaganet and Tudor Reigns* (Chester, 1894).

Mortimer, W. W., *History of the Hundred of Wirral* (1847).

Moss, W., *The Liverpool Guide* (Liverpool, 1796).

Mostyn, Lord and Glenn, T. A., *History of the Family of Mostyn* (1925).

Mountfield, Stuart, 'Captain Greenvile Collins and Mr Pepys', *The Mariner's Mirror* 56 (1970), pp. 85–96.

Muir, Ramsay, *A History of Liverpool* (Liverpool, 1907).

Muirhead, L. R., ed., *Ireland* (1949).

Mumford, Enid, *Chester Royal Infirmary, 1756–1956* (Chester, 1956).

Murphy, Denis, *Cromwell in Ireland* (Dublin, 1883).

Naish, G. P. B., 'Hydrographic surveys by officers of the Navy under the later Stuarts', *Journal of the Institute of Navigation* 9 (1956), pp. 47–55.

*The Navy List* (1820–35).

Newspapers—

| | |
|---|---|
| Chester | *Chester Chronicle* |
| | *(Adam's Weekly) Courant* |
| Dublin | *Faulkner's Dublin Journal* |
| | *Freeman's Dublin Journal* |
| | *Dublin News Letter* |
| | *Saunder's Newsletter* |
| | *Sleater's Dublin Chronicle* |
| | *Dublin Weekly Journal* |
| Liverpool | *Gore's General Advertiser* |
| | *Liverpool Mercury* |
| | *Williamson's Liverpool Advertiser* |
| London | *The Times* (until 1788 *The Daily Universal Register*) |
| Shrewsbury | *Shrewsbury Chronicle* |

Nicholson, George, *The Cambrian Traveller's Guide* (Stourport, 1813).

*Notes and Queries* 7th series, 4 (1887); 10th series, 3 (1905), 191 (1952).

O'Donovan, John, *The Economic History of Live Stock in Ireland* (Cork, 1940).

Ogilby, John, *Britannia* (1675).

Ó'Gráda, Cormac, 'Seasonal migration and post-famine adjustment in the west of Ireland', *Studia Hibernica* 13 (Dublin, 1973), pp. 48–76.

Ormerod, G., *History of Cheshire,* 2nd edn, 3 vols, ed. T. Helsby (1882).

Parkes, Joan, *Travel in England in the 17th Century* (Oxford, 1925).

*Parliamentary Papers: 5th Report from the Select Committee on the Roads from London to Holyhead: Holyhead Mails and Packets,* House of Commons sessional papers, 5 (1819).

Paterson, Daniel, *A new and accurate Description of all the direct and principal cross Roads in Great Britain* (1771 to 18th edn, 1826).

Peet, H., *Liverpool in the Reign of Queen Anne* (Liverpool, 1908).

Pennant, T., *History of the Parishes of Whiteford & Holywell* (1796).

*Pepys, Samuel: A Descriptive Catalogue of the Naval MSS in the Pepsyian Library,* ed. J. R. Tanner, 4 vols, Naval Record Society, 26, 27, 36, 57. vol. 1 (1903); vol. 3 (1909); vol. 4 (1922).

————, *Samuel Pepys' Naval Minutes* ed. J. R. Tanner, Naval Record Society, 60 (1926).

Pilkington, Laetitia, *Memoirs* (Dublin, 1748).

Pimlott, J. A. R., *The Englishman's Holiday* (1947).

*Place, Francis: Autobiography*, ed. Mary Thale (1972).

Place, G. W., 'The Chester high road (A540)', *Bulletin of the Burton & District Local History Society*, 1 (1977), pp. 11–18.

————, *This is Parkgate: its Buildings and their Story* (Parkgate, 1979).

————, 'Neston Park, *Bulletin of the Burton & South Wirral Local History Society* 5 (1984), pp. 15–20.

————, 'John Brindley (1811–1873), Cheshire schoolmaster, the opponent of atheism', *T.H.S.L.C.* 133 (1984), pp. 113–32.

————, 'The repatriation of Irish vagrants from Cheshire, 1750–1815', *J.C.A.S.* 68 (1986), pp. 125–41.

————, 'William and Mary, the tale of two anchors', *The Wirral Journal* (Autumn, 1987), pp. 10–14.

————, 'Parkgate as a port', *J.C.A.S.*, 66 (1983), pp. 47–55.

————, 'Wreckers: the fate of the *Charming Jenny*', *The Mariner's Mirror*, 76, no. 2 (May 1990), pp. 167–9).

Pope, D. J., 'Shipping and trade in the port of Liverpool, 1783–93', Ph.D. thesis, University of Liverpool, 1970.

*Prescott, Henry: The Diary of Henry Prescott, LLB, Deputy Registrar of Chester Diocese*, ed. John Addy, Record Society of Lancashire and Cheshire, 127, 1 (1987).

Priestman, K., *see* P. N. Davies

Prior, Matthew, *The Literary Works of Matthew Prior*, eds H. B. Wright and M. K. Spears (2 vols, Oxford, 1959).

Raistrick, Arthur, *Two Centuries of Industrial Welfare: the London (Quaker) Lead Company* (1938).

Redford, Arthur, *Labour Migration in England, 1800–1850* (Manchester, 1926).

Reilly, Jane Hester, 'A young lady's journey from Dublin to London in 1791', *The Nineteenth Century*, 43 (May 1898), pp. 795–808.

Rhodes, J. N., 'The London Lead Company in North Wales, 1693–1793', Ph.D. thesis, Leicester University, 1970).

Ribton-Turner, C. J., *A History of Vagrants and Vagrancy* (1887).

Rideout, Edna, 'The Chester Companies and the Old Quay', *T.H.S.L.C.*, 79 (1927), pp. 141–74.

Rigby, Thomas, *The Cattle Plague in Cheshire* (Warrington, 1868).

Robinson, Howard, *The British Post Office, A History* (1948).

Robinson, A. H. W., *Marine Cartography in Great Britain* (Leicester, 1962).

de Rochford, Albert Jorevin, 'Description of England and Ireland', *The Antiquarian Repository*, ed. F. Grose, 4 (1809), pp. 549–622.

Rodger, N. A. M., *The Wooden World* (1986).

*Royal Society: The Philosophical Transactions and Collections*, ed. John Lowther (1705; 4th edn, 1731).

*Royal Society of Antiquaries of Ireland: Journal* (1897).

Russell, Richard, *A Dissertation on the Use of Sea Water in the diseases of the glands* (Latin edn, Oxford, 1750; 1st English edn, 1752).

Rutherford, G., 'The King against Luke Ryan', *The Mariner's Mirror* 43 (1957), pp. 28–38.

Savage, H. E., ed., *The Great Register of Lichfield Cathedral* (Kendal, 1926).

Schoelcher, V., *Life of Handel*, translated by J. Lowe (1857).

Schofield, M. M., 'The slave trade from Lancashire and Cheshire ports outside Liverpool', *T.H.S.L.C.* 126 (1977), pp. 30–72.

Scouten, A. H., *see* L. Hughes

*Shelley, P. B.: The Letters of Percy Bysshe Shelley*, ed. F. L. Jones, 2 vols (Oxford, 1964).

Sitchell, Walter, *Emma, Lady Hamilton* (1907).

Sydney, Samuel, *Gallops and Gossips in the Bush of Australia* (1854).

Smith, W. C., *A Short History of the Irish Sea Herring Fisheries* (1923).

Sparrow, James, *Biography of J. M. Skinner Esq., Commander R.N.* (1866).

Speed, John, *The Counties of Britain, a Tudor Atlas* (1988), a reprint of the maps in *Theatrum Imperii Magnae Britanniae* (1616).

Stephens, W. B., 'The overseas trade of Chester in the early 17th century', *T.H.S.L.C.* 120 (1969), pp. 23–4.

*State Trials: A complete Collection of State Trials*, compiled by T. B. Howell, 33 vols (1811–28), vol. 20 (1814).

*Stevens, John: Journal of John Stevens, 1689–91* ed. R. H. Murray (Oxford, 1912).

Stewart-Brown, R., *Liverpool Ships of the 18th century* (Liverpool, 1962).

Story, George, *An impartial History of the Affairs of Ireland* (1691).

Stratton, J. M., *Agricultural Records, A.D. 220–1968* (1969).

Stuart, Alan, 'The growth and morphology of coastal towns in North Wales,' (M.A. thesis, U.C.W. Aberystwyth 1959).

Sulley, P., *The Hundred of Wirral* (Birkenhead, 1889).

*Swift, Jonathan: Journal to Stella* (1766), ed. Harold Williams, 2 vols (Oxford, 1948); Letter 1, pp. 1–2 (vol. 1); Letter 65, pp. 670–1 (vol. 2).

——, *Poems*, ed. Harold Williams, 3 vols (Oxford, 1937).

——, *Works*, ed. Herbert Davis, 13 vols (Oxford, 1962).

———, *Correspondence*, ed. Harold Williams, 5 vols (Oxford, 1963).

———, *Account Books*, ed. P. V. and D. J. Thompson (1984).

Sylvester, Dorothy, *A History of Cheshire* (Henley on Thames, 1971).

Symonds, Richard: *Diary of the Marches of the Royal Army during the Great Civil War*, ed. Charles Long (Camden Society, 1859).

Tait, J., ed., *Chartulary of Chester Abbey* (Chetham Society, N.S. 82, 1923).

*Torrington: The Torrington Diaries*, ed. C. B. Andrews, 4 vols (1936).

Townsend, W. J., Workman, H. B., Eayrs, G., eds, *History of Methodism*, 2 vols (1909).

Townshend, D. *The Life and Letters of the Great Earl of Cork* (1904).

Verney, Margaret, ed., *Verney Letters of the 18th Century*, 2 vols (1928).

Victor, Benjamin, *The History of the Theatres of London and Dublin*, 3 vols (1761).

'An unpublished diary of the Rev. Peter Walkden in 1733–34', *J.C.A.S.*, N.S. 3 (1888–90), ed. H. Taylor, pp. 151–61.

Wardle, A. C. 'Early Steamships on the Mersey, 1815–20', *T.H.S.L.C.*, 92 (1941), pp. 85–100.

———, 'The early Liverpool privateers', *T.H.S.L.C.*, 93 (1942), pp. 69–97.

———, 'Some glimpses of Liverpool during the first half of the 18th century', *T.H.S.L.C.* 97 (1946), pp. 145–57.

Wark, K. R., *Elizabethan Recusancy in Cheshire* (Chetham Society, 1971).

Wassell, John, 'The Lion's Whelp', *The Mariner's Mirror*, 63 (1977), pp. 368–9.

Watson, Edward, *Royal Mail to Ireland* (1916).

Webster, Frank, 'The River Dee reclamation and the effect upon Navigation', *Transactions of the Liverpool Engineering Society* 51 (1930), pp. 63–92.

Wedgwood, Josiah, *The Correspondence of Josiah Wedgwood, 1781–94*, ed. Lady Farrer (1904).

*Wesley, John: The Journals of the Rev. John Wesley A.M.*, ed. N. Curnock, 8 vols (1911–16).

Whitaker, Harold, *A Descriptive List of the Printed Maps of Cheshire, 1577–1900*, Chetham Society, 1942).

White, Gilbert, *The Natural History and Antiquities of Selborne* (1788; Penguin edn, 1941).

Wilkinson, Tait, *Memoirs of his own Life* (1790).

Willan, T. S., *The English Coasting Trade, 1600–1775* (1938).

Williams, Basil, *The Whig Supremacy, 1714–1760* (Oxford, 1939).

Williams, D. M., *see* Lloyd-Jones, D.

Williams, James E., 'Growth and decline of the port of Whitehaven, 1650–1900', M.A. thesis, University of Leeds, 1951.

Williams, Robert (publisher), *Liverpool Memorandum* (1752) (in Liverpool Record Office, ref. 920 MD 407).

Williams, W. R., *The Parliamentary History of the Principality of Wales, 1541–1895* (Brecknock, 1895).

Wilson, K. P., 'The port of Chester in the 15th century', *T.H.S.L.C.* 117 (1966), pp. 1–15.

——, *Chester Customs Accounts, 1301–1566* (Record Society of Lancashire and Cheshire, 1969).

*Wirral Notes & Queries*, ed. F. Sanders and W. Fergusson Irvine (Birkenhead, 1892–3).

Woodward, D. M., 'The Chester leather industry', *T.H.S.L.C.* 119 (1967), pp. 65–111.

——, *The Trade of Elizabethan Chester* (Hull, 1970).

——, 'The overseas trade of Chester, 1600–1650', *T.H.S.L.C.* 122 (1971), pp. 25–42.

——, 'The Anglo-Irish livestock industry in the 17th century', *Irish Historical Studies* 18 (Dublin, 1972–3), pp. 489–523.

——, 'Charter party of the *Grace* of Neston, 1572', *Irish Economic and Social History* 5 (1978), pp. 64–9.

——, 'Ships, masters and shipowners of the Wirral, 1550–1650', *The Mariner's Mirror* 63, no. 3 (1977), pp. 233–47. Also in *Maritime History*, 5, no. 1 (Spring 1977), pp. 3–25.

——, 'The port books of England and Wales', *Maritime History* 3 (1973), pp. 147–65.

Woodward, E. L., *The Age of Reform, 1815–1870* (Oxford, 1938).

Yarranton, Andrew, *England's Improvement by Sea and Land* (1677).

Young, Arthur, *A Six Months' Tour through the North of England*, 2nd edn, 4 vols (1770–1).

——, *A Tour in Ireland* (Dublin, 1780).

Young, H. E., *Perambulation of the Hundred of Wirral* (Liverpool, 1909).

Young, Peter, *The English Civil War Armies* (Reading, 1973).

# Index